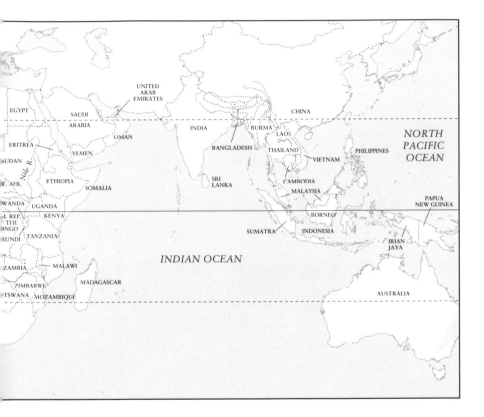

A Naturalist's Guide to the Tropics

Marco Lambertini

A Naturalist's Guide to the Tropics

Translated by John Venerella
With illustrations by Kitty Capua

THE UNIVERSITY OF CHICAGO PRESS / CHICAGO AND LONDON

Marco Lambertini is Director of Network and Programme for BirdLife International, UK, and is also a freelance scientific journalist for several national magazines and newspapers in Italy who has traveled to thirty-five tropical countries. He is author of several books in Italian, including *Safari in Africa,* and is coeditor of *Where to Watch Birds in Italy.*

John Venerella is an active member of the American Translator's Association and is accredited for translation from Italian into English.

The University of Chicago Press, Chicago 60637
The University of Chicago Press, Ltd., London
© 2000 by The University of Chicago
All rights reserved. Published 2000
08 07 06 05 04 03 02 01 00   1 2 3 4 5
ISBN: 0-226-46828-3 (paper)
Printed in Hong Kong

Originally published as *Guida alla natura tropicale,*
© 1992 Franco Muzzio & C. Editore, Padova, Italy.

Library of Congress Cataloging-in-Publication Data

Lambertini, M. (Marco)
    [Guida alla natura tropicale. English]
    A naturalist's guide to the tropics / Marco Lambertini ; translated
by John Venerella ; with illustrations by Kitty Capua.
       p.   cm.
    Includes bibliographical references (p.   ).
    ISBN 0-226-46828-3 (paper : alk. paper)
    1. Natural history—Tropics.   I. Title.
▷ QH84.5.L3613   2000
    508.313—dc21   99-32802
                                            CIP

This book is printed on acid-free paper by C&C Offset Printing Co., Ltd.

This book is dedicated to the eyes of that curious young orangutan.

A wish for those eyes and for their great forest.

Contents

Text Boxes and Tables

Photographs and Color Plates

Color Plates

Foreword

For many years now, I have been well acquainted with the passionate commitment with which Marco Lambertini approaches the important task of the conservation of wildlife and their natural habitats. His is a protective concern that is squarely focused on current, scientific knowledge of today's reality, a concern that is fueled by the conviction that global awareness is the most direct path for achieving this aim.

The present guide to tropical wildlife and their habitats will be a useful instrument for any of the ever more numerous travelers to the extraordinary and fascinating regions described herein.

How many of today's modern travelers are organized and curious enough—or even capable enough—to penetrate the natural world using an effective and cognitive approach? A difficult question to answer. Clearly, though, there are many without this directedness, a distracted mass who miss a tremendous amount in their travels, returning home with only the memory of large hotels and restaurants, or of beaches that all seemed to be about the same. A couple of ritual dances, a few ruins, but little more. Obviously, the organized and curious will benefit more from this guide, but I am also certain—knowing Marco well—that special attention and a careful eye have been devoted to considering those persons whom animals, plants, and nature generally do not interest.

It is, in fact, a major goal of conservationist education to conquer those people, to convince them that they ought to change their attitudes. It is true that these are the persons who are the most difficult to reach—and, among other things, an obvious minority of the potential readers—but what a lucky catch, what a positive result, if some of these were to take the bait! Indeed, it is fundamental to try to convince the skeptical, the inattentive, the disrespectful. There are all too many people who do not consider nature, who do not even see it, or who, irrationally, find cause to fear it— points of view that are founded on ignorance or a cultural upbringing that has been exaggeratedly anthropocentric.

Let us hope, then, that this book, through its being read, will touch not only those of us who already share Marco's concerns, but some of those who have yet to be reached.

Professor Danilo Mainardi
Director of the Environmental Sciences Institute
University of Venice, Italy

1. Floating gardens of the islands of Palau.

Preface

Do you know that strange sensation that strikes you when you first enter a cathedral or a large museum, that induces you to control your movements and lower your voice, that commands your attention and respect? This is what struck me on my first experience with the tropical wilderness, in Sri Lanka.

Penetrating those luxuriant forests, amid their wild and legendary, charismatic protagonists, or sighting my first monkey out in the open or my first enormous jungle tree laden with lianas and epiphytes, or exploring among the variety of forms and colors in the coral gardens, or hearing the geckos chorusing in my bungalow room—these experiences and many others, great and small—remain some of the most powerful marvels of my entire life.

Everyone should visit the Tropics and try immersing himself in that majestic world. It helps us to rediscover a dimension of our being that is well-concealed from the majority of modern men, that of being an integral part of the natural world. Nature is our originator, not our subject—we still depend on it; and when experiencing that grandiose nature of the Tropics, we can discover ourselves to be small and humble—or even a possible prey!

The tropical wilderness amazes us. It is a great laboratory out in the open, and because of the majesty of its forms and the charisma of its protagonists, it attracts our attention and bewilders our senses.

Then, also, there is another beauty concealed within this, less aesthetic, but more intellectual. It is in the awesomeness of the infinite adaptations and specializations making up the admirable and intricate organization of individuals, of species, of life.

Such revealing encounters stir thunderous emotions, and these emotions give rise to an irresistible passion for the natural wildlife of the Tropics. This is a passion that is becoming more and more meaningful to many and that, with all the modern opportunities of traveling, is spreading with a life of its own. In fact, this book is dedicated to all enthusiasts of tropical ecology.

A book that would purport to treat, in a single volume, all the biota of all the tropical regions of the world might seem to be an ambitious work and would run the risk, in wanting to say too much, of failing because of its superficiality. And yet, in spite of the difficulties posed by such a vast topic—and wanting the book still to remain an easy-to-consult manual— it is believed that the principal aspects can be identified and enriched with examples from around the continents, making specific references to fauna and flora, habitats, and general ecological rules. In fact, notwithstanding the enormous diversity of tropical biology, the overwhelming brilliance and wealth of its living forms, and the vastness of a geographic realm that embraces the entire world, it is possible to speak of the Tropics in a larger sense, as a unity. There are rules and relations and some fundamental types of habitats that recur—albeit with local variants—throughout the whole region.

One of the aims of this book is to spark attention and promote knowledge by describing the principal natural laws and essential aspects of the most characteristic of the tropical environments, revealing the rules that— once the animal and plant protagonists have been opportunely changed— are common to all mangrove swamps, whether in Indonesia or in Africa, or those that reappear in every rainforest, in the Democratic Republic of Congo just as in Amazonia, or the rules that unite all coral gardens, be they in Polynesia or in the Caribbean.

Anyone who loves traveling through the tropical latitudes will certainly have noticed these analogies and recurrences, which can be most simply explained by an exceptional climatic homogeneity and the reappearance, in different geographical areas, of ecologically similar conditions. Light, heat, and rain are the three principal components of the tropical formula, the formula that has, after millions of years of evolution, provided for us this feast of the most fascinating and engaging natural life on the planet.

It is time that the natural life of our planet be felt as a common patrimony in the true sense of the word. The principal aim of this work is to promote this understanding, and this is also one of the greatest challenges facing our modern strategies for conserving nature itself.

This is a work that is intended to establish among prospective world travelers a knowledge of the natural life and ecology of the Tropics, to make them seem less distant and unreachable, less unknown and mysterious. It is arranged as a text for orienting oneself, for responding to many of the curiosities and questions that arise spontaneously in the tropical tourist who has an interest in the natural world. A guide to skim before the trip as well as to take along. A stimulus for further and deeper reading.

A work whose text and illustrations are designed to introduce you to the majestic, engaging—and fragile—natural world of the Tropics. Buon viaggio. (Enjoy the journey!)

Guide to Reading the Color Plates

The color plates enhancing the text depict species belonging to various significant categories of tropical flora and fauna. They were chosen as examples, and the reader willing to acquire further expertise in species recognition is addressed to specific field guides, some of which are included in the bibliography. The plates are intended to represent relevant species and families that are typical of the various tropical regions, including indications of the continents where they are to be found. All the examples are distributed tropically, with limited extensions into subtropical areas, especially in Africa and South America. The term "pantropical" is used for a species that is distributed throughout all the continents included in the tropical band. In some cases, the distribution of the more general pertinent family is given along with that of the individual species depicted.

Acknowledgments

A special thanks to all those who have facilitated my visits to the tropical wilderness—often logistically difficult to penetrate! Among the many, I'd particularly like to thank Michele and Gianna Spinelli of Planet Italia (Italy), Willem and Izak Barnard and Alexa MacNaughton of Penduka Safaris (South Africa), Dr. Mike Canton of Charly's Desert (Namibia), Dr. Robert Fincham of the Institute of Natural Resources, University of Natal (South Africa), Ker Downey Selby (Botswana), Madagascar Airtour (Madagascar), Carine van der Merwe of SA Nature Foundation (South Africa), Dr. Clive Marsh of Sabah Foundation (Malaysia), Jorge Martinez Favini, attorney of the National Atomic Energy Commission (Argentina),

Jean Louis Prevost of Safari Vezo (Madagascar), Pierre Moukala of the Italian Embassy of the DRC, and the Italian office of South African Airways.

Proper thanks are also due to the magazine *Airone* and to its director, Salvatore Giannella, who, as a result of his having commissioned reportage on naturalistic themes, has several times permitted the organization of complex expeditions and exceptional experiences in the tropical wildernesses of Africa.

I'd like to express my special appreciation to Professor Massimo Pandolfi, the scientific curator of the series from which this work was translated, to Franco Muzzio Editore, who appreciated my editorial proposal from the very first, and to professor Danilo Mainardi, not only for his having accepted the opportunity to introduce this text with his Foreword, but for the continuing cultural stimulation that—throughout our years of acquaintance and friendship—he has never ceased offering me. To Kitty, the artist responsible for the beautiful drawings in this book, for her enthusiasm and commitment, to Agata, for her stimulating company on some of my most interesting trips, and for the assistance given me in more than one difficult occasion. To John Venerella, for his passionate enthusiasm and efforts in translating and adapting this work for an international audience.

M. L.

I would like to acknowledge my sincere gratitude to Christie and Russell, for the pleasure of working with them and for the quality of their editorial style, to Marco, for the privilege of collaborating with a world-class expert in safaris and tropical wildlife, to Mary, for helping me ever to refocus on my truest aims, and to Janet, for her unconditional love and friendship. As for my contribution to this work—a work written by an ardent lover of birds—I dedicate it to Joseph, who was a pilot.

J. V.

A Naturalist's Guide to the Tropics

2. Sunset on the Indian Ocean, framed by coconut palms. 3. Dawn on the great Selous Reserve.

Chapter 1

Tropical Geography and Biogeography

On any conventional map of the world you can see two parallel lines traced around the planet. These imaginary lines mark the northernmost and southernmost limits on the earth reached by the changing position of the overhead sun, and they join the points where the sun shines in a vertical position on the days of the summer solstices for each of the two hemispheres. The line to the north is called the tropic of Cancer, and the line to the south is called the tropic of Capricorn.

By definition, "the Tropics" or "the Torrid Zone" refers to the geographical area lying between these two lines, which indicate the latitudes 23°27′, north and south, respectively. The equator cuts through this broad intertropical band, at latitude 0°, dividing the earth's Northern and Southern Hemispheres from each other. This is the most astonishing region of any on the planet. It receives such an abundance of solar energy that the most complex of the earth's ecosystems flourish there, and the majority of the various known forms of life are concentrated there.

Considering the variation of the incidence of the sun's rays, and, therefore, of their concentration over a given unit of the earth's surface, we pass from a maximum near the equator, where the sun's rays are closest to perpendicular more often, to a minimum at the poles, where the sun's rays are very oblique. Along this path from the hot to the cold, we can speak of several climatic zones. Within and around the Tropics we can broadly distinguish:

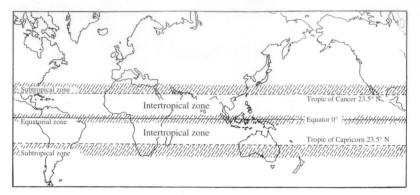

Geographical boundaries of the tropical area. The intertropical zone is defined as the entire area between the tropic of Cancer and the tropic of Capricorn. The portions immediately outside the two tropics are referred to as the subtropical zones. The band centered on the equator is called the equatorial zone.

- the equatorial zone, which is the band extending to a few degrees on either side of 0° latitude;
- the tropical zone, which is the entire region lying between the tropic of Cancer and the tropic of Capricorn; and
- the subtropical zones, which are the regions located immediately outside the tropical zone.

Often when we use the term "Tropics," we mean a concept, rather than a geographical designation. While most people could describe a generic tropical landscape, there would certainly be fewer who have a good idea of which of our world's countries actually lie within the tropical region, or who are aware of the great diversity in the various types of tropical landscapes and habitats. And fewer still would be able to relate the absolutely amazing history of these latitudes—a history filled with cataclysmic upheavals—by tracing through the geological and geographical evolution of the planet.

Continents in Evolution

The world hasn't always looked the same as the way we know it today. Besides the current geographical arrangement, there also exists a geography of the past, or better, a history of the geography of the planet, which tells us of dramatic and extraordinary events, of phenomena so vast

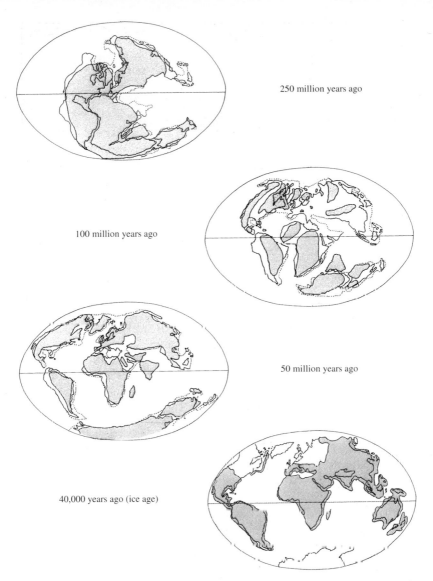

250 million years ago

100 million years ago

50 million years ago

40,000 years ago (ice age)

Some of the principal stages in the evolution of the geography of our planet. Note how certain of the present continents previously had terrestrial points of contact that acted as dispersal corridors. This is the reason for current faunal and botanical analogies among different regions that are widely separated.

Tropical Countries An asterisk (*) indicates countries only partially contained within the tropical belt. A degree symbol (°) indicates countries through which the equator passes.

AFRICA

Algeria*	Gabon°	Nigeria
Angola	Gambia	Reunion (France)
Benin	Ghana	Rwanda
Botswana*	Guinea	St. Helena (UK)
Burkina Faso	Guinea-Bissau	São Tomé and Principe
Burundi	Ivory Coast	Senegal
Cameroon	Kenya°	Seychelles
Cape Verde	Liberia	Sierra Leone
Central African Republic	Libya*	Somalia°
Chad	Madagascar*	South Africa*
Comoros	Malawi	Sudan
Congo°	Maldives	Tanzania
DRC (the Democratic Republic	Mali*	Togo
of Congo, formerly Zaire)°	Mauritania*	Uganda°
Djibouti	Mauritius	Western Sahara*
Egypt*	Mayotte (France)	Zambia
Equatorial Guinea	Mozambique*	Zimbabwe
Eritrea	Namibia*	
Ethiopia	Niger	

ASIA

Bangladesh*	Kiritimati	Sri Lanka
Brunei	Laos	Taiwan*
Cambodia	Malaysia	Thailand
China*	Myanmar*	United Arab Emirates*
Cocos (or Keeling Islands)	Oman*	Vietnam
(Australia)	Philippines	Yemen
India*	Saudi Arabia*	
Indonesia°	Singapore	

CENTRAL AMERICA AND CARIBBEAN

Anguilla	El Salvador	Nicaragua
Antigua and Barbuda	Grenada	Netherlands Antilles
Aruba	Guatemala	Panama
Bahamas*	Guadeloupe	Puerto Rico
Barbados	Haiti	St. Kitts and Nevis
Belize	Honduras	St. Lucia
Cayman Islands (UK)	Jamaica	St. Vincent and the
Costa Rica	Martinique	Grenadines
Cuba	(France)	Trinidad and Tobago
Dominica	Mexico*	Turks and Caicos Isles (UK)
Dominican Republic	Montserrat	Virgin Islands

OCEANIA		
American Samoa	Marshall Islands	Papua New Guinea
Australia*	Micronesia	Solomon Islands
Cook Islands	Nauru	Tokelau (NZ)
Fiji	New Caledonia	Tonga
French Polynesia (France)	Niue	Tuvalu
Hawaiian Islands (USA)	Northern Mariana	Vanuatu
Guam (USA)	Isles	Wallis and Futuna Islands
Kiribati	Palau	Western Samoa
SOUTH AMERICA		
Argentina*	Colombia°	Paraguay*
Bolivia	Ecuador°	Peru
Brazil°	French Guiana	Suriname
Chile*	Guyana	Venezuela

and awesome that they are almost unbelievable. If we could just step into a time machine and run through the past again at will, we would see for ourselves those strange and unexpected facts that geologists and fossil scholars (paleontologists) have reconstructed and demonstrated using scientific induction. Thousands of years ago, for example, or hundreds of thousands, or even millions of years ago, the location of the city we live in may have been a lagoon or a sea, possibly with a tropical or a polar climate. The morphological and climatic aspects of the planet have never been static, but rather they have always been changing, slowly and progressively.

The nature of the origin of our planet, the formation of the seas, and the emerging of the lands will always remain theoretical, and our ideas of these are based on greater or lesser probabilities. Even today, the original layout of the continents is not known with absolute certainty, but paleogeographers generally accept the theory, supported primarily by botanical evidence, that about 250 million years ago, in the late Permian period, all of the continents were united into a single land mass called **Pangea.**

This unified terrestrial formation surrounded by the sea was the one from which the various continental "plates" then began to fracture off and shift. During the Jurassic period (around 180 million years ago), one of the blocks, referred to as **Gondwana,** which included the current Africa, South America, Australia, Antarctica, India, and Madagascar, separated from a second block, known as **Laurasia,** which was the conglomerate of North America, Greenland, and Eurasia. From that point on, various episodes of fracturing and rejoining occurred throughout the ages, up until the composition of the current geographical arrangement of the continents, which are still undergoing a slow process of evolution. The birth of geographical barriers, such as seas and mountain chains, or their successive disappearance, and the splitting off or rejoining of continents down through the various epochs are all phenomena that have profoundly influenced the processes of the distribution and colonization of life on the planet.

The presence of certain of the same botanical families in the flora of tropical forests located in Amazonia (the Amazon River basin), in Malaysia, and in equatorial Africa, for example, is a result of the fact that the ancestors of these modern plant families were once part of the immense, continuous forests that covered the ancient Gondwana.

Continental Drift. The history of geology begins with such fantastic origins that it might seem more like an amusing fable than a scientific explanation of natural processes.

Two hundred million years ago, the continent of South America was still united with Africa. After about 65 million years, these two land masses began to drift apart and separate, so that the "Latin" continent was left isolated, and so it remained for a long period before it joined with North America. The Americas were still separated even as recently as 2 million years ago, at the end of the Pliocene epoch. In the Upper Cretaceous period, about 80 million years ago, Europe was still separated from Asia by the Sea of Obik, which has since vanished, and North America was divided by a long oceanic channel; and while the eastern portion was united with Greenland and Europe, the western part was connected with Asia "via" the present Alaska. At the end of the Cretaceous period (about 70 million years ago), South America finally became detached from Africa, but was still connected to Antarctica, which, in turn, was united with Australia.

One hundred twenty million years ago, Asia was already a single great block, while India was in the process of splitting off from Africa. After traveling 7,000 km (4,400 mi) over a period of 100 million years, India finally concluded its journey about 45 million years ago, colliding with Asia and thus originating the immense Himalayan range, which includes the mountains of Tibet, southern China, Myanmar, and Indochina, one of the most imposing mountain systems in the world today. This occurred at about the same time that Australia became completely detached from Antarctica and Europe separated from Greenland, joining with Asia.

In the Paleocene epoch (60 million years ago) a "strange" looking fauna arrived in South America, coming from the northern continent, across the land bridge provided by Central America. These were the condylarths, the didelphids, and the paleanodonts, distant relatives of our present-day armadillos, opossums, anteaters, and sloths.

In the Upper Eocene epoch (40 million years ago), a second wave of species, including the lemurids and primitive rodents, was able to migrate, despite the discontinuities in the uniting land masses, by passing from one island to another. At the end of the Pliocene epoch (1 to 2 million years ago), a newly reestablished contact with North America allowed access to horses, tapirs, deer, insectivores, bears, and lagomorphs (hares and rabbits). The origins of the faunal composition of South America today actually span a vast time range: we find descendants of the ancient colonizers, like the armadillos, sloths, and marsupials, living together with some of the later island hoppers, like the modern monkeys and rodents, and also with the latest arrivals, which include peccaries, deer, tapirs, and insectivores, among others.

The Ice Ages

Invaders from the North, Glacial Relicts. The glacial periods are another phenomenon of great importance in understanding the natural history of the planet. At the end of the Tertiary and in the Quaternary period, when the world had already become populated by an innumerable series of animals and plants, many cycles of climatic alternations occurred, which included phases of marked reductions in the temperature, or glaciations, followed by warm interglacial stages. One of the most interesting effects of the glacial stages, from the point of view of the colonization of flora and fauna, is connected with the migration of northern species into temperate or even tropical latitudes during those mighty global climatic events, the glaciations. When these "cold tides" withdrew, certain species were left in particular microclimates or mountains that preserved the cold necessary for them, and there they were left stranded as though in refuge

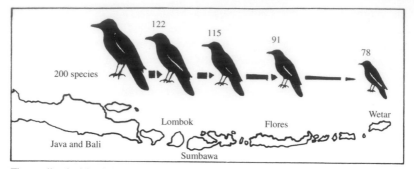

The smaller the islands are, and the farther away from the mainland, the fewer living species they exhibit. This is referred to as the "island effect."

conditions. Many of the great mountains of the Tropics now represent the only areas for the survival of species that once were widespread throughout these latitudes. The beautiful *Dendrosenecio* and giant lobelia, for example, are forms of plant life that today are imprisoned in the high altitudes of some eastern African mountains, such as Mounts Kenya and Kilimanjaro, and they will not venture down from their islands of cold within the hot seas of the underlying savannas.

With the cooling of the climate, the volumes of ice trapped in the upper latitudes increased enormously. In the Northern Hemisphere, perennial glaciers reached and occupied Scandinavia and central Europe, while a thick, wide polar ice pack extended around the continent of Antarctica. The water that solidified into ice was subtracted from the oceans, which caused the sea levels during the ice ages to be as much as 100 m (110 yd) lower than they are today. As a consequence, many stretches of the ocean bottom emerged, and entire chains of islands became united, producing a favorable situation that promoted movements of fauna and colonizations of flora. Later, species were halted again in their migration because climatic conditions changed, and many terrestrial connections were interrupted again by new temperature increases and glacial melting.

The **Wallacea** is not a region that you will find named in a geography book. It belongs to the fascinating discipline of biogeography, the science that studies the relationships and the history of the distribution of life on the planet. Through a study of the ancient relations and positions of the

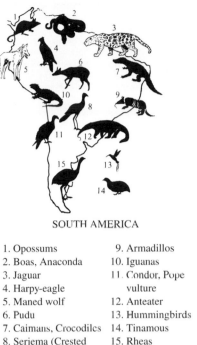

SOUTH AMERICA		AFRICA	

1. Opossums	9. Armadillos	1. Insectivores (shrews,	8. Secretary bird
2. Boas, Anaconda	10. Iguanas	hedgehogs, etc.)	9. Pangolins
3. Jaguar	11. Condor, Pope	2. Pythons	10. Agamas
4. Harpy-eagle	vulture	3. Leopard	11. Vultures
5. Maned wolf	12. Anteater	4. Crowned eagles	12. Aardvark
6. Pudu	13. Hummingbirds	5. Wild dog (or	13. Sunbirds
7. Caimans, Crocodiles	14. Tinamous	Licaone)	14. Francolins
8. Seriema (Crested	15. Rheas	6. Duikers	15. Ostrich
screamer)		7. Crocodiles	

(Animals listed as plurals exhibit multiple species.)

At one time South America and Africa were joined, and to this we can attribute the presence of related species on both continents today, that is, species belonging to the same genera or families. Other similarities between isolated species are attributable to the fact that certain species have occupied the same ecological niches and have adopted the same survival strategies in environments that are similar, such as the rainforests found in Amazonia and in western or central Africa, by the process known as evolutionary convergence.

various regions of the globe, it is possible to understand many apparent enigmas in the present distributions of flora and fauna. "Wallace's Line," named for the English naturalist who described it, clearly demarcates the Australian region from the Indo-Malayan region, or, in technical terms, it separates the Malayan, or continental Asian, plate from the Australo-Papuan, also known as the Sahul plate. Makassar Strait, which passes

The History of the Tapir

The current distribution of the tapir *(Tapyrus)* is a good example demonstrating why bioge-ography (or, in this case, historical biogeography) is so useful for understanding more about tropical wildlife. Today there are three species living in South America and one in Malaysia. Such a scattered distribution can only be explained by knowing their colonization pattern, starting from a common ancestor, the *Paleotapyrus,* which was distributed in Eurasia during the Upper Eocene (40 million years ago). During the first wave of colonization, the animals (which had evolved into a successive genus, the *Protapyrus*) migrated into Europe and to-wards the east, to Siberia, China, and Southeast Asia. These species succeeded even in tra-versing the Bering Strait, and, in the Pleistocene epoch (1 million years ago), they arrived in Canada and the northern United States. From here, as soon as the two Americas were joined, the tapir reached the southern continent, where it still survives.

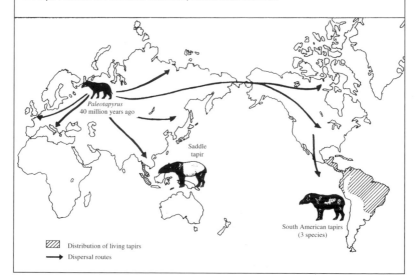

Paleotapyrus
40 million years ago

Saddle
tapir

South American tapirs
(3 species)

▨▨▨ Distribution of living tapirs
➤ Dispersal routes

between the islands of Sulawesi and Borneo and on down between Bali and Lombok, is so deep that it has resisted every glacial period, maintain-ing the separation between these two blocks of land emerging from the ocean. The Indonesian islands, on the other hand, were united to one an-other and to the Malay Peninsula for many years, just as New Guinea was to Australia. Thus, that "simple" strait is responsible for the surprising differences between the flora and fauna existing just to the north or to the

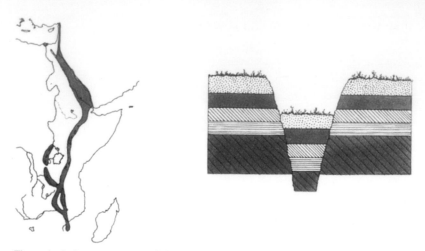

The geological processes responsible for the evolution of continents continue right under our very eyes. The figure illustrates the diagram of the fracture that is opening in eastern Africa, giving rise to the Great Rift Valley, whose fissure coincides with the Red Sea and a long series of lakes. The Horn of Africa could perhaps be starting to move off to become an island. The fracture starts in Turkey and continues on to southern Africa.

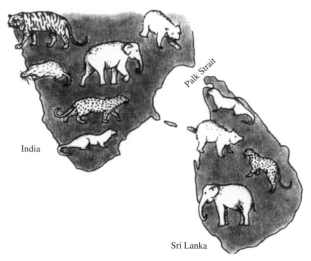

Some of the species characteristic of India, such as the tiger, do not exist in Sri Lanka, despite its closeness to southern India.

Madagascar: 100 Million Years As an Island

What today is the fourth largest island in the world (or the third, if Greenland is, as many think, actually an archipelago covered by ice) enjoys a rather remarkable record: it has been an island for over 100 million years. At one time it was part of the supercontinent Gondwana and later was separated from this by the formation of the Mozambique Channel. This passage of water is very deep and difficult to cross, so life on the island evolved in a prolonged climate of isolation, which is the principal reason for the extraordinary floral and faunal differences on either side of the strait, as well as for today's extremely high percentage of animal and plant species that are endemic, that is, exclusive to Madagascar. With about 30 living species of lemurs, of which about 95% are endemic, Madagascar is rightly termed the island of the lemurs, as it is here that these gentle prosimians have best resisted the evolutionary attack of modern monkeys. Although in Africa and Asia monkeys have entered into competition with the primitive lemurs, superseding them and driving them almost to the point of extinction, no monkeys have ever reached Madagascar, so lemurs have been able to differentiate and evolve there.

Today in Madagascar, there are 50 living species of chameleons, which account for about two-thirds of all the world's species. Some are extremely large, such as the *Chamaleo oustaleti*, a world record holder with its length of nearly 70 cm (28 in); some are extremely small, such as the *Brookesia minima*, another world record holder, at barely 3.2 cm (1.3 in).

The only existing amphibians are frogs, but there are nearly 150 different species of these (98% endemic), as opposed to the 100 present in all of southern Africa. The reptile species number nearly 270, of which about 90% are endemic, and here we find boas and iguanas typical of Asia and America, respectively, although lizards are entirely absent. The bird species are relatively few, with only about 250, of which 40% are endemic, compared to the more than 600 in nearby Zambia.

The floristic field also enjoys an outstanding exclusivity. Of the 133 palms present, 128 are endemic to the island, while 80% of the approximately 12,000 species of Madagascar's flowering plants exist nowhere else.

Despite the apparent contradictions and the doubts that remain, the current composition of the island's animal and plant life appears to date back to the ancient detachment of Madagascar from Gondwana, with additions from the successive colonizations facilitated by land bridges that appeared between islands during the glacial epochs, all of which has contributed to the development of this "promised land" for naturalists and tropical nature enthusiasts.

south of the line. The marsupials that are so typical of Australia are absent in Asia. The parakeets and parrots that are so abundant in Australia have never become widespread in Southeast Asia; and woodpeckers, which flourish there, are scarcely to be found in the Papuan or Australian forests, even though these are equally luxuriant.

New Archipelagoes and Land Bridges. Seventeen million years ago broad expanses of the low seas dividing Africa from Asia dried up, leaving a sort of bridge of dry land that connected those tropical latitudes before

Australian Marsupials

The order of marsupials is distributed throughout South, Central, and parts of North America, Australia, New Guinea, Sulawesi, and other members of the Sunda Islands.

At one time, marsupials were broadly distributed in Eurasia as well, before the placental mammals appeared and asserted themselves as competitors, and it was from this point precisely that they reached the continent of Australia, by means of the Malay Peninsula and the bridge formed by the islands of Indonesia, which were more or less connected then. The Australia of that time was more humid than today, as demonstrated by the fossil remains of kangaroos three meters high and marsupials as large as rhinoceroses, both of which must have required luxuriant vegetation for survival.

The marsupial colonies experienced a great diversification and a rapid distribution throughout Oceania, as they were left in greater tranquility when Australia separated completely from the other continents, about 50 million years ago. There were no great mountain barriers, and those vast spaces were shared only by a few monotremes (relatives of the present-day duck-billed platypuses) that had arrived in the same manner. In fact, it was only about 30 million years ago that the placental rodents and, later, the bats arrived. This is the reason for the great wealth of marsupials in Australia today. Because they occupied different habitats and multiple ecological niches that were devoid of competition, the various species were able to differentiate among themselves in a prodigious manner, based on that process biologists call adaptive radiation. In such a natural scenario, one that was entirely "up for grabs," the marsupial species developed specialized devices that they share in common with many other mammals living in similar environments on different continents. This well-noted phenomenon of evolutionary convergence has given rise to marsupial "moles" and "cats," marsupial versions of jumping mice and flying squirrels, and the cuscus, which reminds us, for all intents and purposes, of a prosimian. The thylacine, or marsupial "wolf," which is also exemplary of this convergence, has been, sadly, extinct since 1934.

Marsupial mouse
Antechinomys spenceri

Marsupial cat
Dasyurus quoll

the glaciations of the late Cenozoic era. Later, following the development of deserts in Africa and the Middle East and the birth of the Red Sea (during the Pliocene epoch), the two continents were again divided.

Later still, in the early Miocene epoch, the sea level lowered between Africa and tropical Asia, favoring an increase of biological transit. The rhinoceroses, elephants, apes, lemurs, lorises, and pangolins that are found on both continents today are a faunal analogy that exists in demonstration of that ancient connection. (Note, also, that there are no apes in tropical America, only monkeys.)

The "typical" fauna of Africa, such as the zebras, buffaloes, antelopes, giraffes, and warthogs, in reality, is more recent. Their predecessors were first noted only after the middle Miocene epoch (about 10 million years ago). At the time India split off from it, eastern Africa, as well, was covered with luxuriant rainforests. Then, in the late Miocene (about 7 million years ago), it shifted up to its current position farther north, taking on its characteristically drier climate. The forests were replaced by scattered woods and grasslands, and the rainy jungles that remained were confined to the western versants of the continent and the upper altitudes of the eastern mountain ranges.

So, we see, it is only in this manner, using our knowledge of the fascinating history of the movements of the land masses on the globe—continents that drift about like rafts, peninsulas and archipelagoes that emerge only to sink again—that we can fully comprehend the differences and similarities between various forms of animal and plant life and their distribution throughout today's geography.

5. *Borassus* palms along the Selous River.

Chapter 2

The Climate

Most of us base our mental images of the Tropics on the deeply rooted perception the general public holds of this region. Whenever we think about the Tropics, we visualize impenetrable, luxuriant vegetation, with palm trees on white beaches and crystalline waters rich with coral gardens. We see "tropical," thus, as synonymous with light and color: Nature at her most exuberant. And when we go to the Tropics, we all go for the hot, shining sun.

Although a part of this may be true, as for all commonplaces, these images may also harbor some errors or suffer from excessive generalization. It would be reductive to maintain such a view of tropical climatology—both reductive and risky. Indeed, many tourists are disappointed by the torrential rains, by low nightly or seasonal temperatures, by the turbidity of the sea, or by the dense blankets of clouds that shatter the stereotypes of azure skies and a scorching sun; but these, too, are part of "the Tropics."

Different Climates from the Equator to the Tropics

Because the Tropics are not just a single geographic band having a uniform climate, it is useful to call attention immediately to the differences among the equatorial, the subequatorial, the tropical, and the subtropical zones.

Along the equatorial band, the climatic conditions are particularly stable and homogeneous, whereas, towards those latitudes that are more properly referred to as tropical, the geographic variations can actually be quite marked. Notable variations exist that are primarily related to the effects of the continental masses, marine currents, and wind patterns. In particular, some of the parameters that vary are humidity, rainfall, temperature, and wind, gainsaying, in certain cases, an apparent geographic or climatic homogeneity.

Consider, for example, the western part of Africa, where the climate is extremely rainy, giving rise to one of the most luxuriant tropical forests in the world. This area is divided into two zones by what is known as the Dahomey Gap, a sort of semiarid wedge that interrupts this land of rainforests. The coast here describes the direction WSW-ENE, so that it forms a very acute angle with respect to the prevailing winds, which thus bear little humidity there.

The term **wet tropics** (or "humid tropics" or "moist tropics") refers to those regions having temperatures that average around 25°C (77°F), accompanied by elevated rainfall. Generally, these extend as far as about 5° to 10° latitude north and south of the equatorial line and tend to cover their greatest latitudinal extensions on the eastern sides of the continents (a highly accentuated case of this is seen in South America) or in certain tracts along the coasts. Exceptionally, however, local morphological factors can also motivate a wet tropical climate, even at a notable distance from the equator. The wet tropics occupy about one-third of the intertropical lands, and in these same areas we can also find deserts, savannas, or mountainous habitats.

Another characteristic of the equatorial zone is the low monthly variation of its high average temperature. Rarely is there a difference of more than 3°C (5°F) between any two months of the year; practically speaking, the seasons do not even exist here.

It is a common error to associate the Tropics with an intense heat. The humidity of the Tropics does maximize the sense of heat, but in actual fact, the maximum seasonal temperatures are much higher in many extra-tropical areas, even if these maximums are reached less frequently. In Amazonia, for example, the average temperature in the dry season is 27.9°C (82.2°F) and, in the wet season, 25.8°C (78.4°F). In Kalimantan (the Indonesian part of Borneo, the south and east part of the island), the temperature varies between 21°C (70°F) and 33°C (91°F) throughout the year, with humidity from 60% to 100%. Compare this with the

40°C (104°F) temperatures easily reached during midsummer in Rome, New York, or Tokyo! Furthermore, the daily variations in temperature can measure excursions between day and night of more than 10°C (18°F). It is one of the peculiarities of the climate at the equator that the daily temperature excursions often exceed the annual variation of maximum temperatures. While the maximal seasonal temperatures in the temperate latitudes can vary as much as 30 to 40°C (54 to 72°F) between winter and summer, at the equator, where no real seasons exist, these variations are often limited to 5°C (9°F). The temperature excursions between day and night at the equator can be far greater than this, and if the geography includes mountains, upland plains, or deserts, these variations can be even more accentuated.

Intertropical Climatic Zones. Between the equatorial region and either tropic, we define the "intertropical zones," where the seasons are more distinct, and, in general, the precipitation is concentrated into certain periods of the year, which are referred to as the "wet" or "rainy" seasons.

Climates within the Tropics

According to certain authors, tropical climates can be divided into five principal zones:

- *Wet (or Humid or Moist) Tropical Zone.* Refers to the equatorial and subequatorial regions, which have climatic homogeneity and precipitation within the range of 2,000 to 10,000 mm (80 to 400 in), or even more.
- *Monsoon Tropical Zone.* Two principal seasons alternate, characterized by marked differences in rainfall. This is the typical climate for the tropical regions around the Indian Ocean or, to a lesser extent, those of the Indo-Pacific Ocean.
- *"Wet and Dry" (or Seasonal) Tropical Zone.* Here seasons exist that are not primarily influenced by an actual monsoon system. This type of climate appears in the majority of the areas that are properly referred to as intertropical, rather than equatorial.
- *Semiarid Tropical Zone.* Has the same pattern as the preceding climate, but this is produced by local conditions related to morphological factors, to the circulation of the winds, or to the presence of mountain ranges or other geographical relief.
- *Arid Tropical Zone.* Coincides, for the most part, with the vast subtropical desert systems encroaching upon intertropical areas. In certain cases, this type of zone can also result from the effects of the presence of major geographic relief or of marine currents along the coasts.

Even though the divisions between one category and the next are not precisely defined, it is possible to distinguish a large number of intermediary subdivisions, each of which is characterized in particular by its annual level of precipitation and by the distribution of rainfall throughout the course of the year.

The annual temperature excursion is still limited here, and does not exceed an average of 8 to 10°C (14 to 18°F). This is a zone where the natural vegetation tends toward savanna or deciduous woods (dry tropical forests). Daily temperature variations are lower during the hot and rainy period and more marked during the dry and colder period. It is often the case that the hottest months are those that immediately precede the rainy season, when precipitation and cloudiness lower the temperatures.

Scorching Sun and Pelting Rains

An equatorial position ensures not only a more direct and constant **insolation** than in subtropical or temperate areas, but also the absence of marked annual variations in the length of the day. This follows logically from the fact that the spherical form of the earth imposes an unequal distribution of the solar radiation over the surface of the globe. Solar rays incident at 90° are at their maximum concentration, so that a given surface area struck perpendicularly by the sun's rays receives more heat than the same area would in the zones that are struck obliquely. In March and September, on the respective equinoxes, the sun's rays strike the equator at exactly 90°, shifting somewhat from this incidence at this latitude during the other months. The point where the rays of the sun have an incidence perpendicular to the ground varies with the seasons, reaching its northernmost latitude at the tropic of Cancer (approximately 23.5° N) in June on the "summer" solstice, and reaching its southernmost latitude at the tropic of Capricorn (approximately 23.5° S) in December, on the "winter" solstice. The changing of this point of the overhead sun describes the so-called solar equator, and no other place on earth gets perpendicular solar rays during the year. It is precisely on the basis of this phenomenon—and on the latitudinal limits reached by the overhead sun—that the Tropics, as a climatic and ecological region, are determined.

Because of the way in which radiation from the sun strikes the earth's surface at the various latitudes, temperatures increase going from the poles to the equator. Insolation at the equator is basically uniform throughout the year, with no major variations, and this results in the fact that seasons, which are characterized by differences in temperature and length of day, do not manifest as they do elsewhere. In fact, one detail that is often little appreciated by tourists at the equator is the early sunset, which occurs about six in the afternoon! This is offset by an equally precocious dawn, which thus accounts for the twelve hours of daylight that are typical at the equator.

The Tropics, we see, experience an elevated and constant insolation, meaning that this region receives more heat than any other on the globe. One of the principal effects of this heating is the circulation up into the atmosphere of this relative surplus of thermal energy produced by the sun. In accordance with a simple theory that was proposed as early as 1735, the air that is warmed at the equator and in the Tropics rises into the atmosphere because of its relatively low density, causing an area of low pressure below itself. Then, after having reached a certain height, the air currents transport these masses of warm air toward the upper latitudes, usually stopping at about 20° to 30°. Along its path through the upper altitudes, the air slowly cools and begins to descend because of its increasing relative density, then forming high pressure areas around the subtropical regions, which is one reason why subtropical latitudes often exhibit desert-like or arid areas, characterized by a significantly reduced rainfall. This air mass then can either move back toward the equator or, alternatively, it can move toward the poles. The model just described is complicated in actual fact by a number of variables, primarily relating to the oceans and continental masses, but, in general, it represents the phenomenon well.

It is not only the intensity of the solar rays that varies in the Tropics, but also their quality. The concentration of **ozone** in the stratosphere decreases from the poles to the equator and, with this, so does its screening effect of the sun's ultraviolet rays. In the tropical areas, therefore, the ultraviolet component of the solar spectrum reaches the soil with a greater intensity, being screened less by this important natural filter. On the other hand, the greater humidity of the Tropics in relation to the temperate or northern areas represents a second ultraviolet screening element, albeit less effective than that of the ozone molecules. Indeed, in the mountains, ultraviolet rays are filtered even less, because of the low air density and the lesser quantity of humidity. It is the greater power of the solar rays and the elevated percentage of ultraviolet rays that are responsible for the deeply rooted stereotype of the "scorching sun" of the Tropics. In effect, sunburn and erythema—sometimes quite serious cases—can easily result from unprotected or prolonged exposure.

The climate of a tropical region is influenced by many factors connected to its terrestrial morphology, and especially to the presence of mountain ranges. Tropical mountains have their own particular characteristics, and, because of their elevated average temperatures, they present an ecology that is notably different than those of mountain ranges in the temperate regions. One aspect of a mountain climate is the prevalence of strong winds, and these winds originate from the motion of the warm air that ascends from below. The atmosphere of the mountains does not heat up as does that of the plains, however, because the rarefied air pressure of the former, which equates to a lower air density, implies a lower water vapor density, as well. These factors cause the heat resulting from solar radiation to be retained to a lesser degree, so that the energy disperses without heating the air. It is for these same reasons that the mountain temperatures can drop so rapidly at night: at 3,000 m (10,000 ft) the temperature can drop by 15 to 20°C (27 to 36°F) during the night, depending upon whether or not there are clouds present.

As a general relation between altitude and temperature, there is an average drop of 0.6°C (1.1°F) for every hundred meters of height above sea level; but this varies greatly depending on many factors, such as the season, the hour of the day, the exposure, and the humidity.

Nighttime Condensation and . . . Evening Rains. A given amount of water moisture in the air will represent a higher percentage of the saturation quantity of water vapor when the temperature is lower, so in the mountains, and especially in the forests, the relative humidity is high. During the night, when it cools, because of an elevated thermal excursion, the condensation point is frequently reached and dew is deposited. The same effect occurs in certain deserts, where, exaggerated by the low humidity, the thermal excursion between day and night is extremely marked. Also, clouds form when rising warm, humid air expands and cools, nearing the condensation point. When this point is reached, it starts raining. This is the reason why the majority of rains form in the afternoon in the wet tropical latitudes, or, alternatively, during the night, after the humidity evaporated during the day condenses and causes precipitation.

During the wet months in the Tropics, clouds will often cloak the mountains all day long for several days in a row. Frequently during the dry months, a ring of clouds will form around 2,000 m (6,600 ft), and then higher up it may be clear again. In many tropical and equatorial regions, the rains are generally scattered throughout the year, particularly the eve-

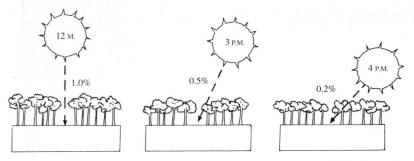

The canopy of a primary tropical forest absorbs the solar rays to an astonishing degree. At noon on a cloudless day, an average of merely 1% of the available light reaches the ground. This value decreases to 0.5% at 3 P.M. and to 0.2% at 4 P.M. These percentages are even lower on cloudy days. The light from the full moon never penetrates below the dense, leafy layer of the canopy.

ning and night rains, although during the rainy season it rains for several hours every day. Before the rain, the air becomes quite sticky, and afterwards it is pleasantly cool, often with sunshine.

Clouds, Mountains, and Rains. In the mountains, there are extreme amounts of rain on the slopes exposed to the prevailing winds. Cherrapundji in Myanmar, which is nestled in a position sheltered by high mountains that promote the gathering of rain-laden clouds, is one of the rainiest places in the world, receiving up to 12 m (470 in) per year. Geographic relief significantly influences the climate, sometimes by promoting "slope rains," or, contrarily, the mountains may impede the passage of clouds. Consider, for example, the south of Sri Lanka, where the mountains at the crest of the island block the monsoon clouds, causing a dry season on the leeward slope and a wet season on the exposed slope, where the clouds gather; the seasons change with the alternation of the monsoons.

In Madagascar, the high crest of the mountain blocks the humid currents coming from the east. To the northeast an extraordinary rainforest flourishes, receiving up to 4,000 mm (160 in) of precipitation (at Sainte-Marie). To the northwest, a dry, deciduous tropical forest flourishes; to the central west, a beautiful baobab savanna opens out; and to the southwest, with barely 300 mm (12 in) of rain per year (at Anakao), the only type of forest able to grow is of the thorny, subdesert sort.

Cyclones and Hurricanes

One of the most well-known and awesome demonstrations of force in the Tropics is the cyclone. Basically, these are closed, low-pressure systems, having diameters of about 600 to 700 km (375 to 450 mi). The inner part of the cyclone is referred to as "the eye," generally measuring some tens of kilometers in width and characterized by weaker winds and relatively clear skies. Cyclones are associated with very violent winds and torrential rains. They have various local names in the areas struck with the greatest regularity, such as "hurricane" in the West Indies, "typhoon" in the China Sea, "willy-willy" in Australia, or "cyclone" in the Bay of Bengal. In order for a cyclone to develop, an elevated atmospheric humidity is necessary. In fact, we often find them in correspondence with the most elevated temperatures on the surface of the sea, such as up to 27°C (81°F), for example, along the western portions of oceans in the late summer. The humidity provides the latent heat necessary to trigger the cyclone and to produce rain. When a cyclone passes over onto land, it quickly disperses. Most frequently, cyclones occur in areas within 5° of the equator. Normally, their average life is one week, and they involve an enormous rainfall (for example, 2,000 mm, or 79 inches, in one day, recorded in the Philippines). Because of the extremely low pressures with which they are associated, they can cause spectacular rises in the sea level. The typhoons that occur in Japan—and, in the United States, the hurricanes—derive from the lower latitudes. The Bay of Bengal and the Ganges delta are highly subject to the development of cyclones, as are the Philippines, the West Indies, and northern Australia. Hurricane winds can blow as hard as 160 km/h (100 mph), usually averaging about 120 km/h (75 mph). Their effects on coasts and islands can be disastrous, both for man and for natural habitats. In 1970, a cyclone in Bangladesh claimed nearly a million victims, while the more recent hurricane Gilbert that ravaged the eastern coast of Jamaica destroyed a large part of the forests there, with winds blowing at 220 km/h (135 mph)

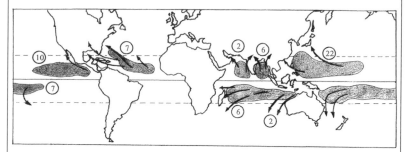

Distribution, frequency, and movement of tropical cyclones. The number indicates the approximate frequency throughout the year.

Seasonal Winds

Soil has a low thermal capacity, which means that it receives and disperses heat from the sun very quickly. Any heat gathered in the soil during the summer is rapidly lost by conduction during the winter, just as the heat gathered there during the day is rapidly lost during the night. Water behaves differently, however, and the heated water in the oceans' large volumes moves by convection and is transported down to the depths, affecting large masses of material. Furthermore, water has a considerable thermal capacity, which means that it tends more slowly and gradually to liberate the heat that it has absorbed. These differences have an enormous influence on the atmospheric pressure. For instance, large continental masses, like Eurasia, tend to have high pressure zones in the winter and low pressure zones in the summer because of the heating of the air and its rising. This, then, influences the direction of the winds and contributes to the various phenomena characterizing the monsoon system.

For centuries, and even millennia, the inversions of the winds and the rains that characterize the climate for a large part of the tropical regions of Asia have aroused interest and attempts at explanations among the local populations. These events are the **monsoons,** or seasonal winds that invert twice a year, changing from humid and inconstant to dry and stable, or vice versa. The term monsoon derives from *mausim,* which means "season" in Arabic. Monsoon-like events are not unique to southern Asia; they also appear, though to a lesser extent, in regions such as the western coasts of Africa and the northern coast of Australia. The Indian monsoon, which is the most typical and the most powerful of these inversions, is actually a gigantic land-sea-land breeze caused by the differences in temperature between the Eurasian continental mass and the Indian Ocean. Out at sea, temperature and pressure variations are mitigated, but on the continent, these variations are amplified.

The tropical zone that ranges from India to Indonesia is bordered on the north by the immense Asiatic continental mass and to the south by the great Indian Ocean. In the winter, the continent cools and generates high pressures, whereas on the ocean, the southern sun heats and generates low pressures. This difference of pressures results in an air current that blows from the land to the ocean, chasing away the clouds; and this is the dry season.

In the spring, the sun returns to heat the land on the continent, and the pressures and air circulation invert. The winds blowing from south-

Climates of Some Tropical Nations

NATION	DRY SEASON	RAINY SEASON
Angola	May–September	October–April
Antilles	February–April	June–November (typhoons)
		August–September (hotter, more humid)
Northern Australia	May–October	November–April (hotter, more humid)
Bahamas	December–March (more wind)	April–November
		September–October (hurricanes)
Bangladesh	December–February (less heat, less humidity)	June–October (cloudier, hotter, monsoons)
Belize	February–April	June–December (typhoons in October)
Botswana	May–September (cooler, more sun)	November–April
	October (more heat)	
Brazil (Amazonia)	June–October (south of the equator)	November–May (constant rain and humidity)
	November–February (north of the equator)	March–October (constant rain and humidity)
Comoro Islands	May–October (less heat, more sun)	November–April (more heat)
Congo	June–September	October–May (local variations)
Costa Rica	December–April (Pacific coast)	Somewhat variable along the Caribbean coast
Cuba	November–March (less heat, less humidity)	April–November
DRC	June–September (southern)	October–May (constant rain and humidity)
	December–February (northern)	March–November (constant rain and humidity)
Ecuador	June–November	December–May (constant rain and humidity)
Philippine Islands	December–February (less heat)	June–October (typhoons)
Gabon	June–September (cloudier)	October–February (more heat and humidity)
Guatemala (Pacific coast)	December–March	May–October
Haiti	December–March	April–October (more heat and humidity)
Hawaii (western coast)	May–September (more sun, hurricanes)	October–April (cloudier, more storms)
India	November–March (less heat)	June–October (monsoons)
	April–May (more heat)	
Indonesia	May–September	November–April

Kenya	July–October	November–December
	January–February	March–June
Madagascar	April–October (less heat, more sun)	November–March
Malaysia	June–September (eastern coast)	August–November (western coast)
Maldives	December–April	June–September (agitated sea, especially for the northern islands)
		October–November (southern islands)
Mauritius	June–November (less heat)	January–March (typhoons)
Myanmar	November–February ("cool" season)	June–October (cloudier, more heat, monsoons)
	March–May ("hot" season)	
Namibia	April–September (more effects to the northeast)	November–March (more effects to the northeast, more heat)
Nicaragua	December–April	June–October
		September–October (typhoons in the Atlantic)
Peru (Amazonia)	June–July (more coastal fog)	August–May (constant rain and humidity)
Polynesia	May–October (less heat)	November–March (more heat, more humidity)
Puerto Rico	January–March	May–December
Reunion	May–November	December–April
Seychelles	May–June	July–August
	September–November	December–April (more wind)
Senegal	October–May	June–September (coast and south)
Somalia	May–September (torrid heat along the north coast)	April–August (east coast)
Sri Lanka		
Southwest coast	January–March	April–December
North, east coasts	February–September	October–January
Tanzania	June–September	March–May
		November–January
Thailand	November–February	March–October
		September (typhoons)
Vanuatu	June–October (less heat)	December–May
Venezuela	December–April (less heat)	May–November
Zambia	May–October (more heat)	November–April
Zimbabwe	April–September (less heat, more sun)	November–March
	October (more heat)	

Note: Since any generalizations must necessarily involve approximations, the reader is invited to consider this chart to be indicative and to consult a guide specific to the destination for more precise information.

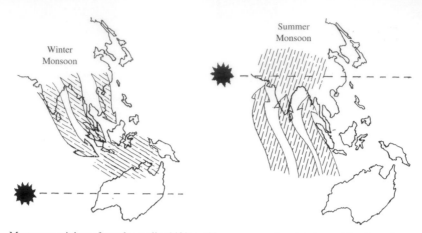

Winter
Monsoon

Summer
Monsoon

Monsoons originate from the cyclic shifting of large masses of moist air, resulting from the differences in temperature and air pressure between the oceans and the continent of Asia. The seasonal rainfall deriving therefrom influences the climate and ecology of these areas.

southwest bring rains that fall primarily in the summer. Between August and September, the climate changes markedly.

There are no monsoons along the coasts from Vietnam to Malaysia, nor, for the most part, in Indonesia. Here, the rains are more evenly distributed and not so markedly seasonal. To the east of Java, monsoons begin to appear again in certain areas. Indonesia experiences two yearly monsoon winds. The southeast monsoon brings dry weather (the *musim ponas,* or "dry season"), and the northwest monsoon brings rain (the *musim hujan,* or "rainy season"). In Indonesia, perhaps because of recent deforestation, the seasonal rains are becoming more unpredictable, with serious consequences for wildlife and people.

The flora and fauna of an area depend, in large part, on the climate. And it is therefore in the climate of the Tropics, with its abounding light, heat, and rain, distributed more or less uniformly throughout the course of the year, that we find the explanation for the great biological wealth exhibited there, as well as for the differences between its most characteristic and its most unique environments. Taking the time to learn about the climate of a region before undertaking a voyage, we see, becomes doubly important: first, in order to avoid unpleasant climatic surprises, and second, to know at what stage the flora and fauna of a location are in their yearly ecology.

Chapter 3

The Soils

W hen passing over the Tropics, whether overhead, in an airplane, or overland, aboard a jeep or pick-up, the dirt roads and trails that branch out through the dazzling green forests or golden yellow savannas appear, shockingly, like blood-red arteries penetrating this strangely colored "connective tissue." When the season is dry, these byways are the factories of an extremely fine and literally inescapable dust, and during the rains, they change into veritable rivers of mud.

Even though there are a number of exceptions and variations, on the whole, the soils of the Tropics can be generalized because of certain recurring characteristics they exhibit as a group. They are defined, specifically, as being lateritic (from the Latin *later*, "brick"), as they are very frequently of a bright red color.

Absence of Humus and Surface Decay or Litter. The high temperatures and elevated rainfall of the Tropics exaggerate the speeds of chemical and biological processes. These are the primary reasons for the intense and rapid bacterial decomposition of the majority of the fallen organic material that, in temperate areas, by contrast, would be deposited to make up humus and surface litter. In fact, one of the typical aspects of soils of the wet tropics is the absence or the greatly reduced quantities of organic material on the ground surface. Even in the most majestic and luxuriant of rainforests, all you need to do to encounter the red color of the soil is to lift the very first layer of decaying leaves. Although this may seem to be a contradiction, in reality, it is the logical consequence of the augmented activity of the bacteria and soil microfauna, which is facilitated by the constantly high temperatures and humidity.

Without colloidal elements such as humus, the nutritive elements have a difficult time withstanding the **leaching** and **washing away** that occurs—often violently—because of the abundance of the rains. This is the reason for another apparent contradiction. The soils of the wet tropics, those very soils we see housing the most imposing forests on the planet, are, all told, extremely poor in nutrients—in fact, nearly sterile. Just dig down a little bit. In spite of the fact that the soil is moist and seemingly inviting for a rich variety of hypogeal fauna, the poverty of the nutrients is such that earthworms and other typical subterranean detritivores (those creatures that consume and digest detritus) are extremely scarce. Because of this, the majority of the soils of the wet tropics are not fertile at all, and therefore are inadequate for long-term cultivation. The indigenous peoples of the rainforest areas have, in fact, throughout the millennia, developed the technique called **shifting cultivation.** Using this system, an area of small dimensions is deforested and cultivated for two or three years, thus taking maximum advantage of the naturally low level of fertility; the area is then abandoned in favor of another plot.

Certain agricultural practices that are used successfully in temperate regions, such as maintaining stable cultivations in the same area for a long time, instead produce serious erosion and promote desertification of the soil in the Tropics.

As noted above, it is possible to generalize tropical soils according to their flaming red hue. This color is one of the characteristics of soils that are properly lateritic, owing to the elevated presence of sesquioxides of iron and aluminum. In technical terms, these **red soils,** which are typical of about two-thirds of the wet tropics, are **oxisols** or **ferralsols,** which, indeed, are highly lateritic. The higher temperatures of the tropical soils render the mobilization of iron and aluminum more difficult, so that they remain concentrated on the surface. The leaching spares quartz, clay, and oxides of aluminum and iron, but it transports the calcium, magnesium, and sodium on down into the depths. Acidity, also, is usually extremely scarce in these soils.

Gray or black soils on alluvial plains do not share these characteristics, as recent and continuous sedimentation bear a great quantity of nutritive substances and minerals there.

The hot and dry desert and sub-desert regions, by contrast, have soils that are typically calcified and often saline, called **aridisols.** These are soils typical of areas having scarce precipitation and elevated evaporation. Here, the precipitation is sufficient to penetrate the first surface layer and to dissolve the soluble mineral salts, taking them farther down into the depths. The rains are insufficient, however, to leach out the insoluble mineral salts, and the quickly evaporating water leaves deposits, such as calcium carbonate.

The **ultisols** or **acrisols** are another category of tropical soils, and these develop in areas with high levels of summer humidity and high temperatures alternating with a season of water shortage. These soils, distributed throughout several intertropical areas, are of a nature that is significantly oxidized and lateritic, constituting a sort of transition toward oxisols.

Chapter 4

The Flora

It is generally recognized that the colonization of plant life on the earth had a beginning, as well as a consequent evolution, but little is yet known regarding the details of this process. In their progressive adaptation to life on dry land, members of the plant kingdom have developed life processes, that is, their "biology," in specific relation to the local availability of water and light, the two fundamental elements necessary for the process of photosynthesis. We must add, also, to this list of basic requirements, the proper supply of nutritive substances from the soil and a sufficient environmental temperature. For the most part, the geographic distribution of vegetation throughout various regions in the world, or within a given habitat, is based on the relative predominance of heat or cold, rain or drought, and light or shade. The vegetation of a given region, in other words, depends primarily on its climate.

Water, Heat, and Light: The Winning Formula in the Tropics

With such a premise, we can quickly deduce that the vegetation in a climatic zone like the Tropics—which is characterized by a considerable insolation, high temperatures, and a generally elevated rainfall—will enjoy one of the most favorable conditions on the entire planet.

As regards water, heat, and light, a great difference will be noted immediately between the **wet tropics** and the **dry tropics.** In the first case, the available water and heat are literally unlimited, so that vegetation develops prodigiously, and competition between individual plants is primarily for the gathering of light and nutrients. By contrast, in desert environments, the sparse plant cover allows for a great abundance of unobstructed light, and it is essentially the availability of water, as well as the successfulness of strategies for conserving it, or for resisting prolonged periods of drought, that selects the species.

Evergreen or Deciduous. In the equatorial or humid tropical areas, most of the plants are always green. In the intertropical areas, there is a more markedly seasonal aspect to the rains, and leaves may fall in the dry seasons, just as they do in the winters of the temperate zones. In this case, it is the absence of rain, and not the diminution of the temperature, that stimulates the loss of the leaves and the quiescence of many plants.

In spite of its generally poor soils, the vegetation of the wet tropics is astoundingly luxuriant, and it exhibits exceptional examples of specialization for dealing with these poor soils that recur on the different continents.

One of these is the high concentration of **roots** at the surface, favoring the more important task of gathering nutrients before they can be washed away by the rains. Plants and trees in the richer soils of regions with a more pronounced seasonality, by contrast, have very deep, stabilizing roots, serving the purpose of seeking into the depths for moisture, which can be extremely reduced at the upper levels of the soil during certain periods of the seasonal cycles. Another very important adaptation typical of wet tropical forests is the **elevated recycling** of the nutrients that are lost with the falling of leaves or with the death of a plant. Various experiments have proved that the absorption of these nutrients is close to 90%.

Although the elevated rainfall of the Tropics represents one of the main factors contributing to the outstanding plant diversity in these regions, this exaggerated surplus also provides the undesirable effect of a washing agent for many trees and ground plants. The rains, in fact, are constantly washing nutrients out of the soil, either sending them deeper underground or carrying them away, down rivers and streams. As in many cases in the natural world, what is a problem for some turns out to be an opportunity for others, and, indeed, the pouring rains constitute an excellent vehicle for nutrients for the forms of vegetation that live far away from the soil. Such is the case for the many **epiphytes** and **epiphyllous plants**—which include herbaceous or ligneous plants, lichens, and mosses—that make their homes clinging onto the trunks, branches, and leaves of other trees or shrubs. These all benefit immensely from the opportunity to absorb nutrients suspended in the rainwater that runs along their outer surfaces. Some trees even have special aerial roots that protrude from the trunks and

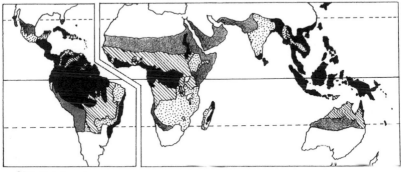

■ Rainforests
▨ Deciduous or semievergreen forests
▧ Savanna
▨ Arid or semiarid deserts

Distribution of the principal typologies of tropical vegetation.

branches, appearing almost to be lifting their nutrient-absorbing append-ages directly into the critical zone of the running rainwater.

From the point of view of forest economy, the "primary production," or photosynthesis, depends enormously on the "secondary production," meaning the **decomposition** or transformation of organic material that has died or has been eaten, involving the reduction of these to composts ready to be recycled through their absorption into plants. The quantity of organic material available for decomposition in a rainforest is immense. Near Manaus in the Amazon River basin, the weight of leaves alone fallen among the ground litter has been estimated at about 7 tons per hectare (3 tons per acre) each year. To this figure are also added fallen fruits, branches, and entire trees.

Poor Soil and Rich Vegetation. The tropical moist forests are particularly noted for their efficient recycling of nutrients. The soils themselves are poor, and the entirety of the nutritive organic and mineral resources of the zone is housed within the living forest. Another conservation mechanism used by the plants is that often the nutrients are stored within the leaves and utilized in photosynthesis for long periods of time, so that they are protected from the washing of the rains. In many cases, essential nutrients are reabsorbed by the main body of the plant before the leaves are allowed to fall.

Analogies and Differences among Continents

Species, genera, and families are often considered to characterize a continent. For example, the Dipterocarpaceae family dominates the Southeast Asian rainforests, accounting for about 80% of all the large trees there, while only about ten species of this family are found in Africa, and just a few have been recently discovered in South America. By contrast, the forest giants—those trees emerging over the canopy layer—of the Leguminosae family are well distributed among all three of the major rainforest blocks of the planet. These trees belong to the genera *Mora* in America, *Koompassia* in Asia, and *Cynometra* in Africa.

All the continents have epiphytes, such as orchids and ferns, but the epiphyte bromeliads, of the family Bromeliaceae, live only in the Americas. There is a single known species of bromeliad in Africa, but it is not an epiphyte. In Indo-Malaysia, the principal families of epiphytes are

the Rubiaceae (including the "ant plants," *Myrmecodia* and *Hydnophytum*), the Gesneriaceae, the Asclepiadaceae, the Orchidaceae, and many Bryophyta.

The botanical affinities noted between Africa and Asia are the strongest among the continents, followed by those between America and Asia (amphi-Pacific), then those between the Americas and Africa.

Many tropical leaves have particular forms, venations, types of surfaces, and prominent tips ("drip tips") that facilitate the dripping away of the intense and frequent rains.

Ficus religiosa

Medusandra richardsiana

What is "Biodiversity"?

The term "biodiversity," or biological diversity, indicates the variety of living beings existing in the world. This includes, also, consideration of the genes, species, populations, ecosystems, and ecological processes of which living creatures are a part.

The importance of biodiversity is enormous. It is the product of the evolution of life on the planet and is the basis for the process of future evolution. Biodiversity sustains ecological functions that influence and determine global and micro-climates, oxygen production, fixing of carbon dioxide, regulation of water cycles, bio-geo-chemical processes, nutrients, and energy flows—all the processes that are crucially important for the support of our current life on earth. Human beings are part of the world's biological diversity, and we are ever dependent upon on biodiversity—for what it offers us in the form of wild or domesticated animals and plants for food, fibers, and medicines, and, not least importantly, for emotional support and recreation. Biodiversity is also valuable in safeguarding watersheds, protecting soil from erosion, etc. To most people, living animals and plants communicate interest, attraction, curiosity, and positive emotions, which is why we have plants and flowers in our houses, keep animals as pets, or enjoy relaxing in the garden. We take a walk for relaxation in the city park or the countryside, among the woodlands or mountains, or look for natural landscapes and beautiful scenery as holiday destinations. It seems that we need to be in touch with nature, perhaps as a consequence of our past history—about two million years in strict dependence on wildlife and the natural world. To an increasing number of people, biodiversity also has an intrinsic value, by the mere fact that it can exist—that it has the right to exist.

genes→organism→species→population→ecosystem→ecological processes

About 1.7 million different types of life forms are currently known in the world, but it is estimated that their total number is somewhere between 5 to 50 million. On the basis of the number of new insects discovered in small sample areas of tropical forests, certain entomologists estimate that there are over 30 million belonging to this category of animals alone. Ten million species is currently accepted as a broad "working figure," but, even so, this still implies that 80% are not yet known to science.

BIOSPHERE

Biodiversity		Evolutionary and Ecological Processes
Genes		Cycles of nutrients
Individuals		Cycle of water
Species	↔	Photosynthesis
Populations		Predation
Ecosystems		Mutualism
Ecological processes		Speciation and evolution

The Structure of a Tropical Forest. Despite their floristic differences, meaning differences between the botanical species constituting a given forest, there are certain unexpected structural analogies among the forests of the three principal tropical blocks: Central and South America, Africa, and Indo-Malaysia. These are demonstrated to be examples of convergence, as the species have evolved in parallel, even though isolated by thousands of kilometers of distance, due to their developing in situations that are environmentally and climatically similar. In general, the many tropical moist forests present similar structures, with trees that are 30 to 40 m (100 to 130 ft) high, from among which certain emergents of 50 to 70 m (160 to 230 ft) may stand out. Certain morphological aspects recur with extreme frequency, even among different species and genera. The trees in tropical forests throughout the world tend to be elongated, with thin trunks that are vertical and straight, allowing them to tend toward the light and to avoid (or to vanquish) competition. Smooth trunks and oblong leaves, with an appropriate, apical tip (the "drip tip") are adaptations to the rain, as these reduce the friction from the washing of the rain and favor dripping. Many grass species (Poaceae, formerly known as Gramineae or Graminaceae) also, which are typically elongated and ribbon-shaped in temperate areas, thus often have oval leaves in the Tropics. The bases of the trees often have "buttresses" or are supported by curved "stilts" that are braced on the ground, providing stability for these giants that frequently have no deep, supporting, underground roots.

The Richest Botany in the World

The enormous diversity of plant life is another peculiarity of the tropical latitudes. For example, 300 different species of trees can be found in just 2 square km (500 acres) in Brazil, compared to a few dozen species in an extensive woods in the temperate or boreal zones.

In tropical moist forests, many plants are distributed in patches, while others are sparse, as a consequence of different dispersal mechanisms. As a general rule, it is difficult to find species that actually dominate. Often, in order to find a second plant of the same species, it is necessary to walk for many hundreds of meters within the forest. In savannas and seasonal tropical forests, however, there are species that dominate in terms of abundance, even though the floristic diversity still remains highly elevated.

10. Detail of the network of the "trunk" of a strangler fig.

Palms

Palms are a typical botanical family, with distribution limited primarily to the Tropics. The principal centers of differentiation are the tropical regions of the American and Asian continents. In the tiny nation of Singapore, there exist more native palms than in all of Africa. Coconut palms *(Cocos nucifera)*, as well, originate in Southeast Asia and the Indo-Pacific region. The tropical distribution of palms is principally explained by their sensitivity to the cold. Some adult desert and mountain palms can tolerate temperatures below zero, but these must never be too acute nor too prolonged. In fact, palms have only one single vegetative apex, positioned at the top of the stalk, or trunk, and damage to this by the cold, especially in the plant's younger years, will cause the death of the entire plant by rendering it incapable of growing and developing.

Ravenala madagascariensis
(not a true palm, but related to the banana family)—Madagascar

Some examples of palms from
the different continents.

Borassus flabellifer—Africa

Nypa fruticans— Southeast Asia

Cocos nucifera—Indo-Pacific

Hyphaene thebaica—Africa

Maurizia flexuosa —South America

Licuala grandis— South America

Phytelephas macrocarpa—South America

Top Ten Countries for Diversity in Higher Plants

Country	Number of Species	% of World's Diversity
Brazil	50–56,000	22.5%
Colombia	45–51,000	20.5%
China	27–30,000	12.0%
Mexico	18–30,000	12.0%
South Africa	23,000	9.0%
Ecuador	17–21,000	8.5%
Papua New Guinea and Venezuela	15–21,000	8.5%
Peru and India	17–20,000	8.0%
USA	19,000	7.5%
Australia and Malaysia	15,000–16,000	6.5%

Certain areas of the eastern African savannas, for example, are dominated by the acacias (*Acacia* spp.) that are so very characteristic of the landscapes of those environments, with their umbrella-shaped leafage. At least forty different species of acacias have been described.

Stable and Ideal Climate. One of the most generally accepted hypotheses explaining the phenomenon of the extremely elevated biodiversity of the Tropics makes reference to the fact that these latitudes have been less affected by the relatively recent and frequent climatic changes

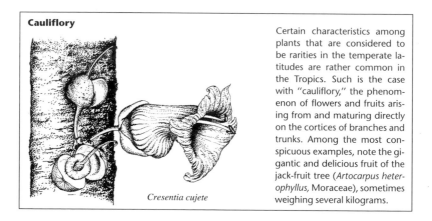

Cauliflory

Cresentia cujete

Certain characteristics among plants that are considered to be rarities in the temperate latitudes are rather common in the Tropics. Such is the case with "cauliflory," the phenomenon of flowers and fruits arising and maturing directly on the cortices of branches and trunks. Among the most conspicuous examples, note the gigantic and delicious fruit of the jack-fruit tree (*Artocarpus heterophyllus,* Moraceae), sometimes weighing several kilograms.

(glacial stages). During those events, the tropical forests were reduced, but they never disappeared completely, and they represented important islands of refuge for many species, which then had the possibility of enjoying new expansion once the original climatic conditions were re-established. The ecosystems of the Tropics must have had more time to evolve and to differentiate, without the interruptions or mass extinction that affected the more peripheral latitudes. The forests of western Africa, with their refugia in Gabon and the DRC, have been estimated to have flourished through an

---

A Surprising Wealth

The Tropics play host to a wealth of living forms unequalled throughout the globe. In 23 hectares (57 acres) of forest in Malaysia, there are more than 375 different species of trees having diameters greater than 90 cm (35 in), in contrast to barely 40 in the richest of the temperate woods. Overall, in Malaysia, about 20,000 botanical species have been described, compared with only about 2,000 for Great Britain, which is about two-thirds the size of the former. In Great Britain, *Carex* is the plant genus having the most different species, about 75, while in Malaysia, again, genera such as *Solanum* or *Vernonia* have over 1,000 species each. The primary forest of Borneo produces up to 750 tons per hectare (350 tons per acre) of wood, five times more than a mature wood of conifers in Canada or Siberia. Again, in Borneo, which has about 126,000 square km (50,000 square mi) surface area, there are more than 2,500 endemic plants, compared to about 40 in Great Britain, with nearly twice the surface area. In the 2,100 square km (800 square mi) of the Amistà National Park in Costa Rica, there are 900 species of birds, the same number of bird species populating the entire continent of North America, which has over 20 million square km (7.7 million square mi) of area.

In scanning a list of nations having the greatest number of angiosperm plants, meaning those plants having flowers and seeds enclosed in their fruits, we note the predominance of countries that are entirely or partially tropical; for example, Brazil alone hosts over 50,000 higher plant species. The Tropics are home to about two-thirds of all the known plants in the world, and approximately 45% of these live in the forests.

Countries	Angiosperm Species (flowering plants)
Brazil	55,000
Colombia	45,000
China	27,000
Mexico	25,000
Australia	23,000
South Africa	21,000
Indonesia	20,000
Venezuela	20,000
Peru	20,000
FSU (former Soviet Union)	20,000

unchanging development for over 65 million years. Similarly, though there was, about 18,000 years ago, an enormous reduction of even the tropical forests of South America, numerous small "islands" survived—within Amazonia, to the eastern slopes of the Andes, and to the more equatorial regions of Venezuela and Guyana. These areas represented extremely important refuges for thousands and thousands of life forms, both animal and plant, which were, thereby, afforded the possibility of propagating anew. A further hypothesis suggests that the optimal climatic conditions for the development of plant life in the Tropics resulted in inciting a greater level of competition, thus accelerating the diversification of species.

And yet another important factor in the diversification of species, suggested by ecologists, is that of **predation,** a factor of great significance in the Tropics as a consequence of the climatic stability. What often happens in the temperate latitudes is that many prey (and this includes those plants that are "preyed upon" by herbivores) disappear or become unavailable during the inclement seasons, reducing opportunities for predators, whether carnivorous or herbivorous. This is not the case in the Tropics, where, for example, it is estimated that the quantity of leaves in the foliage cover of a rainforest that are eaten by herbivores amounts to no more than 15%.

As a consequence of this elevated predation in the Tropics, even within the plant world, we witness the development of the diversification of species and the appearance of **defensive adaptations** of various sorts. Some plants, for example, have leaves that are very coriaceous and bear a wax, tending to discourage the attacks of parasites and herbivores. Other plants protect themselves through the use of poisonous or irritating substances, or appendages for defense such as thorns or tubercles, or associations with animals (for example, with ants, in myrmecophilism). To demonstrate this, certain species of acacias in Central America were experimentally rid of the ants that occupy them, with the rapid result that their foliage was eaten by herbivores or that the trees were covered with lianas.

Time, space, resources, competition, and predation, therefore, all contribute to explain the diversity of life in the Tropics.

Human Use of Tropical Plants. A logical consequence of this great wealth and diversification of species within the tropical plant universe is that man, as well, has discovered many plants from which to draw alimen-

Tropical Plants and Termites

Termites are animals that are not very visible, because they move primarily among rotting vegetation or within their nests. They are extremely abundant, however, and to such a degree that it has been calculated that in Malaysia the weight of the termites and ants together is greater than that of all the ungulates in the forest. Termites live on dead vegetation and have the peculiarity of being able to digest wood. Much of this dead and rotting vegetation scavenged by the termites is deposited within their subterranean nests, the **termitaria**, or termite mounds, which often emerge above the ground as earthen accumulations having fantastic shapes. The vegetation deposited in the termitaria represents an alimentary excess that has not been completely digested. Thus, when a colony abandons the nest—and this occurs often: in Peru, it has been calculated that the frequency is 165 nests abandoned per hectare (67 per acre) per year—the vegetation remains underground, and, together with the earth of the termitarium, this becomes a fertilizer exceptionally rich in nutrients for the development of the fortunate seeds that are deposited there.

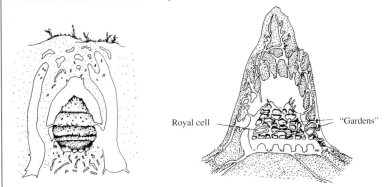

Royal cell   "Gardens"

Two sections of a *Bellicositermes africana* termitarium: in the process of formation under the surface of the soil (left); and completely developed (right). At the center of the base and, often, still below ground level, the most delicate and important parts of the termitary are housed. These are protected from the surrounding environment by tens of thousands of soldiers ready to attack any aggressors and by workers, which repair any damages to the structure.

tary advantage, or advantages of other types. Two-thirds of the world's plants that are cultivated for alimentary use originate in the tropics. Ninety-nine percent of the natural rubber produced in the world comes from a single tree species originating in the Amazon, the *Hevea brasiliensis*.

Here are a few examples of products that are consumed throughout the world today, which derive from the immense biodiversity of tropical

Fruits

Banana
Musa paradisiaca

Durian
Durio zibethinus

Eugenia
Eugenia javanica

Mangosteen
Garcinia mangostana

Papaya
Carica papaya

Rambutan
Nephelium lappaceum

Passion fruit
Passiflora laurifolia

Guava
Psidium guajava

Mango
Mangifera indica

Jack fruit
Artocarpus heterophyllus

Pineapple
Ananas comosus

Coconut
Cocos nucifera

Carambola (or starfruit)
Averrhoa carambola

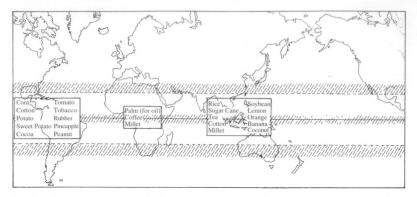

Origins of some of the most typical alimentary plants from the Tropics. Eighty percent of the alimentary plants utilized by man come from the Tropics. Additionally, 85% of human food derives from only twenty species of cultivated plants (and from three of these especially: rice, corn, and wheat). Throughout history, man has used 7,000 species of plants, in contrast to the more than 75,000 that are comestible but still living in a wild state, and this is not even counting those used for producing fibers or medicines. While indigenous communities tend to have a deep knowledge of how best to take advantage of the biodiversity of the wild, our modern society tends to focus more and more on the selection of just a few species for domesticated crops. We should understand, therefore, the immense potential that the botanical diversity of the Tropics offers in terms of new resources for the future. Each year deforestation extinguishes hundreds of higher plant species; about 250,000 are currently known to exist in the world.

flora, some even proving to be of vital importance for humanity: cotton (*Gossipium* spp., from southern Asia and South America), rice (*Oryza sativa,* from Asia), corn (*Zea mays,* from Latin America), potato (*Solanum tuberosum,* from South America), pepper (*Capsicum* spp., from South American and southern Asia), cacao (*Theobroma cacao,* from Central America), coffee (*Coffea arabica,* from Africa), tomato (*Lycopersicon esculentum,* from Latin America), vanilla (*Vanilla planifolia,* from Madagascar), and cane sugar (*Saccharum officinalum,* from New Guinea). The same can be said for certain delicious fruits that, by now, have become commonplace because of their cultivation in the temperate regions, such as oranges, mandarins, grapefruits, and other citrus fruits (*Citrus* spp., and related genera, from Indo-Malaysia), watermelons (*Cucurbita* spp., from India), bananas (*Musa paradisiaca,* possibly originating in the Afro-Asiatic tropics), pineapple (*Ananas comosus,* from Central and South

America), coconut (*Cocos nucifera,* from Southeast Asia and the Indo-Pacific), papaya (*Carica papaya,* from Mexico and Costa Rica), mango (*Mangifera indica,* from India and Indo-China), and many, many others.

It is the extraordinary floristic variety of the vegetation of the Tropics, particularly that around the equator, which, more than any other element, characterizes the ecology of these latitudes; and it is this variety, indeed, that first impassioned and astonished the early botanical explorers, and which still, today, strikes even the most careless and distracted of tourists.

Chapter 5

The Fauna

Try to name ten wild animals, just off the top of your head, and you'll see that most of them are from the Tropics. When you try to imagine the vast African savannas, the dense Asian jungles, or the endless rainforests of the Amazon, doesn't your mind go naturally to the large and charismatic animals we know live in those wildernesses? The exciting flagship species living there have always stimulated the fantasies, not just of those who live far from the Tropics, but of the local populations as well.

During the age of modern exploration a few centuries ago, when some of these unusual animals first arrived at the ports of Europe after having traveled across the world, sometimes for months and months aboard sailing ships, they caused quite a commotion, inspiring thoughts about mysterious and faraway countries, the homelands of those and other formidable beings. That was the same time that the first zoos were organized in Europe, in Vienna and Madrid, during the second half of the eighteenth century, probably to satisfy some of that burning curiosity.

One could think   and, certainly, a part of this would be true—that the fauna of the Tropics impressed, and continues to impress, the inhabitants of the Northern Hemisphere of the planet because they are curiously unfamiliar. But there's more; and even a preliminary glance at the variety within tropical zoology says a lot about the enticing universe of exotic species, the diversity of their adaptations, and the extravagance of their shapes and specialized behavior, all of which contribute to the extraordinary originality and spectacular character of tropical fauna.

An Extraordinary Wealth

As we've already seen regarding tropical vegetation—or perhaps even more so—the fauna of the Tropics exhibits an astounding level of diversity and specialization.

Henry Bates, the English naturalist, first began visiting Amazonia in 1848; and over a period of eleven years of study, he was able to classify some 14,000 different animal species, of which 7,000 were yet unknown. Invertebrates make up by far the largest percentage of species that are yet unknown to science. It is estimated that from 6 to 30 million arthropods live in the tropical forests, and the great majority of these are yet unknown to science. This estimate represents over 96% of the total number of arthropods hypothesized to live on the planet. About one-third of the world's birds live in tropical forests, and many others use these habitats during migration or as wintering grounds. Some of the most reliable and generally accepted estimates recognize that the tropical latitudes may host up to 80% of all living animal species in the world.

Three Principles regarding Tropical Wildlife. The extraordinary

---

The Systematics of Living Beings

Biologists classify life on the earth into a generally recognized and accepted hierarchical scale that reflects the evolutionary relationships among organisms. The branches of natural science that deal with the naming and the classification of organisms are called taxonomy and systematics. The principal systematical categories are, starting from the individual organism and proceeding through ever broader groups:

species→genus→family→order→class→phylum

Organisms are further distinguished into two large "kingdoms," the animal kingdom and the plant kingdom. For example, the sea crocodile belongs to the species *porosus,* to the genus *Crocodylus,* to the family Crocodylidae, to the order Crocodylia, to the class Reptiles, to the phylum Chordata, and to the animal kingdom.

Each organism is characterized by a basic binomial denomination in Latin that includes the genus and species names. This is the scientific name of the species it belongs to, such as, for example, *Crocodylus porosus.* A species includes organisms that are very similar, to the degree that they can couple among themselves and give rise to fertile offspring. Nonetheless, the "species" concept is a human one, and, to be sure, there are some fertile hybrids coming from different species or, conversely, some separately isolated populations of the same species that show marked differences in their gene pools. In reality, each species is more or less part of a dynamic process that continues to select and evolve in response to environmental changes, opportunities, and ecological disturbances.

---

wealth and variety of living forms lead us to consider the three primary characteristics of tropical zoology:

1. the extremely high diversity of species;
2. the relative scarcity of individuals of each species; and
3. the great variety and diversification of specialization techniques, survival strategies, and morphological, physiological, or behavioral adaptations.

These principles find their fullest expression in the humid areas, and most especially in the rainforests. When you read that there are seventy six different species of serpents in tiny French Guiana alone, as contrasted with about twenty in all of Europe or a hundred throughout North America, you begin to imagine that you might step into a tangle of ophidians as soon as you started into their forest! In actuality, the high diversity leads to a relatively low density of individuals of a given species, so even though there are a large number of species, the number of individuals of each species is not necessarily high. Indeed, you might even enjoy a long excursion through the forest without observing one single reptile.

Great Diversity and Unexpected Look-Alikes

One of the biological factors markedly influencing the distribution of every individual species of living being on the planet, or even within a given

11. American crocodile.

12. Wild peacock.

13. Family of lemurs.

habitat, is **interspecific competition,** or competition with other species for food and space. The success of a given species in terms of its expansion, resistance, or colonization within an environment depends upon how well it succeeds in overcoming or avoiding competition with other species that are present or attempting to colonize. For many animals, competition is a concern, not only for food, but also for territory, reproduction sites, and areas for refuge or repose.

Competition is best avoided by specializing. There are species that hunt during the day and others that hunt at night, for example, or those that hunt different prey, some larger, some smaller. Sometimes, when such "adjustments" have not been made, competition between species has caused widespread extinction. This was the case when monkeys appeared and came to colonize the African continent, clashing with the more primitive lemurs there. The latter have survived in Madagascar alone, and this is because the monkeys have never been able to cross the Mozambique Channel.

A high degree of competition, combined with a high availability and diversity of resources, stimulates species to differentiate their diets and habits, with the result that, from a few common progenitors, numerous distinct species originate over time, in a process referred to as **adaptive radiation.** When opportunities for specialization and differentiation are increased as a consequence of a complex environmental structure and favorable ecological conditions, as is the case in many tropical habitats, we are witness to a veritable explosion of different living species, each with its own exclusive forms and habits.

One further fascinating aspect regarding tropical zoology, again, is linked to the climatic stability and homogeneity of many tropical areas, even though they may be separated from one another geographically. This is the phenomenon known as **evolutionary convergence,** which occurs when two species that are isolated from one another evolve, by chance, to the point that they assume appearances, ecological roles, or behavior patterns that are extremely similar. This depends, logically, on their living in analogous habitats, having become adjusted to the same environmental characteristics, and having adopted the same strategies. The chance nature of the phenomenon is clearly demonstrated by the fact that, quite often, instances of evolutionary convergence involve species that have no relation to one another and no common ancestors. Cases of this type of

Prosimians, Monkeys, and Apes

The order of Primates includes all the species that are commonly called monkeys. These are divided into prosimians and actual monkeys. Within this order, there is also a superfamily, Hominoidea, made up of all the so-called anthropomorphous monkeys, or apes, and man. Recent studies on genetic similarities between apes and man have even led some scientists to include the two within a single family, Hominidae. The apes are distinguished from other simians by their lack of a tail, their larger dimensions, their greater thoracic development, and their longer arms, which they can rotate on the joints of their shoulders. Apes are distributed into two families, Hylobatidae (gibbons), and Pongidae (orangutans, gorillas, chimpanzees, and bonobos, or pigmy chimpanzees). Prosimians are primitive simians, and many species are now extinct on most continents because of competition with the later-evolving monkeys.

Distribution of the Primates of the World

PROSIMIANS	TARSOIDS	MONKEYS and APES (or ANTHROPOIDS)
Lorisids (family Lorisidae)	**Tarsids** (family Tarsidae)	**Cebids** (family Cebidae)
Loris (southern and southeast Africa)	Tarsier (Southeast Asia)	Capuchin (South and Central America)
Galago, or bushbaby (family Galagidae, sometimes included with Lorisidae) (Africa)		Titi monkey (South America)
		Saimiri or squirrel monkey (South and Central America)
		Uakari monkey (South America)
		Saki monkey (South America)
		Spider monkey (South and Central America)
		Howler monkey, or howler (South and Central America)
		Night monkey (South and Central America)
		Woolly spider monkey (South America)
		Woolly monkey (South America)
Potto (Africa)		**Callitrichids** (family Callitrichidae)
Lemurids (family Lemuridae)		Pigmy marmoset (South America)
		Tamarin (South and Central America)
Lemur (Madagascar)		Marmoset (South America)
Mouse-lemur (Madagascar)		**Cercopithecids** (family Cercopithecidae)
		Guenon (Africa)
Daubentonids (family Daubentonidae)		Mangabey (Africa)
		Drill-mangabey (Africa)
		Langur, or leaf monkey (southern and Southeast Asia)
		Macaque (northwest Africa, southern and Southeast Asia)
Aye-aye (Madagascar)		Colobid monkey (Africa)
Indrids (family Indridae)		Guereza (Africa)
		Baboon (Africa and southwest Asia)
Indri (Madagascar)		Mandrill (Africa)
Sifaka (Madagascar)		Proboscis monkey (Borneo)
		Red guenon, or patas monkey (Africa)
		Hylobatids (family Hylobatidae)
		Gibbon (Southeast Asia)
		Pongids (family Pongidae)
		Gorilla (western and central Africa)
		Orangutan (Borneo and Sumatra)
		Chimpanzee (western, eastern, and central Africa)
		Bonobo, or pigmy chimpanzee (western and central Africa)

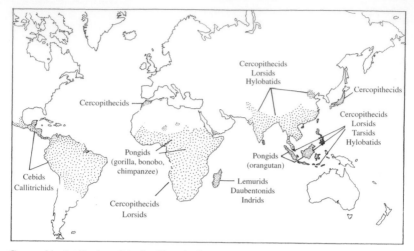

Geographic distribution of the families of primates.

convergence are very numerous in the Tropics. For some of the most striking examples, let us recall the South American toucans and the Afro-Asian
hornbills, with their great, curved beaks, powerful yet light, used to feed
on fruits and seeds. Or else, the similarity of the body structure and habits
among ungulates in the African forest and Amazonian rodents, both of
which are adapted to moving or running among the dense vegetation of the
glades or the underbrush of primary jungles. And again, the myrmecopha-
gous, or ant-eating, animals of the five continents: the Amazonian anteaters,
the pangolins of the Asian forests and African savannas, the African aard-
varks, and the Australian echidnas. All of these have forward-leaning
carriage, prominent snouts, and extremely long, sticky tongues.

Also surprising are the instances of evolutionary convergence between
the marsupials of Australia and placental mammals of the other continents. Having colonized Australia at a time when there were no competitors, the progenitor marsupial species differentiated profusely, so as to
occupy the available space and numerous ecological niches. Examples of
this are seen in the convergence between marsupial rats and the homologous rodents, the false marsupial "flying squirrels" and the true variety,
the now extinct marsupial wolf and the canids, or the cuscus and the Neo-

tropical sloth, and there are many other examples. Because of this, there are species belonging to widely different faunal categories all over the world that have remarkably similar counterparts in Australia, all belonging to the same order of marsupials!

A Thousand Strategies for Survival

The complexity of tropical ecology and its elevated biological diversity have pushed the process of adaptation to the extreme, giving origin to living beings with bizarre or even astonishing appearances. A couple of examples of these are seen in the four-eyed fishes of South America (*Anableys* spp.), with their two pupils and divided retinas, for seeing above and below the surface at the same time, and the electric eel *(Electrophorus electricus),* from the Amazon, which hunts by discharging powerful electric jolts in the water. The strength of these electrical jolts depends upon the length of the fish, because the negative and positive poles of the "battery" are located on the head and the tail, respectively—fish 90 cm (35 in) long can emit discharges of about 350 volts. The same fish uses somewhat weaker discharges for orienting itself, for echolocating enemies, prey, or obstacles, or for communication (!) among its kind. Brightly colorful Central American poison dart frogs (genus *Dendrobates*) are more or less poisonous in accordance with the degree to which their "warning" colors are accentuated.

Then there is the universe of insects: there are carpenter wasps, which are capable of forcing entry into certain closed flowers; leaf-cutting ants, or weaver ants, which construct great nests by gluing and sewing plant cuttings to size; caterpillars that resemble the excrements of small birds; and butterflies, such as the plume moths of the Alucitidae family, which appear just like the small feathers lost by birds; or leaf butterflies, which are perfectly similar to green or dry leaves; or butterflies whose flight resembles the falling of leaves from the canopy layer. There are stick insects that are covered with protrusions exactly like the moss on which they live; treehoppers that pass the hours of the day fixed to branches or trunks, and which look like the thorns on a plant due to the odd form of their dorsal protuberances; "orchid" praying mantises of Borneo, whose lateral appendages are shaped and colored like the petals of their very beautiful epiphytic namesakes; and others, like the Amazonian *Choeradodis,* whose

Woolly spider monkey
Brachyteles arachnoides
Cebidae, South America

Dusky titi monkey
Callicebus moloch
Cebidae, South America

Gibbon *Hylobates lar*
Hylobatidae, Southeast Asia

Catta or ring-tailed lemur
Lemur catta (female)
Lemuridae, Madagascar

Chimpanzee *Pan troglodytes*
Pongidae, Africa

Orangutan *Pongo pygmaeus* (male) Pongidae, Borneo and Sumatra

Gorilla *Gorilla gorilla* Pongidae, Africa

Macaque *Macaca nemestrina*
Cercopithecidae, Southeast Asia

Yellow baboon
Papio cynocephalus (female)
Cercopithecidae, Africa and southwest Asia

Langur *Presbytis entellus*
Cercopithecidae, southern Asia

Collared mangabey
Cerocebus torquatus
Cercopithecidae, Africa

Proboscis monkey
Nasalis larvatus (male)
Cercopithecidae, Borneo

Guereza *Colobus guereza*
Cercopithecidae, Africa

Green guenon *Cercopithecus aethiops* Cercopithecidae, Africa

Some of the most representative species of the living primate families.

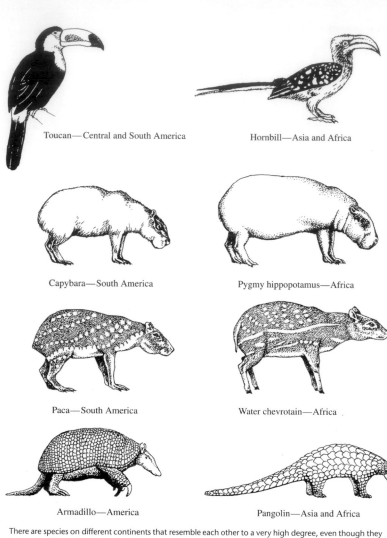

Toucan—Central and South America

Hornbill—Asia and Africa

Capybara—South America

Pygmy hippopotamus—Africa

Paca—South America

Water chevrotain—Africa

Armadillo—America

Pangolin—Asia and Africa

There are species on different continents that resemble each other to a very high degree, even though they belong to different families and orders. This has resulted from the phenomenon of evolutionary convergence, by which unrelated species that have evolved in similar environmental conditions exhibit convergence of form and behavior.

forms perfectly mimic the leaves of certain small climbers—and this is just a brief selection of a few of the more striking examples.

Diversification among Neotropical Bats. A wonderful example of the accentuated diversification of forms and behavior within the fauna of the Tropics can even be found within a single animal group: the order of Chiroptera. It is true that the Tropics are an important center of differentiation for bats, and in South America, this reaches its maximum level. Although there are none of the megachiropterans (such as flying foxes or fruit bats) that are so abundant in Africa, Asia, and Oceania, we do find incredible examples of specialization among the microchiropterans.

As far as regards their alimentary strategies, it is believed that the ancestor of the current bats, that first mammal that succeeded in colonizing air space with its own active flight, was insectivorous, as are many currently living species, which feed upon flying insects using their exceptional "radar system" for echolocation. From one common progenitor, different species have evolved, exhibiting quite different instances of adaptation. Considering diversification in the diet alone of the bats of the American Tropics, we find those of the genus *Noctilio,* which emit sounds, not for echolocating insects within the air, but for finding fish and amphibians on the surface of the water. They have developed long claws and sharp teeth that are neatly adapted for capturing their prey. Vampire bats *(Desmodus)* are notoriously hematophagous. They detect their prey using eyesight and sense of smell, and often they approach by moving along the ground until they reach the preferred areas of the body (the hooves, ears, or muzzle), where they inflict wounds measuring about 5 by 10 mm ($\frac{3}{16}$ by $\frac{3}{8}$ in), using

14. Male impala enjoying acacia flowers.

their extremely sharp incisors. Utilizing an anticoagulant liquid, they extract about 15 to 25 ml (½ to 1 oz) of blood. False vampires—some of these have large dimensions, such as the *Vampyrum spectrum,* whose wingspans can reach 75 cm (30 in)—catch prey such as small birds and mammals by surprising them while they sleep, possibly using their sense of smell to detect them. The *Glossophaga* are specialized in a totally different field, the gathering of pollen, and they have developed long, retractile tongues. The *Macrophyllum* and the *Ectophylla,* by contrast, are expert frugivores, while the *Phyllostomus* demonstrate, by their incredible and monstrous facial, foliaceous protuberances, an alimentary spectrum that is quite broad, including fruits as well as insects and animal prey of larger dimensions. Just as surprising are the adaptations involving the sites chosen for refuge and repose during the day. Among the South American species alone, those that belong to the genera *Artibeus* and *Uroderma* have the habit of weaving palm leaves into a comfortable sack. Many species choose grottos, caverns, or cavities in tree trunks, such as the *Desmodus* vampires. Bats of the *Lasiurus* genus conceal themselves simply among the leaves, and *Hipposideres* choose from among the numerous cavities at

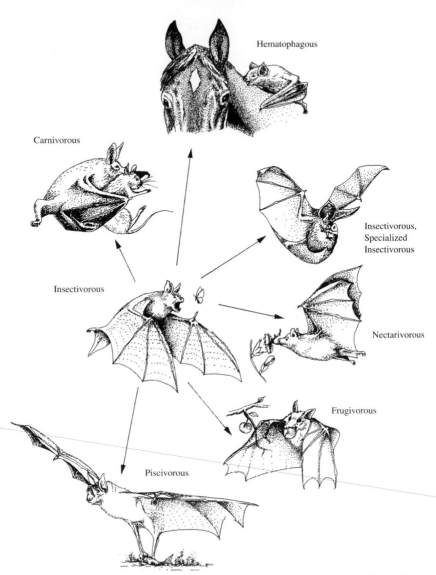

Hematophagous

Carnivorous

Insectivorous, Specialized Insectivorous

Insectivorous

Nectarivorous

Frugivorous

Piscivorous

South American bats have evolved from their common insectivorous progenitors into various species, resorting to multiple strategies and specialized behavior adaptations in order to take best advantage of the available resources and avoid alimentary competition among themselves.

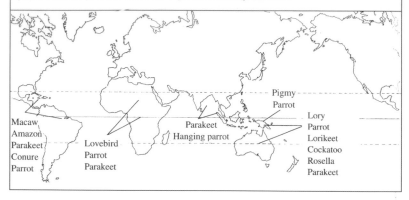

Parrots

The tropical zones are inevitably associated with their many brilliantly colored parrots. In fact, with the exception of the few species whose habitats extend into the temperate latitudes, parrots are mainly distributed in the tropical and subtropical zones.

Pigmy Parrot

Macaw
Amazon
Parakeet
Conure
Parrot

Lovebird
Parrot
Parakeet

Parakeet
Hanging parrot

Lory
Parrot
Lorikeet
Cockatoo
Rosella
Parakeet

the bases of large forest trees. Equally innovative is the tiny Asiatic bat, which specializes in passing the entire day in the trunks of great bamboo plants. Meanwhile, the fruit bat and flying fox (*Pteropus,* which do not exist in South America) are famous for clinging onto the highest branches of trees, in clear view, in such a manner as to appear like hanging fruit.

In accordance with ecological rules, such an abundance and diversity of species has, as a response, predators of a superior degree. In the case of bats, these predators are the raptors, or birds of prey. There are falcons *(Machaerhampus alcinus)* that become active around twilight, which are specialized in hunting bats at the moment they leave their diurnal shelters. The technique is rather simple, in theory: they drop suddenly upon their prey from behind, taking advantage of the one "blind spot" within the bats' extremely sensitive radar range. Bats are mammals capable of such lightning-quick swerves and veers that, unless they are unaware of their danger, they are virtually ungraspable.

Accentuated specialization often restricts species to particular ecological niches, microhabitats, or periods of activity. Spider monkeys (genus *Ateles*) of the Central and South American rainforests are agile climbers that move among broad expanses of the jungle in nuclear families. They inspect the trees in search of food, fruits, and leaves. If, however, we

Leaf-Cutting Ants

It is impossible to travel through a tropical landscape without encountering ants. They are everywhere, in the savannas as well as in rainforests, but also in deserts or mangrove forests, either on land or in the trees, and moving by the hundreds, by the thousands, by the millions. Some species are solitary, although many others are highly social, and collectively, they swarm like living rivers that run across paths before disappearing among high grasses, into luxuriant vegetation, or on high, in the canopy layer of the trees. Among the many species of ants, those of the genus *Atta*—besides being distributed throughout the entire tropical region (some even extend their habitats into the temperate latitudes)—have the peculiar habit of collecting vegetation. It is easy to distinguish the workers of these ants, otherwise known as leaf-cutters, by the slices of green leaves they transport towards their underground colonies. The impact of these insects upon vegetation can be enormous. In the forest of Barro Colorado Island (Panama), it has been calculated that the ants consume something like 0.3 t of vegetation per hectare (0.1 tons per acre) each year, the same quantity consumed by all the vertebrate herbivores in the same forest, from monkeys to rodents to ungulates. The different species of ants within a given forest often consume different types of plants, selecting among forms of vegetable life so as not to enter into competition with each other.

A truly surprising fact is that the *Atta* do not consume the leaves themselves, but rather they use them for nourishing a special culture. Microscopic fungi develop on the masses of leaves that are borne underground by the workers, escorted by soldiers armed with powerful jaws. These fungi are adapted to living in these underground fungus gardens alone and nowhere else among the surface litter or dead tree trunks of the forest. Furthermore, the *Atta* select, among the plants they use in this manner, with the intent of improving upon their cultures. For example, they avoid plants containing substances that are harmful to the fungi, such as the terpenoids that numerous plants have as defense mechanisms. When a colony grows to the size of several million, often it will divide, and a new queen followed by her many "faithful," will migrate and build another nest. Even in the excitement of the move, though, nobody forgets the most important thing: to transport a fragment of the fungus and its pabulum. Only thus will it be possible to reconstruct a culture for feeding the new colony.

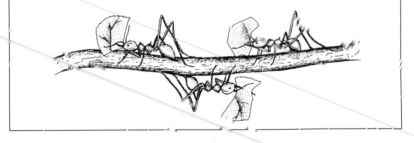

observe them for a bit of time, we will discover rather easily that they pass the larger part of their time and perform the majority of their patrolling in the lowest stratum of the forest canopy, especially on the small, peripheral branches. The motive for this is simple. Their alimentary adaptation — their diet — is composed principally of fruits and nuts that only grow on

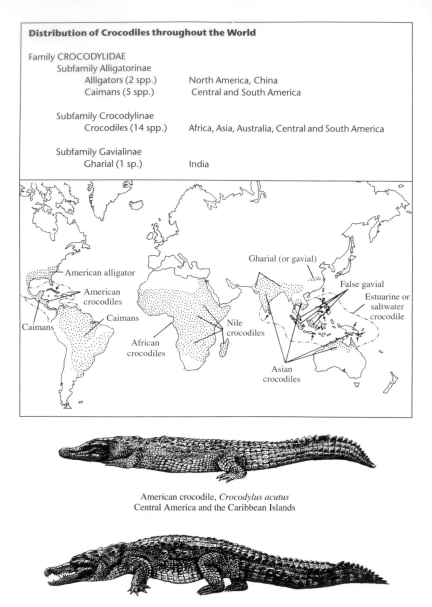

Distribution of Crocodiles throughout the World

Family CROCODYLIDAE
    Subfamily Alligatorinae
        Alligators (2 spp.)   North America, China
        Caimans (5 spp.)   Central and South America

    Subfamily Crocodylinae
        Crocodiles (14 spp.)   Africa, Asia, Australia, Central and South America

    Subfamily Gavialinae
        Gharial (1 sp.)   India

American crocodile, *Crocodylus acutus*
Central America and the Caribbean Islands

Mugger or marsh crocodile, *Crocodylus palustris*
India

Gharial, *Gavialis gangeticus*
India and Indochina

Nile crocodile, *Crocodylus niloticus*
Africa

Cuvier's dwarf caiman, *Paleosuchus paleobrosus*
South America

False gavial, *Tomistoma schlegelii*
Southeast Asia

American alligator, *Alligator mississippiensis*
Eastern subtropical North America (Florida, Georgia, southern Louisiana)

Some species of the various categories of living crocodiles. Crocodiles first evolved about 200 million years ago, belonging to the subclass of Arcosauri, the same as the dinosaurs and pterosaurs.

the young, lateral branches. This part of the forests represents, for the *Ateles,* a habitat within a habitat, a small preferred portion within the larger environment of the forest.

A dangerous place to live . . . Still more amazing is the true microhabitat of certain forest insects, which choose as a habitat the "pitcher" of a special carnivorous plant, the *Nepenthes,* living in Asia, Oceania, and Madagascar. This pitcher plant has a cylindrical flower covered with a flap that acts as a sort of half-closed cover. Sacchariferous substances attract the insect prey, and, once they have oriented themselves facing the inside, they slip down along the edges and remain trapped within the chamber, ending up snared within the dense digestive liquid at the base of the chalice. The *Nepenthes* flower, a death trap for most, is, however, also the favorite habitat for certain super-specialists, making this an eerie microcosm of life and death. Within the liquids where the prey are slowly decomposed live numerous insect larvae that are able to resist the digestive enzymes. Many draw nutrients directly from the substances resulting from the plant's digestion, while others prey upon the bacteria and protozoa that abound in these highly specialized chemical conditions. Other, larger larvae prey upon the smaller larvae. Near the opening of the pitcher plant's flower, certain thomasiid spiders wait patiently, and the predatory larva of the mycetophilid fly is capable of extending its tiny nets to capture the incoming insects before they fall into the deadly liquids. There are even certain parasitical wasps that enter into the flower to deposit their eggs on these larvae, upon which the newly hatched wasps will feed and nourish themselves. Two-thirds of the animals found in the *Nepenthes* live nowhere else. Others are also able to live apart from the plant, though they simply exhibit a predilection for this habitat, which, despite its being a deadly trap for some, provides food and shelter to a variety of others. A study in Sumatra and Singapore registered the presence of twenty-five different species of insects and three species of spiders living in just three species of *Nepenthes.* This is truly an exemplification of the difficult struggle for survival, waged through invention and adaptation, all enclosed within the restricted and hostile environment of the flower of a "fearsome" carnivorous plant.

Living on Decay. One ecological category that is well represented in the tropical latitudes, and distributed somewhat throughout all habitats, is that of the decomposers, meaning those organisms that feed by degrading organic matter. The great biomass of plants, in particular, offers food to an immense number of small organisms, from bacteria to insects, that are capable of decomposing, absorbing, and permitting the recycling of this precious source of nutrients. Among the insects, both ants and termites exhibit an enormous number of different species, passing their lives and building nests either on the ground or in trees, and with habits that are either predatory, herbivorous, or parasitic. One single, huge tree of the Leguminosae family, towering above the Amazonian forest, has been found to play host to forty-three different species of ants, nearly the same number existing in all of Great Britain.

Termites are even more closely bound to the decomposition of dead vegetation, and in particular, with ligneous structures. Thanks to their symbiosis with flagellate protozoa living in their intestines, they are able to digest and decompose lignin, something that few animals in the world can do. Besides performing the role of decomposing agents, these social insects, which group in colonies varying from a few hundred to millions of individuals, constitute an alimentary source for numerous species of

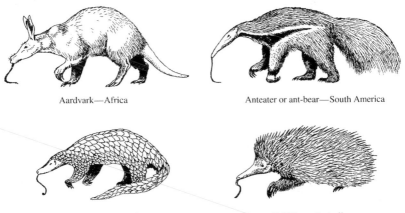

Aardvark—Africa

Anteater or ant-bear—South America

Pangolin—Africa, Asia

Echidna—Australia

The abundance of ants and termites is a constant throughout the entire tropical region. This is why there are animals on the various continents that specialize in this form of nourishment (myrmecophagy). These animals exhibit a high degree of similarity, both in form and behavior.

Biodiversity in Brazil

Brazil, with its 8,511,965 km^2 (3,286,473 mi^2), nearly thirty times the size of Great Britain, is probably the single nation hosting the greatest degree of biodiversity on the entire planet. It is first for wealth of species in certain faunal and floral groups, such as mammal diversity (524 species), plant diversity (over 50,000 species, of which about 30% are endemic), primate diversity (77 species, over one-fourth of the world's total and more than double that of the next highest country), and freshwater fish diversity (over 3,000 species, three times more than any other country in the world—consistent with the fact that about 20% of the world's fresh water flows through the Amazon basin). Brazil holds the record for highest terrestrial vertebrate diversity (over 3,000 species, of which about 300 are globally threatened), as well as that for terrestrial invertebrate diversity, with perhaps 10–15 million species of insects alone. And it is second in parrots (70 species) and amphibians (517 species, of which over half are endemic), third for birds (1,622 species, of which 191 are endemic) and palms (387 species), and fifth for reptiles (468 species).

Brazil also possesses the world's largest extent of tropical forest, with 357 million hectares (145 million acres), equivalent to one-third of the world's total, and three times that possessed by Indonesia, the nation in second place. Brazil has more forest than all of Asia, all of Africa, all of Central America, and all of the remaining South America combined. Sixty-two percent of the Amazonian forest belongs to Brazil, and about 70% of it is still reasonably intact. The northern and western portions of Brazilian Amazonia host the largest pristine block of rainforest wilderness on earth. Deforestation, which is effected primarily to make space for cattle ranching, agriculture, mining, and timber exploitation, is an extremely serious and continuing agent of destruction. A satellite-based analysis has demonstrated that, in 1987 alone, more than 8 million hectares (3.2 million acres) of forest were felled or burned. Despite the increase in public awareness on an international scale and Brazil's improvements in commitment, planning, and legislation, satellite images show that the last few years have been the worst ever in terms of deforestation in Brazil!

Biodiversity in Indonesia

Indonesia is by far the nation with the richest flora and fauna of all of Asia. The country is composed of about 17,000 islands of various dimensions dispersed along the border between two great biogeographical regions: the Indo-Malaysian and the Australian. The Indonesian archipelago stretches for more than 5,000 km (3,100 mi), roughly the distance between Oregon and the Bahamas.

With 1,150,000 km^2 (450,000 mi^2) of tropical forest—about 500,000 km^2 (or 200,000

myrmecophages on the different continents. The previously noted South American anteaters (Myrmecophagidae family) for example, have morphology and habits that are similar to the African aardvark *(Orycteropus afer),* to the pangolins of the African and Asian continents (Manidae family), and to the Australian echidnas (Tachyglossidae family). As a further consequence of their adaptation for hunting ants and termites, and in order mi²) of lowland rainforest—it possesses more forested land than any other Asian or African country, surpassed on a world level only by Brazil and the DRC. Indonesia is host to the greatest diversity of parrots (75 species, of which 38 are endemic) and palms (477 species, of which 225 are endemic) in the world. Indonesia also hosts more monkeys than any other Asian nation, with 33 species, more than half of which are endemic. It is also first for swallowtail butterflies (with 121 species, of which about half are endemic), second for mammals (515 species, about 40% of which are endemic), fourth for reptiles (511 species) and higher plants (about 40,000 species), and fifth for birds (1,531 species, of which about 400 are endemic). The flower with the largest blossom, the rafflesia, and the largest lizard on Earth, the Komodo dragon, are from this region, as are the unique and charismatic orangutan and Javan rhinoceros.

Indonesia probably has the world's highest degree of marine biodiversity, with the largest coastal surface area of any tropical country (5,500,000 ha, or 13,600,000 acres), its huge expanses of mangroves, and its vast wonderlands of coral reefs.

Biodiversity in the DRC (formerly Zaire)

The DRC possesses the largest expanses of wild tropical forest on the African continent and the second largest block on the planet after Brazil, about 1,190,000 km² (460,000 mi²), of its total 2,346,000 km² (906,000 mi²), divided into three main categories: 100,000 km² (39,000 mi²) of swamp or flooded forest; 900,000 km² (347,000 mi²) of lowland rainforest; and more than 50,000 km² (19,000 mi²) of African montane forest. The DRC hosts the second largest river system in the world, the Zaire River, as well as the largest forest park, the Salonga National Park, and it shares the second deepest lake in the world, Lake Tanganyika. Its central basin (Cuvette Centrale) is the second largest block of undisturbed rainforest on earth after northern Amazonia.

The DRC has the highest mammal diversity in Africa, seventh in the world (415 species), the highest bird diversity on the continent, tenth in the world (1,094 species), and the highest number of primates in Africa (32 species). It also hosts very high numbers of freshwater fish (sixth place, with 962 species) and higher plants (more than 11,000 species, of which over 3,000 are endemic). Zaire also hosts important populations of some charismatic and threatened species, such as the chimpanzee; the bonobo, or pigmy chimpanzee; three subspecies of gorillas (the highly threatened mountain gorilla, the declining eastern lowland gorilla, restricted to eastern DRC, and the more abundant western lowland gorilla); the northern white rhinoceros, the most endangered of all rhinos; and the forest-dwelling okapi, a close relative to the giraffe, restricted to the vast, largely pristine Ituri rainforest block to the east of the country.

to reduce competition, certain species of anteaters and pangolins live and feed on the ground, while others are tree dwellers. One pangolin can eat about seventy-five million ants and termites in one year, which is equivalent to about two hundred thousand a night! On the other hand, there is no lack of prey: a single nest of the African termite *Atta cephalotes* can occupy as much as 150 square meters (180 square yards) of surface area and

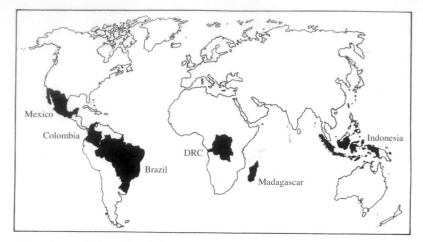

The nations with "megadiversity"—the planet's countries richest in animal and plant species, often including high percentages of endemic species (those that are typical of a restricted locality or region and found nowhere else).

house many millions of workers. Moreover, termites are an extremely nutritious source of food: 1 kg (2.2 lb) of termites is equivalent to 0.75 kg (1.7 lb) of fresh meat!

Many faunal groups are facilitated by advantageous climatic conditions. **Amphibians,** for example, are extremely widespread and diversified in the wet tropics, where, quite often, they do not even need to have direct contact with the water, except for when depositing their eggs and raising their tadpoles, because the elevated humidity of the atmosphere and of the microhabitats where they often live is sufficient for them. This is the case for the tree frogs (family Hylidae) or the poison dart frogs (family Dendrobatidae), of which there exist some striking species, such as the marsupial tree toad (genus *Gastrotheca*), which guards first its eggs and then its tadpoles within a dorsal pouch, until complete development. The *Hyla faber* is so named because of the metallic sound that it emits, which recalls the beating of a hammer upon an anvil. Within the ponds of water, the male constructs a bank of mud, often circular, within which he couples with the females, which then deposit their eggs. The tadpoles develop within this

Birds of Africa

Blue-naped mousebird
Urocolius macrourus
Africa
Coliidae, Africa

Green-crested touraco
Tauraco persa
Africa
Musophagidae, Africa

Regal sunbird
Nectarina regia
Africa
Nectariniidae, Africa, southern and Southeast Asia

Glossy starling
Lamprotornis nitens
(formerly *Lamprotornis splendidus*)
Africa
Sturnidae, Africa, Europe, Asia, Australia

Fork-tailed drongo
Dicurus adsimilis
Africa
Dicruridae, Africa, Asia, Australia

Crested barbet
Trachyphonus vaillantii
Africa
Capitonidae, Africa, Asia, Central and South America

Yellow-vented bulbul
Pycnonotus barbatus
Africa
Pycnonotidae, Africa, southern Asia

artificial bay, sheltered from the many predatory fish, until their metamorphosis into adults.

Homeland of the Great Fauna

Beyond these and an infinite number of other marvelous instances of specialization, the Tropics are characterized by great, legendary, and charismatic animals. The greater part of the largest felines in the world have mainly a tropical distribution, such as do the great reptiles, and, to a certain degree, all of the largest terrestrial species: elephants, rhinoceroses, hippopotamuses. Simians and prosimians are exclusively tropical, with the very few exceptions of some Asian macaques and langurs. The same exclusiveness applies to an innumerable list of species, families, and orders of birds, some among the most beautiful and striking on the entire planet: from the New Guinea birds of paradise to the toucans of Central and South America, from the African and Asian hornbills to the pantropical parrots, from the majority of the American hummingbirds to the African and Asian sunbirds (Nectariniidae).

With their privileged climate and luxuriant vegetation—and above all, thanks to these animals—the Tropics have consolidated the image of the exotic and the attractive. And this, more than anything else, evokes fascination and stimulates the imagination, whether of locals or visitors.

Nations with the Greatest Number of Species, for Selected Categories of Animals

An obvious display of the wealth of species found in the tropical latitudes is offered by a graded list of the world's nations exhibiting the highest numbers of species in certain faunal categories. The majority of these countries are entirely tropical, or else they are countries whose geographical extent is so vast that they also include tropical portions (for example, China and the United States).

		Mammals				Birds	
Rank	Country	Species	% Endemism	Rank	Country	Species	% Endemism
1	Brazil	524	26 %	1	Colombia	1,815	8 %
2	Indonesia	515	39 %	2	Peru	1,703	6 %
3	China	499	15 %	3	Brazil	1,622	12 %
4	Colombia	456	6 %	4	Ecuador	1,559	2 %
5	Mexico	450	31 %	5	Indonesia	1,531	26 %
6	USA	428	24 %	6	Venezuela	1,360	3 %
7	DRC	359	7 %	7	India	1,258	4 %
8	India	350	13 %	8	Bolivia	1,257	1 %
9	Peru	344	13 %	9	China	1,244	8 %
10	Uganda	315	?	10	DRC	1,094	2 %

		Amphibians				Reptiles	
Rank	Country	Species	% Endemism	Rank	Country	Species	% Endemism
1	Colombia	583	63 %	1	Australia	755	82 %
2	Brazil	517	57 %	2	Mexico	717	51 %
3	Ecuador	402	34 %	3	Colombia	520	19 %
4	Mexico	284	60 %	4	Indonesia	511	29 %
5	China	274	64 %	5	Brazil	468	37 %
6	Indonesia	270	37 %	6	India	408	46 %
7	Peru	241	37 %	7	China	387	34 %
8	India	206	53 %	8	Ecuador	374	30 %
9	Venezuela	204	37 %	9	Papua New Guinea	305	30 %
10	Papua New Guinea	200	67 %	10	Madagascar	300	91 %

		Butterflies					
Rank	Country	Species	% Endemism	Rank	Country	Species	% Endemism
1	Peru	3,550	10 %	6	Mexico	2,250	9 %
2	Brazil	3,150	6 %	7	Ecuador	2,200	9 %
3	Colombia	3,100	10 %	8	Indonesia	1,900	37 %
4	Bolivia	3,000	7 %	9	DRC	1,650	?
5	Venezuela	2,300	5 %	10	Cameroon	1,550	?

Sources: Mittermeier, et al., 1997, *Megadiversity* and BirdLife International, 1998, *Endemic Bird Areas of the World.*

Tropical Saurians (Lizards) (In most cases, the number of species is indicative rather than exact. Certain authors adopt slightly different systematics for the families.)

Order Squamata
Suborder Sauria

Family	No. Species	Distribution
Gekkonidae (geckos)	ca. 830	Asia, Africa, South and Central America, Australia, Madagascar, many oceanic islands
Pygopodidae (snake lizards)	ca. 30	Australia, New Guinea
Iguanidae (iguanas)	ca. 650	North, Central, and South America, Antilles, Galapagos, Madagascar, Fiji, Tonga
Agamidae (agamas)	ca. 300	Africa (excepting Madagascar), Australia, central, southern, and Southeast Asia, 1 sp. in Europe
Chamaeleontidae (chameleons)	ca. 85	Africa, Madagascar, southern Asia, southern Europe
Lacertidae (lizards)	ca. 200	Asia, Africa excepting Madagascar
Teiidae (whiptails)	ca. 225	North and South America, Antilles
Xantusidae (night lizards)	ca. 16	North and Central America, Antilles
Scincidae (skinks)	ca. 1000	Everywhere, especially Southeast Asia, Africa, Australasia
Cordilidae (plated lizards)	ca. 70	Africa, Madagascar
Dibamidae (blind lizards)	ca. 10	Southeast Asia down to New Guinea, 1 species in northeast Mexico
Anguidae (legless lizards) and Anniellidae (glass lizards)	ca. 75	North and South America, Antilles, southern and Southeast Asia, Europe
Xenosauridae (xenosaurs)	4	Mexico, China
Varanidae (monitors)	ca. 30	Africa, Australasia, Southeast Asia
Helodermatidae (beaded lizards)	2	North, Central, and South America

Tropical Mammals Listed below are the principal groups of mammals that are characteristic of the tropical latitudes and, in certain cases, extending only marginally into subtropical latitudes. The entries show common name, order and/or suborder, and/or family. When only the order or the suborder is indicated, this means that all families included are tropical.

Flying lemurs or colugos	Order Insectivores Family Cynocephalidae	Asia
Flying foxes, fruit bats	Order Chiroptera Suborder Megachiroptera	Asia, Africa, Australia
Vampire bats	Order Chiroptera Family Desmodentidae	America
Tree shrews	Order Primates Family Tupaiidae	Asia
Lorises, tarsiers, lemurs	Order Primates Suborder Prosimians	Africa, Asia
Monkeys	Order Primates Suborder Monkeys	Pantropical
Anteaters and three- toed sloths	Order Edentata Families Myrmecophagidae and Bradypodidae	America
Pangolins	Order Pholidota	Asia, Africa
Capybaras	Order Rodentia Family Hydrochoeridae	America
Pacarana, pacas, etc.	Order Rodentia Family Dinomyidae, Dasyproctidae	America
Spiny rats	Order Rodentia Family Echimyidae	America
Civets, genets, mongooses	Order Carnivores Family Viverridae	Africa, Asia
Hyenas	Order Carnivores Family Hyaenidae	Africa, Asia
Aardvarks	Order Tubulidentata	Africa
Elephants	Order Proboscidea	Africa, Asia
Hyraxes and dassies	Order Hyracoidea	Africa
Dugongs	Order Sirenia Family Dugongidea	Asia, eastern Africa
Manatees	Order Sirenia Family Trichechidae	Eastern America, western Africa
Tapirs	Order Perissodactyla Family Tapiridae	Asia, America
Rhinoceroses	Order Perissodactyla Family Rhinocerotidae	Africa, Asia
Peccaries	Order Artiodactyla Family Tayassuidae	America
Hippopotamuses	Order Artiodactyla Family Hippopotamidae	Africa
Asian chevrotains or mouse deer	Order Artiodactyla Family Tragulidae	Africa, Asia
Giraffes and okapis	Order Artiodactyla Family Giraffidae	Africa
Antelopes	Order Artiodactyla Subfamily Antilopidae	Africa, Asia

Birds of the Americas

Anne's humming bird
Calypte anna
Central America
Trochilidae — North, Central, and South Ame

Keel-billed toucan
Ramphastos sulfuratus
Central and South America
Ramphastidae — Central and South

Blue-crowned mot-mot
Motmotus motmota
Central and South America
Momotidae — Central and
South America

Blue cotinga
Cotinga nattaririi
(formerly *Cotinga amabilis*)
Central America
Cotingidae — Central and
South America

Collared puffbird
Bucco capensis
Central and South America
Bucconidae — Central and South America

Black-faced ant thrush
Formicarius analis
Central and South America
Formicariidae — Central
and South America

Hocco or black curassow
Crax rubra
Central and South America
Cracidae — Central and South America

Gray-winged trumpeter
Psophia crepitans
South America
Psophiidae — South America

Birds of Australasia

Long-tailed broadbill
Psarisomus dalhousiae
Asia
Eurylaimidae—Asia, Africa

Bar-bellied pitta
Pitta ellioti
Asia
Pittidae—Asia, Africa, Australia

Diard's trogon
Harpactes diardii
Asia
Trogonidae—Central and South America, Africa

Raggiana bird of paradise
Paradisea raggiana
New Guinea
Paradisaeidae—New Guinea, Australia

Asian fairy bluebird
Irena puella
Asia
Irenidae—Asia

Greater coucal
Centropus sinensis
Asia
Cuculidae, subfamily Centhropodinae
Africa, Asia, Australia

Indian pied hornbill
Antracoceros coronatus
Asia
Bucerotidae—Asia, Africa

Tropical Birds

Families of birds with tropical distribution. After the name of the family, the common name is indicated in parentheses. The last two columns indicate numbers of species and genera.

AFRICA

Anhimidae (screamers)	America	3 spp.	2 gen.
Anhingidae (darters)	Pantropical	4 spp.	1 gen.
Aramidae (limpkins)	America	1 sp.	1 gen.
Artamidae (wood swallows)	Asia, Australia	10 spp.	1 gen.
Balenicipitidae (shoebill stork)	Africa	1 sp.	1 gen.
Bucconidae (puffbirds)	America	32 spp.	10 gen.
Bucerotidae (hornbills)	Asia, Africa	44 spp.	12 gen.
Campephagidae (cuckoo-shrikes)	Africa, Asia, Australia	72 spp.	9 gen.
Capitonidae (barbets)	Asia, Africa, America	78 spp.	11 gen.
Cariamidae (seriemas)	America	2 spp.	2 gen.
Casuaridae (cassowaries)	Australia	3 spp.	1 gen.
Coliidae (mousebirds)	Africa	6 spp.	1 gen.
Cotingidae (cotingas)	America	79 spp.	28 gen.
Cracidae (curassows)	America	44 spp.	8 gen.
Dicruridae (drongos)	Asia, Africa	20 spp.	2 gen.
Dromadidae (crab plovers)	Asia, Africa	1 sp.	1 gen.
Estrildidae (waxbills)	Africa, Asia, Australia	133 spp.	28 gen.
Eurilaimidae (broadbills)	Asia, Africa	14 spp.	8 gen.
Eurypygidae (sunbitterns)	America	1 sp.	1 gen.
Fragatidae (frigate birds)	Pantropical	5 spp.	1 gen.
Galbulidae (jacamars)	America	15 spp.	5 gen.
Heliornithidae (finfoots)	Africa, Asia, America	3 spp.	3 gen.
Hemiproctydae (crested swifts)	Asia	3 spp.	1 gen.
Indicatoridae (honeyguides)	Africa, Asia	14 spp.	4 gen.

Irenidae (leafbirds)	Asia	14 spp.	3 gen.
Jacanidae (jacanas)	Pantropical	7 spp.	6 gen.
Leptosomatidae (cuckoo-roller)	Madagascar and islands	1 sp.	1 gen.
Mesenatidae (mesites)	Africa	3 spp.	2 gen.
Momotidae (motmots)	America	8 spp.	6 gen.
Musophagidae (turacos)	Africa	22 spp.	5 gen.
Nectarinidae (sunbirds)	Africa, Asia, Australia	118 spp.	5 gen.
Nictybiidae (potoos)	America	5 spp.	1 gen.
Numiddidae (Guinea fowls)	Africa	8 spp.	4 gen.
Opisthocomidae (hoatzin)	America	1 sp.	1 gen.
Paradisaeidae (birds of paradise)	Australia	40 spp.	20 gen.
Phaethontidae (tropic birds)	Pantropical	3 spp.	1 gen.
Philepittidae (false sunbirds)	Madagascar	4 spp.	2 gen.
Phoeniculidae (wood hoopoes)	Africa	6 spp.	1 gen.
Pipridae (manakins)	America	53 spp.	39 gen.
Pittidae (pittas)	Asia, Africa, Australia	26 spp.	1 gen.
Podargidae (frogmouths)	Asia, Australia	12 spp.	2 gen.
Psophiidae (trumpeters)	America	36 spp.	1 gen.
Pycnonotidae (bulbuls)	Africa, Asia	118 spp.	16 gen.
Ramphastidae (toucans)	America	38 spp.	5 gen.
Rhynchopidae (skimmers)	Africa, Asia, America	3 spp.	1 gen.
Sagittariidae (secretary birds)	Africa	1 sp.	1 gen.
Scopidae (hammerheads)	Africa	1 sp.	1 gen.
Steatornithidae (oilbirds)	America	1 sp.	1 gen.
Struthionidae (ostrich)	Africa	1 sp.	1 gen.
Todidae (todies)	America	5 spp.	1 gen.
Trochilidae (humming birds)	America	315 spp.	114 gen.
Trogonidae (trogons)	America, Africa	36 spp.	8 gen.
Vangidae (vanga shrikes)	Madagascar	13 spp.	9 gen.
Zosteropidae (white eyes)	Africa, Asia, Australia	79 spp.	11 gen.

Chapter 6

Mangroves

W here the crystalline salt waters of the ocean meet with the turbid fresh waters of tropical rivers, loaded with their mud and sediments dragged away from the hinterland, one of the most unusual types of vegetation on the planet develops. These are forests that become submerged periodically by the waters of the sea or when the rivers rise or overflow. The base of such forests is an interminable interlacing of adventitious aerial roots, sometimes having forms that are fantastic or haunting, but always and continually emerging from and sinking into the mud that is rhythmically flooded or exposed by the tides.

We do not yet have a clear and concise definition of these associations of trees that have such an exceptional **resistance to salinity,** or, as botanists would call them, halophytes. "Mangrove" can refer either to these luxuriant evergreens themselves or to the tidal salt-marsh communities, as a group, that are dominated by this type of trees and shrubs. Mangroves prosper under extremely specific conditions. Waters that are more or less brackish, a muddy soil that is highly saline, and the frequent presence of anaerobic sediments represent the inevitable components of the mangrove forest. The mud is extremely fine, with particles having a granular measure of between 20 and 200 microns (8 to 80 millionths of an inch), as compared with the 200 to 800 microns (8 to 30 hundred-thousandths of an inch) of common grains of sand; and this gives rise to an incoherent and yielding soil (where one could sink perilously deep!). During the high tides, the salinity is equivalent to that of the sea, with values of about 3%. With intense rains, this value lowers to around 1.5%, and with evaporation, the level can rise to as high as 5%. Obviously the local concentration of salinity depends upon the distance from the sea and the balance between the salt and fresh waters.

The Nonexistent Mangrove Tree

In reality, the mangrove as a tree does not exist: it does not correspond to one precise species, but rather to many, taken together. The term "mangrove" is a sort of collective name given to trees that are characteristic of this habitat, and although each has its own specific identity, they are thus generically grouped. Further, the mangrove forest is formed not just of trees, but also of many different palms, bushes, and ferns of various species, all associated, in a manner of speaking, in the formation of this peculiar ecosystem that is typical of sheltered, muddy coasts.

The Trees of the Mangrove Forest. Among the most commonly found trees that are exclusive to the mangrove forest, we find the various species of *Avicennia* and *Rhizophora* distributed throughout the world. *Bruguiera, Xylocarpus, Ceriops,* and *Sonneratia* are typical of Southeast Asia, Australia, and, to a lesser extent, eastern Africa. Examples of some other, less widespread species are the *Pelliciera rhizophorae* of western America or the *Laguncularia* of America and western Africa. Less numerous are the bushes, such as *Acanthus* and *Aegialitis* of Southeast Asia and Australia. There are about sixty trees and bushes that are typical of mangrove forests; and there are other species present, but these are not characteristic—they are colonizers, but not dominant. The epiphytes, climbers, and parasites

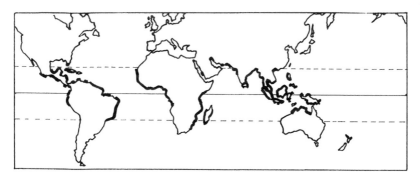

World distribution of mangrove vegetation.

17. Young mangrove, pioneer of the seawaters.

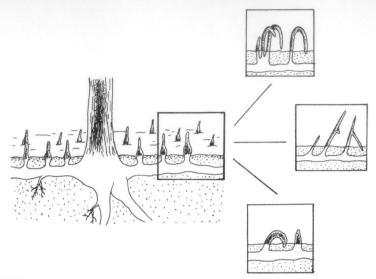

Different types of pneumatophores emerging from the surface roots of flooded forests.

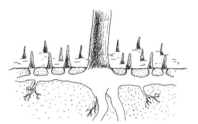

Spike roots of the *Sonneratia* spp.
and *Avicennia* spp.

Stilt roots of the *Rhizophora* spp.

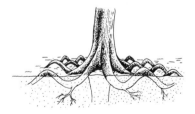

Knee roots of the *Bruguiera* spp.

Typical aerial roots for support of some of the most characteristic mangrove trees.

that populate the more mature and developed mangrove forests are also significantly represented and well-diversified.

Therefore, there is no single systematic definition of a mangrove tree. Mangroves are those plants, broadly speaking, that are associated, in an exclusive manner, with the forming of a mangrove forest. Fortunately, however, a mangrove forest is as simple to recognize as it is difficult to define.

Original Architecture and Adaptations

The architecture of a mangrove forest is unmistakable and highly characterized by the base structure. The **aerial roots,** or pneumatophores, whose function has not yet been entirely understood, create plays of fantastic and disquieting forms, practically incarnating the difficulty of life in this frontier habitat. Various species have characteristic aerial roots allowing their identification.

Trees of the genera *Sonneratia* and *Avicennia* have roots that issue forth horizontally at shallow depths and, from time to time, send out shoots emerging into the open air, like spikes. In the *Rhizophora,* the supporting architecture has characteristic, long "stilt" roots that issue from various levels of the trunk and drive into the ground after designing a "flying buttress," which, itself, can be further ramified at the base. The *Bruguiera,* on the other hand, propagates its "knee" roots horizontally, in a long, tortuous form, often appearing briefly above the surface before descending anew into the mud.

One of the functions of the mangroves' aerial roots is of course for support, given such an incoherent substratum. At the same time, they also

The trees forming the mangrove forest are distributed, starting from the coast and moving inland, in bands that can be distinguished on the basis of the degree of their resistance to salinity and immersion.

function to favor the accumulation and retention of rubble and mud, which are submitted to the erosive forces of periodic flooding. And in all probability the aerial roots also have a respiratory function, though this has not been fully demonstrated. But if aerial roots become covered with mud, they quickly generate new growth that provides access to the atmosphere, indicating a vital function, here, for the plant.

The reason why many other plants die in saltwater is that, with salinity, the osmotic potential of liquids in the interstices of the soil increases, and it becomes more difficult for the roots to absorb water and mineral salts. In these conditions, the accumulation, the exclusion, or the excretion of salt by the plant increases its consumption of energy. The ability to function under such conditions distinguishes the mangroves from other plants, but the degree of resistance also varies according to the given species in the mangrove forest.

In relation to tolerance to salinity, different mangrove species arrange themselves in parallel bands along the coast, reflecting zones of greater or lesser contact with marine or brackish water.

The genera *Sonneratia* and *Avicennia* are the true vanguards, pushing all the way to the coast, sometimes even colonizing the sands that are always submerged by the sea. Their roots are almost continuously immersed, and often branches and leaves of the young trees can end up entirely underwater during high tide, giving rise to strange underwater woods. In these conditions, the trees do not develop much, and die with a certain frequency, living at the very threshold of ecological and physiological tolerance. Farther inland are the *Rhizophora,* frequently bathed by the medium tides or even pioneering along the coastlines of creeks and lagoons filled with brackish water. Finally, the *Bruguiera* colonize the innermost areas, those that are reached only by the syzygial (that is, the highest) tides. Even farther inland, the forest opens up; however, the succession can vary in relation to the local situation and microenvironmental factors.

Optimal conditions for the development of mangroves are those in which there is a continuous supply of fresh water from inland, giving rise to a brackish environment influenced by the sea. This occurs when.

- rivers or marshes or broad basins provide an inflow of fresh water, and
- annual precipitation exceeds evaporation.

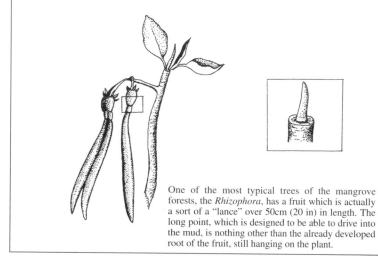
In any case, the effect of fresh waters is that they directly reduce salinity, while that of the tides is that they prevent the concentrations of salt promoted by evaporation. Therefore, the washing action of the soil by these waters is very important.

Mangroves can live in environments with fresh water, and, in fact, some species are even found along river banks and fluvial islands, swamp forests, and marshes, and they are cultivated in fresh waters in botanical gardens. Therefore, salinity is not a necessary condition for many trees of the mangrove forest, which are defined as nonexclusive halophytes, probably being constrained to occupy this difficult environment because of competition with other forest trees.

The two principal environmental factors that support the ecology of the mangrove forest are varying influxes of salt waters from the **marine tides** and fresh waters from **rivers and rains.** The volume and the frequency of these water supplies are very significant. The fresh waters from rivers are cast into the marine waters, giving rise to a brackish mixture that the tidal movements cause to flood the soil of the mangrove forest and then to retreat, exposing it. It is a powerful and impressive spectacle to find oneself in a boat near the mouth of a river, or even a few kilometers (or a couple of miles) upstream from the mouth, and observe the course of the current inverting suddenly between waves and eddies, until it overspills the shores and rapidly inundates the mud, submerging the mangrove roots.

Where the tide washes through at least once a day, the salinity of the soil of the mangrove forest will be similar to that of the neighboring estuary, lagoon, or ocean. If the tides are less frequent, the salinity will rapidly rise in response to the elevated temperatures.

Tides are vital to the mangrove forest. They normally occur twice a day (the interval between the high and the low tides is about 12 h 30′) and are caused by the gravitational attraction of the moon, and, to a lesser extent,

---

The Estuarine, or Saltwater, Crocodile

The mangrove environments in Asia, Australia, and the other oceanic islands, such as Fiji and the Solomons, host a legendary and fearsome species, the great estuarine crocodile *(Crocodylus porosus)*.

Like all animals that are able to live both in fresh water and in salt water, the crocodile can regulate the osmotic pressure of its blood by changing the concentration of salts in its vital liquids using physiological mechanisms. In the marine environment, it conserves its water by reabsorbing it into the kidneys and intestines, eliminating a urine that is highly concentrated and feces that are basically dehydrated. Sodium chloride, further, is excreted through a special nasal gland, which can be compared to the salt gland typical of marine birds. This large reptile can reach some rather impressive dimensions, as evidenced by the fact that estuarine crocodiles up to 9 m (30 ft) long have been captured.

The female constructs a large nest, where it lays its eggs and covers them with decomposing plant material. She guards the nest and, if necessary, cools it with sprays of water. When they have hatched, the young emit cries, which stimulate the female to help them to get out of the pile of vegetation. They are then transported into calm, shallow pools (just like taking them into a nursery), where they are followed for the first couple of months and defended with decisive aggression.

Several other species of crocodiles live in the mangroves as well: the false gavial *(Tomistoma schlegelii),* in Southeast Asia; the Nile crocodile *(Crocodylus niloticus),* in Africa; and the *Crocodylus acutus* and a number of different caimans, in Central and South America.

of the sun. The tides having the greatest amplitude are those occurring when the earth, the sun, and the moon are all on the same directrix. These occur during the full moon or new moon, and here the tidal range can exceed 3 m (10 ft). The lesser tides occur when the sun and the moon form a 90° angle with the earth, at the first and last quarters of the moon. The inundation is, in any case, influenced notably by the coastal conformation.

Nourishing Waters. When navigating in a mangrove forest, one appreciates the great wealth of this habitat, even when just observing the golden reflections from the turbid waters, or the comings and goings of the tides that uncover or flood vast areas of mud, baring the tangled masses of roots typical of these trees. The meeting of two rich and beneficial environments, such as the delta of a river and the tropical sea, cannot help but give rise to an exceptional habitat. And the mangrove forest, in a certain sense, can be considered to be a transition habitat that, in this mixture, finds its unmistakable peculiarity.

The principal nutrients used in the mangrove forest come from the flows of fresh and tidal waters, which distribute the organic detritus produced by the decomposition of plant and animal material within the ecosystem. It has been calculated that, on average, only 7% of mangrove leaves are eaten by herbivorous animals. All the remaining biomass of the leaves, once fallen into the water or onto the mudflat, is quickly restored into the life cycle by means of the decomposition promoted by the army of microorganisms and invertebrates, especially crustaceans and mollusks, which perform that indispensable ecological role.

The great quantity of bacteria, microorganisms, and invertebrates enormously accelerates the decomposition of the organic material imported or produced by a given mangrove forest, and this liberates great quantities of ionic minerals that are then made available for the plants. Thus, the mangroves receive organic materials, both from the sea and the land, and these enrich the coastal waters with their loose nutrients, dissolved or dispersed among the tidal waters.

The Army of Specialist Crabs

Tactics for an Amphibian Life. If the cycle of life in the forest is measured by the alternations between light and dark, or day and night, here it all depends on the tides. High waters or emerging mud. The twice-daily cycle influences the living organisms of the mangrove forest, which have developed strong capacities for dealing with environments that are sometimes dry and sometimes submerged. Swimming monkeys and felines, fish that "walk" and remain in the open air, marine mammals that are slow, for moving in low waters. Then there are the crabs. Indeed, these ought to have been named first, because these are truly the main protagonists of the mangrove ecosystem. Millions of individuals within dozens of species, organized basically into colonies with varying populations and densities (up to 50 individuals per m², or 60 per yd²), where each individual has a den, a gallery down into the mud, and a small, surrounding territory. The crabs breathe the air by means of their highly vascularized branchial chambers. There are some terrestrial species, such as *Cardiosoma* and the coconut crab (*Birgus latro,* the "thief of the coconut palms"), which have perfected this capacity and always live in the open air, entering the water only for reproduction.

Each species has its own shapes and colorings, and these are generally bright. When they feed on the dry land during low tide, they enliven the uniform, obscure colors of the mud and turbid wells, standing out like carnival confetti or shining, colored glass. The aquamarine hues of the *Sesarma,* the violet tints of the *Metapograpsus,* the sparkling appendages of the *Sarmantium,* and the red claws of the *Macropthalmus.* Such bright colors lead us to deduce that their function is for territorial warning and sexual attraction. The same holds true for the most striking of the crabs in the mangrove forest, the fiddler crab, of the genus *Uca.*

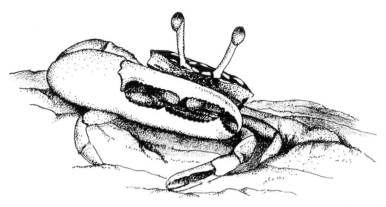

Male fiddler crab *(Uca* spp.) demonstrating the typical disproportion between the two claws.

Fiddler Crabs. Only the males have an enormously developed chela, which is as large as the entire body. This "super chela" is absolutely useless for striking or for feeding, and, as for its alimentary utility, a male requires twice as much time for feeding as a female, who can successfully utilize both chelae. From this derives a general stress, which probably also causes a reduction in the average life of the "stronger" sex. That abnormal appendage has sacrificed any alimentary functionality in order to become, instead, a means of communication. The only direct use made of it is during the course of combat, when the two competitors face off, grasping each other by the chelae until the weaker of the two surrenders. Flaunting its great uplifted, colored chela, and rotating it continuously (from which the association with the fiddle), the crab waves its "banner" of maleness and territorial ownership.

With the high tide, many of the crabs take refuge in their dens, waiting for the waters to recede again before emerging into the open. In the innermost portion of the mangrove forest, where inundation is more rare, there are fewer species. Among these are the large *Sesarma,* which is carnivorous, or the previously mentioned *Cardiosoma,* herbivorous, both of which are able to dig tunnels several meters (or several yards) deep, until reaching subterranean water. A colony of crabs in the dry mangrove forest provides an ever-changing spectacle. Skirmishes, attacks, territorial invasions, attempts to occupy the dens of other crabs—and the rapid responses of the owners! A thousand signals and an intense, ritualized visual communication, choreographed with bizarre undulations and mysterious gestures. Fiddler crabs are also capable of emitting sounds, using the method of stridulation that is common among arthropods. They rub one claw against their carapace, producing sounds with different meanings, many of which are still unknown. The crabs are involved continuously with feeding, defending their territory, or courting females, and, notwithstanding this whirl of activity, they are always on the alert and ready to flee into their dens at the slightest danger. This diffidence is a vital adaptation against the numerous predators that are not only ready to take advantage of such an abundant alimentary resource—but are rather well specialized at doing so.

A Fish out of Water . . . or In

Characteristic of the mangrove expanses are the fish of the Gobiidae family, relatives of the temperate sea and river gobies *(Gobius).* The **mudskip-**

pers, of which the genera *Periophthalmus* and *Boleophthalmus* are the most widely distributed from Africa to Oceania, are exceptionally well adapted to this environment, which requires strong tendencies towards an amphibian lifestyle. They are striking because of their humorous, almost impertinent appearance, with an enormous head and their great protruding, practically telescopic eyes. Their pectoral fins can be folded into a sort of joint simulating an elbow and these are used—neither more nor less—like a seal's flippers, for supporting themselves or for advancing, dragging the passive body behind. When frightened, the pushing of the tail contributes as well, and they are capable of skipping about on the mud or across the surfaces of the water with admirable rapidity. The ventral fins are located right under the pectoral fins, in a close position that facilitates their perambulation, or, in the case of the *Periophthalmus,* they are united to form a single, circular "suction cup" that permits it to adhere onto and climb rocks, aerial roots, or trunks. Their eyesight is excellent, as is demonstrated by the details of the colors used in intraspecific communication, such as the spots on the throat or the ocelli dispersed on the body, which are sometimes quite brilliant or even phosphorescent. The eyes have perfect monocular or binocular vision, according to how they are oriented, and the directions of the eyeballs can be changed with broad movements.

Mudskippers can often be observed in the open, and indeed, it is certain that they pass the greater part of their life outside of water, all the while

Mudskippers are typical fish of the mangrove forests. They pass the majority of their time almost completely out of water.

The archer fish *(Toxotes jaculator),* which lives among the mangrove forests and Asian coastal waters, captures its small prey by striking them with a jet of water. It has learned to obviate the problem of refraction by positioning itself nearly perpendicularly to the water surface.

maintaining the anatomy and physiology of a fish. Two tactics, or adaptations, therefore, become essential. The most important addresses how to survive in contact with the air, and here the strategy employed is simple but efficient. Their branchial chambers retain a quantity of water by means of the hermetic closure of their lateral opercula, and this water is replaced after it has been deoxygenated. Secondly, since fish have no eyelids, their eyes need regular moistening, which mudskippers accomplish by periodically retracting their eyeballs back into the ocular sacks from which they protrude, where there is sufficient moisture and water for this purpose.

Territories in the Mud. Communities of mudskippers are no less lively and bustling than are the crab colonies. Indeed, among mudskippers, communication is even more intense, especially when engaged in the defense of their small territories or when courting females. The males will often face off with their dorsal fins raised in a threatening manner, opening their mouths wide in provocation or to bite each another, jumping and chasing after one another with postures and gestures that are more or less ritualized according to the species. And then they spend hours feeding, the *Periophthalmus* by capturing small invertebrates, and the *Boleophthalmus* by gathering mud and water into its mouth and then expelling it all after having filtered it, using a mechanism that is still not completely understood.

The *Toxotes jaculator,* or archer fish, lives in the Indo-Pacific mangroves and even though it can be found in fresh waters or coral barriers as well, it elects the waters of the mangrove forest as its ideal habitat. It also feeds on small aquatic organisms, and the specialization with which it integrates its diet is, to say the least, surprising. If you happen to observe a jet of water droplets rising out through the surface of the water, possibly even arching up as high as 2 m (80 inches), look right under the surface, and if you're quick enough, you may catch a glimpse of a small light fish with a dark back and irregularly striped flanks, still in its "shooting position," perpendicular to the surface of the water. By means of this technique, it strikes small insects that fly or rest on small protruding branches or hanging leaves. The jet of water causes the prey to fall, and the fish rushes over to devour it. This technique is particularly ingenious, because by positioning itself at almost 90° with respect to the surface, it avoids the usual error due to visual refraction between the water and the air.

The Strategy of Being Amphibian

Many terrestrial or winged species frequent the mangroves in a rather assiduous manner, if not exclusively. In Asia, there are two monkeys that are particularly bound to this environment, namely, the magnificent, herbivorous proboscis monkey *(Nasalis larvatus,* endemic to the island of Borneo), which feeds on the flowers of the *Nipa* palm and leaves of the *Sonneratia,* and the crab-eating macaque *(Macaca irus),* whose diet is based primarily on invertebrates—crabs in particular. Both of these monkeys have social habits and are able swimmers, reflecting the requirements imposed by their habitats. The same tendencies are found in other mammals as well, such as certain viverrids, like the crab-eating mongoose *(Herpestes urva),* or the civet otter *(Cynophaga bennettii,* equally aquatic and arboreal), both of which are Asiatic. Several species of otters and the elusive fishing cat *(Felis viverrina)* also frequent this aquatic habitat, although they can also live in rivers, lakes, or marshes.

Those who approach the mangrove by flying over it resolve a large part of the "technical" problems imposed by the mud and the tides. Some species of **flying foxes,** the large frugivorous and nectarivorous bats, visit the mangroves by night to feed on flowers of the *Sonneratia,* for which they perform an essential pollinating role, while many aquatic birds, such as

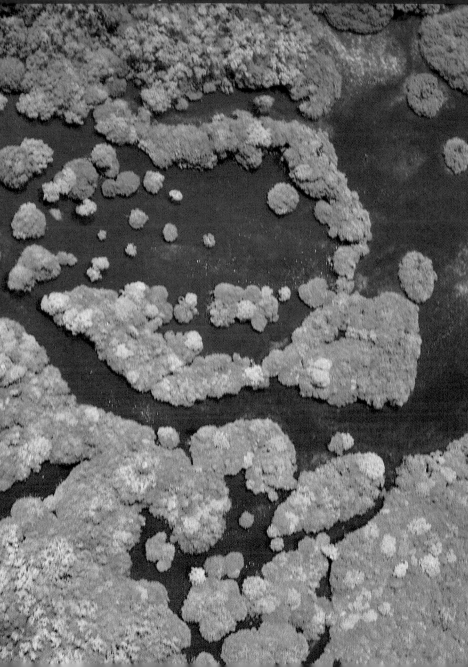

19. Green crowns of mangrove trees dot the characteristically turbid and nutrient-rich waters at the mouth of the Rufiji River.

The Horseshoe Crab

Their appearance is that of a strange armored crab, capable of launching who knows what kind of attacks. These are the limuli, or horseshoe crabs. They are marine animals related to spiders and crustaceans, but belonging to the class of Merostomata, a faunistic group that dominated during the Paleozoic era, 250 million years ago. The fossils that have been dated back to about 200 million years ago are almost indistinguishable from the five species that still survive today. Distributed throughout the Atlantic and Indo-Pacific and representing several genera, they prefer tropical latitudes. They like to go into low muddy waters of the mangroves for reproduction; the females, which are larger, are followed by the males, the two hooked together, one behind the other. The females lay their eggs, taking advantage of the high tide during a night with a full moon, and the males fertilize the eggs externally. After about a month, with the return of the high tide, the hatched larvae are dragged out into the sea, and, during the first stages of development, they contribute to the makeup of the plankton.

In areas with many horseshoe crabs, you can gather their empty shells on the beach. Since the carapace is rigid, as with most crabs, they must change their "container" when it becomes too tight, in order to be able to continue to grow, so they periodically abandon their outgrown shells.

herons, cormorants, and raptors use the trees for repose or to pass the night. You will also see kingfishers, with various species throughout the continents, fishing for crabs, and in the open waters, there are **raptors** that fish, such as white-tailed eagles (*Haliaetus* spp.), ospreys *(Pandion haliaetus),* the Asian Brahman *(Haliastur indus)* and other kites, and the fascinating fish owl *(Ketupa zeilonensis),* a nocturnal raptor specialized at capturing fish and aquatic invertebrates.

Where the tides do not inundate the forest floor as frequently, the mangrove recedes more, and here stagnating pools linger, which are renewed from time to time. This is the kingdom of the many species and genera of **mosquitoes,** some of which, like the *Anopheles, Aedes,* and *Haemagogus,* are vectors of dangerous diseases, such as malaria and yellow fever. The aquatic larvae of some mosquito species can survive in remarkable concentrations of salinity and can often tolerate huge salinity fluctuations, from below 1.5%, when the rains and river waters flood the mangrove during low tide, to over 3% during the high tide.

The trees, for their part, host some fearsome sentinels, in continuous surveillance along the trunks, branches, and leaves. The **weaver ant** *(Oecophylla smaragdina)* is exceptionally aggressive and can inflict ex-

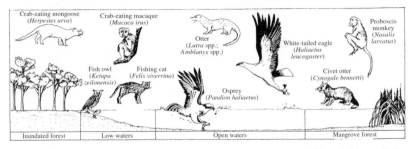

Many species of animals in the mangrove forest have developed amphibious habits, as is the case with Asian birds and mammals, among which we find felines, viverrids, and monkeys.

tremely painful bites to humans as well as to other animals. Their nest is constructed of leaves that are assembled and entwined with strands of silk that only the larvae are able to produce. The adults, then, when dealing with the construction or maintenance of their arboreal nests, take a larva between their chelae and move it up and down in contact with the edges of the leaves, as though it were a tube of quick-drying adhesive. A tree infested with these ants represents a dangerous trap for any unaware insect.

In Borneo, which has marvelous and vast expanses of mangrove forests, the **fireflies** of the genus *Pteropteryx* (the Dayaks call them *kelip-kelip*) have devised an efficient and striking strategy for communication. At nightfall they take flight and start their intermittent luminous signals, flying in sparse array until one finishes by alighting on a small mangrove branch. Its light no longer being in motion attracts the attention of its companions who watchfully evaluate its duration. If the light stays steady long enough, then, one after the next, the other fireflies alight beside the first. In short, a luminous flow directs itself toward the tree, and, extraordinarily, that disarranged intermittence becomes ordered and synchronous. Each firefly lights up in time with the others, and all together they seem to light and extinguish a large, luminous sign. The first to take its position is the most temerarious, because, in fact, one out of three of the trees hosts the dangerous predatory ants. If the light signal persists, this means that the plant is disencumbered of predators and a secure venue for the amorous pyrotechnic spectacle.

Aquatic Birds

Hammerkop
Scopus umbretta
Africa
Family Scopidae, Africa

Pied kingfisher
Ceryle rudis
Africa and southern Asia
Family Alcedinidae, worldwide

Pelican
Pelecanus onocrotalus
Southern Europe, Africa, southwest
Family Pelecanidae, worldwide

Comb-crested jacana
Irediparra gallinacea
Australia
Family Jacanidae, pantropical

Oriental darter
Anhinga melanoga
Asia
Family Anhingidae, pan

Greater flamingo
Phoenicopterus ruber
Southern Europe, Africa, western Asia
Family Phoenicopteridae,
southern Europe, Africa, Asia,
Central and South America

Sacred ibis
Threskiornis aethiopica
Africa
Family Threskiornitidae,
worldwide

An Exciting Habitat—An Important Resource

Mangroves support a moderate diversity of terrestrial fauna, but an extremely varied wealth of invertebrates and (although to a lesser extent, but still considerable) aquatic vertebrates. Further, they provide refuge and areas for reproduction for a very large number of marine animals, including commercial species, such as fish and crustaceans. In Fiji, about half of the fish upon which human consumption and commerce depend require the mangroves for at least part of their life cycle, whether this be reproduction, coupling, weaning of the fry, or their successive growth in size. In Australia, the percentage is even greater, as high as 67%.

The renowned **king prawns** that are served as a delicacy in many tropical restaurants come from calm lagoons that are nourishing and low, surrounded by mangroves.

The mangroves are one of the most productive ecosystems of the entire planet. They represent formidable barriers against erosion by stabilizing the shorelines with their intricate root systems, reducing the effects of waves, and acting as natural barriers against coastal storms. In many cases they produce more wood for fuel per hectare than any inland forest.

About 240,000 km^2 (93,000 mi^2) of mangrove habitats have been mapped throughout the world, and the greatest expanses are found first in Southeast Asia, then in Africa, and then South America. The most extended mangrove forest in the world is that of the Ganges delta between India and Bangladesh, the so-called Sunderbans, famous also for its particularly aggressive tigers.

Such peculiar environmental characteristics, and their cosmopolitan distribution within the tropical zone, make the mangrove forests a rather uniform and recurrent habitat, although there may even be marked geographical variations, as have been briefly described. Someone traveling from the coasts of Venezuela to those of the Gulf of Guinea in western Africa, from the Malagasy or Kenyan coasts to those of Southeast Asia, or even as far as the islands of Oceania and northern Australia, would recognize a mangrove formation anywhere. Luxuriant evergreen forests, admirable pioneers of the interface between sea and land, tenacious colonies of the river mouths and lagoons, where the bizarre and disquieting, contorted aerial roots sink into a deep mud that yellows the tidal waters as they periodically flood and ebb.

Within this erroneously negative stereotype of "unwholesome" marshes thrives an eye-opening wealth of biological variety, as well as an irreplaceable ecological function. The whole forms a magical and fascinating environment, one that anyone traveling through the Tropics absolutely must try to visit.

Chapter 7

Forests

Impenetrable vegetation, thick and luxuriant, enwrapped with lianas and climbing vines, is part of the idea we all share of what a "jungle" is. It is easy to understand that the most successful tropical vegetation is in turn the product of the most unique climate: the moist, rainy one of the equatorial and wet tropical zones. The most famous tropical vegetation is that of the rainforests, which house a wealth of species and adaptations, a magnificent array of structures, and dimensions perhaps unequalled by any other floral community on the planet. In an earlier chapter, we said that the soils of the wet tropics are extremely poor in nutrients and that they are defined as lateritic, being of a brick-red color, typical of the majority of rainforests. And yet, on these poor soils, some of the lushest and most imposing vegetation in the world develops. The solution to the apparent contradiction is found in the fact that in a tropical moist forest, the nutrients are transferred from the soil and stored within the living material. The plants themselves act as reservoirs of nutritive substances and are equipped with sophisticated mechanisms for conserving them. One well-known example of this is the way many plants transfer the principal nutrients from their leaves shortly before losing them.

Absorption and Recycling. The absorption system is extremely efficient. In certain forests, it has been calculated that 99% of the products of decomposition at the soil level return into the circulation of the forests' animal and plant biomass. It has also been calculated that less than 0.1% of these nutrients at the soil level penetrate beyond 5 cm (2 inches) depth. The grandiose green production is, then, the principal manure of the forest itself and is constituted, by weight, of approximately 70% leaves, 20% branches, 5% flowers and fruits, and 5% various other materials. In majestic primary forests, such as those of Malaysia and Indonesia, or in Amazonia, as much as 10 t of leaves can fall per hectare (4.5 tons per acre) per year.

Virgin Forests and Secondary Jungles

Probably deriving from adventure books and documentaries, from Kipling to Salgari or from Sandokan to Tarzan, some commonplaces and stereotypes regarding tropical forests induce us into macroscopic errors. The image of a dense and impenetrable vegetation, a green wall that rises from the soil to the canopy is, in reality, a characteristic of secondary or riparian forests. The actual primary forest is another thing entirely. By "primary," we mean a natural, virgin forest that is intact and unspoiled by influences from man or alterations from natural cataclysms. It is estimated that the forest around the great temples of Angkor in Kampuchea was cut about 600 years ago, and it still does not appear to have been completely reconstituted since that time, if compared with the structure and the wealth of other virgin forests of the same region. It is estimated that after a disturbance such as a wide-scale deforestation—and this can vary based on the environmental conditions—that 500 to 1,000 years are necessary to have a true primary tropical forest anew. A part of one forest that is considered primary in Guatemala has revealed Mayan archeological findings dating back more than 1,000 years. And in Central America and on the Yucatan, the abundance of certain trees in the mahogany family would appear to be related to the promotion of these prized woods by local populations many centuries ago.

The virgin **primary forest** is truly a special environment. A place where the trees unite their crowns to create a canopy suspended at a height of about fifty meters, where the ground is as dark as though in an eternal twilight, and where half of the life on the entire planet lives: this is the primary tropical forest. The ground is practically devoid of any vegetation because of the scarceness of the light filtering through the canopy layer, and it is extremely rare to need a machete in order to proceed on foot. The plants of a primary rainforest are 80% trees or shrubs, and only 20% are herbaceous, since a large part of the light (sometimes over

90%) does not reach the soil and the lower strata of the understory. For the same reason, the plants of the **undergrowth** on the floor, including the young, newly growing trees, have many broad leaves, in order to gather the maximum possible light from the little that filters through. Many trees are only able to flower after having reached the canopy layer, where there is more light. Only where the fall of a great tree creates an opening (a light gap), do the sunrays produce an exuberant, luxuriant growth, an intricate vegetation growing rapidly in the opportunistic attempt to emerge and reach the stratum of the crowns of the "tropical vault," thus to guarantee their survival even after this temporary gap becomes filled again with mature forest growth.

Profile of a Tropical Forest

Besides the humidity, the violent and frequent storms, the size of the trees, and the luxuriance of the vegetation, there are some other components that recur in all the rainforests of the globe, without (or nearly without) distinction among the continents, and these generalizations are even more particularly true if we focus on the equatorial belt. This is the result of the adaptation to a climatic and environmental situation that is among the most homogeneous and constant in the world, so it is understandable how the structure and functions of these ecosystems can resemble each other, even at thousands of kilometers (or thousands of miles) distance.

In particular, some of the typical and recurrent **characteristics of rainforests** are:

- evergreen trees;
- abundance of woody and herbaceous lianas and epiphytes;
- presence of climbing stranglers (*Ficus*—pantropical, *Clusia*—Neotropical, *Wightia*—Indo-Malaysia);
- scarcity of ground litter, because of the high degree of decomposition and recycling;
- involvement of animals, including insects, birds, and mammals, in the plant mechanisms of pollination, predation, and dispersion, more than in any other vegetation system on the planet.

A further structural characteristic of trees of the rainforests is the presence of stilt roots and **buttresses,** those unmistakable wide, winged ribs that start from the broad bases of the trunks. Their function has been hypothesized as support for the large trees in a moist, yielding terrain. These

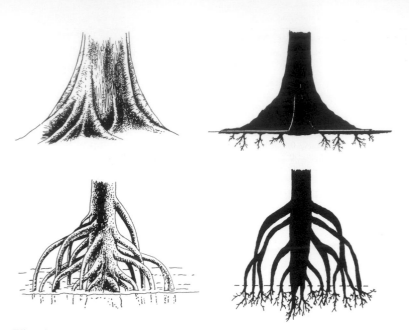

Winged roots, or buttresses (above) are typical of many trees in the tropical moist forests. These are actual ribs that widen at the base of the trunk, exceeding its radius by as much as 5 m (16 ft) in the largest trees. Some trees that live in zones that are often flooded have developed "stilt roots" (below). In both examples, the sections show the distribution of the roots near the surface: a recurring characteristic of many plants of the rainforests.

structures also compensate for the absence of deep taproots, substituted largely in tree species of tropical forests by roots that are primarily superficial. According to research conducted in a sample of Malaysian forest, 41% of the trees had winged ribs at the base. It has recently been suggested that there may be a correlation between the presence of buttresses, which correspond to the occupying of a greater basal area, and the growth of a smaller number of other plants in the nearby vicinity of the tree. An additional function would therefore appear to be competition with other trees, besides that of support for the plant.

From the floor to the canopy. The structure of a tropical forest is not as easy to define or schematize as it can sometimes be for certain temperate woods. The grassy stratum is present and sufficiently dense only in forests that are characterized by a certain seasonality, and thus it is almost entirely

Countries Having the Most Extensive Rainforests

Country	Country Size	Total Forested Area	"Virgin" Primary Forest	% of the World's Tropical Forests
Brazil	8,500,000 km² (3,280,000 mi²)	3,500,000 km² (1,350,000 mi²)	2,800,000 km² (1,081,000 mi²)	30.5
DRC	2,350,000 km² (910,000 mi²)	1,190,000 km² (459,000 mi²)	800,000 km² (309,000 mi²)	10.5
Indonesia	1,900,000 km² (734,000 mi²)	1,130,000 km² (436,000 mi²)	390,000 km² (151,000 mi²)	10.0
Peru	1,300,000 km² (502,000 mi²)	700,000 km² (270,000 mi²)	350,000 km² (135,000 mi²)	6.0
Colombia	1,150,000 km² (444,000 mi²)	500,000 km² (193,000 mi²)	350,000 km² (135,000 mi²)	4.5
Bolivia	1,100,000 km² 425,000 mi²)	450,000 km² (174,000 mi²)	180,000 km² (69,000 mi²)	4.0
Papua New Guinea	480,000 km² (185,000 mi²)	350,000 km² (135,000 mi²)	130,000 km² (50,000 mi²)	3.0
Venezuela	900,000 km² (347,000 mi²)	300,000 km² (116,000 mi²)	80,000 km² (31,000 mi²)	2.5
Myanmar	680,000 km² (263,000 mi²)	300,000 km² (116,000 mi²)	140,000 km² (54,000 mi²)	2.5

Sources: A. Newman, 1990. *Tropical Rainforest*. R. A. Mittermeier, P. R. Gil, C. G. Mittermeier, 1997. *Megadiversity.*

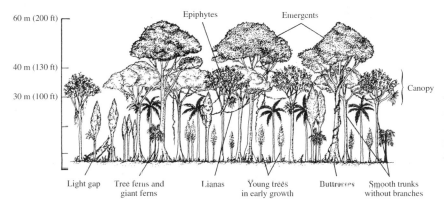

60 m (200 ft)

40 m (130 ft)

30 m (100 ft)

Epiphytes   Emergents

Canopy

Light gap   Tree ferns and giant ferns   Lianas   Young trees in early growth   Buttresses   Smooth trunks without branches

Schematic representation of the structure of a lowland tropical moist forest, with its principal characteristics. *On the forest floor:* Absence of sun (with the exception of light gaps), absence of wind, 28°C (82°F), 90% humidity. *In the canopy layer:* direct or filtering sun, wind, 32°C (90°F), 60% humidity.

absent in the primary rainforests. The intermediary strata are occupied by young trees in early stages of growth and bushes and ferns, which are rather rare or highly scattered in primary rainforests, but well developed in secondary rainforests and in light gaps; these are medially present in seasonal forests. These plants usually occupy the first 10 m (or about 35 ft) of vertical space, and there is often a void from there to the beginnings of the crowns, which start at 20 m or higher. Many young trees, in fact, die before reaching more than 10 m, while bushes and ferns never become very tall. Where the vegetation is less dense, whether because of the seasonal nature of the rains that determine critical periods of dryness, or after the fall of large trees, or because of influences from man, it becomes luxuriant and intricate, without properly identifiable strata. In undisturbed conditions, on the other hand, the crowns of trees constitute a dense layer of vegetation suspended above the ground level, between about 25 m and 50 m (80 to 165 ft), depending on several factors, and this is called the "canopy layer." From the canopy, which is distributed on a rather homogeneous plane, some large trees protrude, which is very typical in such forests, and these are called the "emergents," veritable giants, as high as 70 m (230 ft) and beyond. The crowns of young trees tend to be monopodial, that is, having one single principal stalk around which the foliage is distributed. This arrangement probably has the function of investing the majority of the tree's resources into a vertical, rather than circumferential, expansion, thus allowing the tree to reach the canopy layer more efficiently, giving it a better chance to survive. Mature trees, on the other hand, are sympodial, that is without a principal stalk, but with ramifications that give rise to a broad, umbrella-like foliage that reaches its maximum development in the great emergents, which are no longer hampered by adjacent foliage.

The Ecology of a Green Universe

The Most Imposing Forests. The dimensions of a forest depend only to a slight extent on the type of soil. The type of soil has more influence on the selection of the species than on the vigor of the trees themselves. In rainforests in Asia, for example, it seems that the trees of the Dipterocarpaceae and Leguminosae family prefer sandy soils, while the laurel, sapodilla, and mahogany families (Lauraceae, Sapotaceae, and Meliaceae, respectively) prefer lateritic soils.

More important are factors such as rainfall, humidity of the soil, and seasonality of the rains and temperature. The tallest forests are found in the lowlands or hilly areas below 1,200 m (4,000 ft), where there are alternations between a relatively dry season and a more humid one, well-drained soils, and rainfall around 2,000 mm (80 inches) per year or more. Finally, factors relating to the biogeography of the zone and to the type of evolution undergone by entire ecosystems through the millennia play a part. In Amazonia, the canopy is at 30 to 40 m (100 to 130 ft) with emergents of the genera *Mora, Bogassa,* and *Tetragastris* and Brazil nut trees *(Bdertholletia excelsa),* at about 50 m (165 ft). In Asia, the crowns are distributed at around 50 m, with emergents at 60 m (200 ft) and higher. The tallest recorded tropical tree has been measured at 83.82 m (275 ft), in Sarawak, the Malaysian part of Borneo: this is the tall, green titan *Koompassia excelsa* (Leguminosae), noted as being one of the most frequent emergent giants of the tropical forests of these regions.

There are many types of tropical forests that cannot be clearly classified on the basis of the species of the dominant tree or trees, as can generally be done for temperate forests, and this is because of the extremely high diversity of species. In Guyana, in 2 km² (0.75 mi²) of forest land, there are about 3,000 plant species, 190 in 2 hectares (10 per acre). From Malaysia to New Guinea, 30,000 species have been described, over a tenth

of the total known plants in the world, which are estimated at about 250,000. These are only a few examples of the incredible **floristic diversity** of tropical forests, which are often characterized by a low number of individuals within a given species. The record for floristic diversity seems to be held by the forests of Costa Rica, where, in only 100 m^2, 233 different species of plants have been classified (equating to about 280 per 100 yd^2), followed by those of Borneo, with 700 species of trees in 10,000 m^2 (or about 585 in 10,000 yd^2).

Roger Heim, a renowned botanist, defined the Amazon forest as an undisciplined army where nobody commands or obeys, underlining the extreme mixture of species in comparison with the homogeneous expanses of spruce, fir, oak, or pine forests of the temperate regions. Nevertheless, there are some general differences among the families of large trees that distinguish the three principal blocks of rainforests in the world (Central and South America, western and central Africa, and Indo-Malaysia). In the southeast of Asia, one characteristic family dominates, that of the Dipterocarpaceae, while the Cesalpinaceae are present, in numerous species, in Africa and South America, along with the Cariocaraceae, Chrysobalan-

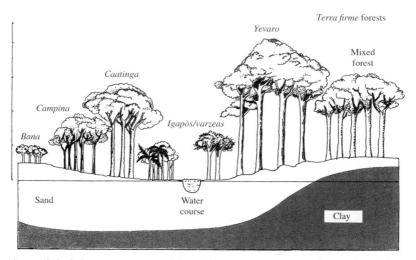

Amazonia includes numerous types of forest formations, depending on the soil, the presence of water courses, and the frequency of flooding. In order to give an idea of the variety, here is the succession of the various typologies of forest in a typical section near the Rio Negro.

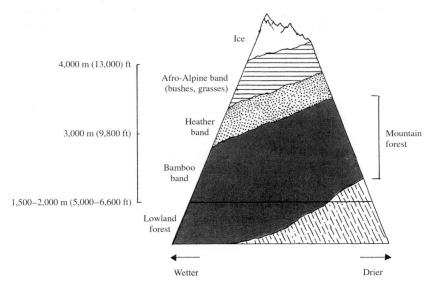

Due to the very hot climate, tropical mountain vegetation reaches higher altitudes than vegetation at temperate latitudes. Distribution of the vegetation in a mountain in equatorial Africa (above) and in Venezuela (facing). In this latter case, the vegetation varies along a north-south gradient in accordance with how the rainfall of the nation varies (expressed in mm [and inches] per year).
Source: A. Goudie, 1989.

aceae, and Dichapetalaceae. Tropical America hosts the maximum plant diversity, with nearly 80,000 species of vascular plants. Africa maintains the "lowest" wealth, with the still remarkable figure of approximately 30,000 species, and Asia, an intermediary value, with about 45,000 species. The forests of the Pacific, since they are located in very remote, insular environments, exhibit only 4,000 species, but a very high rate of endemism.

Rainforests are evergreen and hygrophilous, at least 30 m (100 ft) tall, rich with lianas and ligneous and herbaceous epiphytes. They develop in areas having at least 2,000 mm (about 80 inches) of annual precipitation, but normally with values that are double this, triple, or even beyond, and with no more than two "dry" months (those characterized by a marked diminution of rainfall). In general, botanists consider the lowland rainforests to be those with elevations of up to 1,200 m (4,000 ft) above sea level, beyond which the structure alters somewhat, to assume the characteristic features of **mountain forests.** The higher the altitude, the less majestic the tropical forest becomes. The lowland forest, in fact, presents a canopy at 25 to 40 m (80 to 130 ft), with frequent emergents, while, in the mountains, the crowns develop at 15 to 30 m (50 to 100 ft), without obvious emergents. On the other hand, the great abundance and variety of mosses, lichens, and epiphytes in the mountain rainforests make these habitats, as well, very special and fascinating places.

The **monsoon forests** (or **seasonal tropical forests**), are not as tall in general, nor as imposing, and in these, the precipitation can even be rather elevated during the rainy seasons, but this is interrupted by a period of over three months of reduced rainfall. These are rich with lianas and epiphytes, for the most part herbaceous. Normally, the trees are not evergreens, but deciduous, losing their leaves in the dry season.

The Many Other Forests of the Tropics. The name **tropical moist forest** was recently proposed by tropical ecologist Norman Myers to characterize wet forests of the Tropics that are evergreen or partially evergreen, in areas receiving no less than 1,200 mm (about 47 inches) of rain

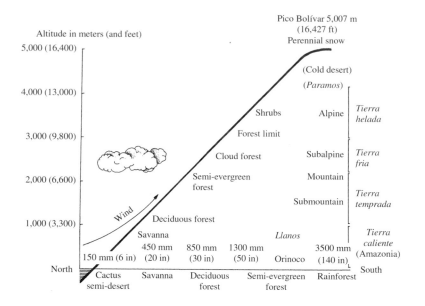

per year, for two years out of three, with an average annual temperature of over 24°C (75°F), and located below 1,300 m (4,300 ft) altitude. This category includes the **gallery** or **riparian** forests, the **swamp** and **bog forests** (and other flooded forests of various typologies), and finally, the classical **lowland rainforests.** The **cloud forests** of the high hills and mountains are also referred to as tropical moist forests, because of their high rainfall and humidity.

In the alluvial plains, broad tracts of forest near great water courses that overflow during the rainy seasons are flooded for long periods. The floristic diversity in these conditions is poorer than in the forests of the dry lowlands or the low hills. As in the mangrove forests, only the plants that are specialized in managing the root damage caused by prolonged periods of immersion can survive. The broadest expanses of flooded forests today are found in New Guinea, along the Sepik and Fly rivers, and in various areas of Kalimantan, where the sago palms dominate *(Eugessona utilis).* The Congo basin in central Africa also hosts large areas of flooded forests.

In **Amazonia,** the forest formations in areas subjected to flooding depend upon the types of waters. The *vàrzea* forests develop in conjunction with the large rivers that descend from the Andes, such as the Madeira and Amazon Rivers. Enormous quantities of suspended sediments become trapped by the root systems, thus becoming constituents of the soils of these forests that are flooded by the so-called white waters (in reality, these would more correctly be called yellow or orange waters, because of their roiled sediment). In areas having sandy soil, by contrast, *igapò* forests grow, which are flooded almost continually by the "black" waters of rivers like the Rio Negro, the Tapajos, and the Arapiuns. The waters are transparent and bear coarse material of plant origin, but not the large quantities of suspended sediment typical of white waters. The floors of *igapò* forests can be submerged by water for four to seven months of the year, with a depth of up to 12 m (39 ft). In Amazonia as well, these forests are rich with palms of various species, and, among the trees, the kapok *(Ceiba pentandra)* dominates, with its enormous buttresses and its seeds that are similar to cotton, hence its common name, the silk-cotton tree. In flooded forests, *igapò* forests especially, some slow-growing trees may be submerged for the greater part of the year and pass the first twenty-some years of life seeing sunlight only through the surface of the water and only for a few, brief periods.

The *igapòs* are characterized by the presence of many ferns, with trees that are not very tall, having bases with ribs and stilts to support the plant, numerous epiphytes because of the extremely high humidity, and sparse lianas. Dry, or *terra firme,* forests, by contrast, occupy interfluvial areas and have tall trees, lianas, and epiphytes that are diffuse, but not extremely abundant. And finally, the *vàrzeas* are forests that are flooded temporarily, with a typical presence of many palms, such as the *Pachiuba,* with their showy stilt roots, or the *Geonema,* which is small and very thorny.

The Collapse of Giants and the Feast of the Colonizers

An integral part of a primary forest is the presence of many light gaps, both real and potential. Despite a life span of several centuries in some cases, trees are not immortal and, with age, they become more subject to attacks from fungi and insects. Additionally, the development of epiphytes, lianas, and stranglers can provoke the fall of large branches or entire trees. The sounds of falling trees or parts of trees echo with alarming frequency in a primary forest. In Malaysia, 10% of the forest area is covered by gaps of various ages. The ecology of the recolonization is fascinating. The array of ecological opportunities produced by the formation of a light gap induces responses that differ according to the species. There are many plants that grow slowly, tolerating the darkness of the understory while waiting for such an event (the shade-bearers), and others are actually stimulated to germinate by the opening of a light gap (the pioneers). Many pioneer trees have vertical or inclined stalks, which, in any case, are very light and spongy as a consequence of their very rapid growth. The *Trema micrantha* (Ulmaceae) in Costa Rica grows 9 m (30 ft) in its first year, and in eight years, it can measure taller than 30 m (100 ft). Some pioneers have short lives, linked to particular stages of recolonization of the light gap, while others are persistent and become forest giants, such as the kapok (*Ceiba pentandra,* Bombaceae) of the African and American jungles. Some, like the traveler's palm (*Ravenala madagascariensis,* endemic to Madagascar and not a palm at all, but a relative of the banana family), are pioneers whose seeds can remain quiescent for many years, awaiting the opportunity to germinate and grow.

Normally a light gap measures from 20 to 700 m^2 (25 to 850 yd^2) or even more, depending on the size of the fallen tree and the number of other

Epiphytes on the Three Continents

The number of epiphytes in a tropical moist forest is extremely high. Botanists have verified that one-fourth of all the lowland forest plants are epiphytes, and this proportion is even greater in the mountains. Tropical America counts over 15,550 species of epiphytes. Africa has a smaller variety of these because it suffered more under the stress of the glacial period. Forty-seven different species of epiphyte orchids have been classified on one single emergent of the African jungle. Colombia is the world leader in orchid diversity, with between 300 and 500 of the world's total number of species, which is estimated to be between 2,500 and 3,500.

Epiphytes are distributed throughout the various strata of the forest. Those that live in the canopy are adapted to resisting the scorching sun and the violence of the direct downpours. In the understory, by contrast, the epiphytes are resistant to the constant humidity and the shortage of light.

In the three principal blocks of tropical moist forests on the planet—Indo-Malaysia, central western Africa, and Central and South America—there are analogies and peculiarities between the categories of epiphytes present:

Neotropics—ferns, orchids, bromeliads, cacti.
Africa—ferns, orchids.
Indo-Malaysia—ferns, orchids, Asclepiadaceae, Rubiaceae.

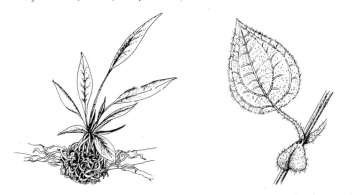

Many plants referred to as "myrmecophiles" (friends to ants) derive advantage from the hospitality they offer, in various modes, to established colonies of ants, which liberate them from parasitic and herbivorous insects. *Anthurium gracile* (left), an Amazonian epiphyte, welcomes the ants *Pachycondyla goeldii* into the network of its supporting roots; *Clidemia tococoidea* (right) has actually developed sacks that are favored by the ants of the genus *Azteca*.

Parrots

Saint Vincent Amazon
Amazona guildingii
Lesser Antilles

Grey parrot
Psittacus erithacus
Africa

Sun conure
Aratinga solstitialis
South America

Masked lovebird
Agapornis personata
Africa

Collared parakeet
Psittacula krameri
Africa, Asia

Hyacinth macaw
Anodorhynchus hyacinthus
South America

Eastern rosella
Platycercus eximius
Australia

Black-winged lory
Eos cyanogenia
New Guinea

Greater yellow-tufted cockatoo
Cacatua galerita
Australia, New Guinea, and nearby islands

Rainbow lorikeet
Trichoglossus haematodus
Australia and nearby islands

Blue-faced parakeet
Psephotus haematogaster
Australia

Red-crowned dwarf parrot
Micropsitta bruijnii
New Guinea

trees involved. The density of the plants in the light gap increases greatly in the first two to four years. The immobilization (meaning the conversion of an element from an inorganic to an organic state by an organism) of the nutrients occurs rapidly. Young regenerations of eight or fifteen years are as capable of immobilizing phosphorus as is a fifty-year old forest.

A Universe of Fruits and Flowers

The Strategy of Flowering. In a climate as homogeneous and constant as that of many tropical areas, particularly those around the equatorial belt, an obvious question is what, if any, is the periodicity of the flowering or the fructification, because the seasons are not as distinctly pronounced as in the ecology of temperate areas. Among the most celebrated comestible tropical fruits are the papaya *(Carica papaya),* the banana *(Musa paradisiaca),* and the pineapple *(Ananas comosus),* which bear fruit throughout the entire course of the year. Durians *(Durio zibethinus),* mangosteens *(Garcinia mangostana),* mangos (*Mangifera* spp.), and lansehs *(Lansium domesticum)* have specific seasons. In lowland rainforests, it is difficult to establish exact rules for fructification, which, rather, are linked to many changeable factors, and the infinite strategies and modalities vary from species to species. Some plants, such as the *Dillenia suffruticosa* in Malaysia, flower continuously, from sprouting stage on through to death. The *Homalium grandiflorum* (Flacourtiaceae), again in Malaysia, flowers once every 10 to 15 years. In Southeast Asia, many trees of the Dipterocarpaceae family and, in Amazonia, the *Tapirira guaianensis,* for example, adopt the strategy of the "big bang," with exceptional aesthetic impact: all the tree's flowers open simultaneously, loading the branches with an enormous floral mass. In this manner, the plant guarantees that a certain number of flowers, fruits, and seeds will be able to resist the predatory action of insects, birds, and arboreal mammals. A contrasting strategy is that of the "steady state," adopted, for instance, by plants of the genus *Gurania,* again in Amazonia, which provides for a flowering that is well distributed through time, opening only one or two flowers per day, in order to give the opportunity to its pollinators (which are solitary, nomad bees) to locate the plant and to find some available flowers. At the forest floor, flowers are often showy and have a long individual life, or they are highly perfumed and are produced at longer intervals.

In forests that are more seasonal, the flowers often open at the end of the dry season, giving rise to the hypothesis that it is the stress of the lack of water that stimulates the flowering. There are many strategies utilized by the various species in regard to fructification as well. One of these is known as monocarpism. Trees such as the Amazonian *Tachigalia mirmecofila* take many years to grow, and after the first and only flowering and dispersion of seeds, they conclude their existence. Every strategy has a motive and conceals an adaptive advantage. In this case, it seems that the death of the plant immediately after fructification serves to create a light gap in the forest, so as to facilitate the birth and development of its own recently dispersed seeds.

Some plants flower and bear fruit at regular intervals, but the majority do so without any relation to time or climate.

Considering the forest community, and despite the many specific variations, it is possible to distinguish a peak in the production of leaves and flowers, which normally occurs at the end of the dry season, and a second, smaller cycle, in the more humid season, which also includes fructification.

The Microcosm of the *Ficus* Flower. Figs (genus *Ficus*) are extremely important plants in the forest ecology, as they supply food to many animals. In accordance with correct botanical terminology, figs are not fruits, but syconia, which actually are inflorescences, even though, ecologically speaking, they have the value and function of true fruits. They are edible, in fact, and rich with nutritive substances. The wall of the flower is curved, forming a small, half-closed bowl. The pollinators for the figs are small fig wasps (Agaonidae, about 1 mm long, or 4 hundredths of an inch). Quite often, each *Ficus* species has its own pollinating wasp. The female flowers develop first, and the female wasps, which are winged, force an entry into several of the "fruits." In so doing, they often end up losing their wings and antennae. With their ovipositors, they deposit an egg into the ovary of the flower. The wasps, thus, are pollinators, but also predators of seeds. Thirty percent of the seeds, in fact, are killed by the wasp larvae, which nourish themselves on these in order to develop. The apterous males develop first, which seek out the female larvae and inseminate them before they transform into adults. Then they dig a tunnel to exit from the fig and go to die nearby or within the fig itself. The tunnel allows a reduction of the concentration of carbon dioxide within the fig (from 10% down to

Strangler Plants

Some of the plants of the genus *Ficus,* distributed throughout all three of the principal geographical blocks of the tropical forests, possess very special habits. Their exceptional biology has merited them the name of "stranglers."

The seed germinates above, in the canopy, wedged into the bifurcation of a branch, or within a crack or cavity of the tree trunk—having arrived there by chance or transported there by a squirrel, a monkey, or a bird. The young plant adheres to the wood and receives nutrients from the rainwater that runs along the trunk. This is what botanists define as a typical semiepiphyte. In fact, as soon as its survival has been assured, long aerial roots begin to sprout from the plant, and these grow, fluttering in what little wind is able to penetrate into the canopy layer and the understory, until they reach the soil. Here, they fix themselves solidly, enlarge, and become woodier, multiplying in the meantime. About the host trunk, a cage of ligneous sticks begins to form, which finally all merge together in the attempt to acquire solidity. Meanwhile, the small, originally epiphytic plant receives nutrients directly from the soil and develops abundant new foliage that invades the crown of the host. The result is normally the death of the large host tree, which comes about through the suffocation of the trunk and the obscuring of the crest. At first sight, the luxuriance of the leaves of the strangler fig mask the crime, and even the aerial roots are melded so adherently as to appear to be the actual trunk, rather than the appendages of a parasite. With a bit of attention one can recognize the skeletal, or suffering, branches of the host tree amid the tangle of the climber. Once the tree is dead, the fig penetrates, with its aerial roots, into the decomposing wood, and then it takes on the role of a saprophyte. After many years, when the host trunk has rotted completely, a great crash signals the fall, and the end, of this extraordinary, profiteering fig.

Besides the genus *Ficus,* there are other plants with "strangling" habits, no less specialized or amazing. There are the genera of *Spondias* (cashew family, Anacardiaceae) in the Philippines, *Fagraea* (Loganiaceae) and *Timonius* (Rubiaceae) in Papuasia, and *Clusia* and *Coussapoa* (Urticaceae, or nettle family) in America. Not all necessarily cause the death of the host (for example, the *Clusia* does not).

Jungle Cicadas

One of the most curious experiences while trekking in the jungle is connected to the variety of sounds, songs, and cries that come out of the vegetation, in particular from the canopy layer of a primary forest. Among the yells of the monkeys, the songs of birds, and the screeching of the insects, the stridulations of the cicadas, as well, stand out for variety and originality. Cicadas are homopterans and make up part of the huge order of Hemiptera, better known as bugs (or *true bugs*). Of the more than 2,200 species, the majority live in the Tropics, and it is logical to think that in such a universe of plant variety these animals, as well, would be diversified, as they depend on the vegetation both in their larval state under the soil, and as adults among the branches and leaves. Each species emits a characteristic noise, thanks to a complex sound production apparatus used by males to attract females. Some are simple croaks, and they recall, although usually louder, the typical chirring of the cicadas of the temperate areas. On the other hand, some species are capable of emitting sounds that would be difficult to impute to cicadas: actual whistles, steady or modulated, or sounds identical to those of an organ pipe, and other cadenced or variable noises. One species, the six o'clock cicada of the forests of Borneo, begins its song every day at precisely six in the afternoon!

0.03%), equalizing it to atmospheric values and thus stimulating both the development of the male flowers and of the female larvae. Further complicating the scenario, there are other wasps that are parasites of these fig wasps, which deposit their carnivorous larvae onto those of the fig wasps. The adults, in general, have large, long ovipositors, with which they perforate the syconium in search of the larvae, using a method of individuation that is yet unknown to science. Other wasps prey or are parasites, in turn, upon these parasites, with the result that together they constitute an unexpected microcosm about and within the small fruit of the jungle fig. This is yet another surprising example of the complexity of tropical ecology.

Climbers, Lianas, and Epiphytes

Lianas characterize a tropical forest in an unmistakable way. They crisscross the forest, usually climbing up trunks and extending from crown to crown, with lengths reaching up to 200 m (650 ft) and diameters up to 20 cm (8 inches) in their aerial stalks. At the bases of their trunks, certain species can have a diameter as large as a man. Some are straight from the start, others are tortuous. When they reach the light, often they produce leaves and flowers that can even be quite conspicuous and colorful. The liana *Clusia* has seeds that, like those of epiphytes, germinate on high. They cause their roots to fall, and as soon as these touch ground, they develop and lignify.

Often the liana will end up suffocating the plant upon which it rests, or cause it to fall. There seem to be no limits to the fantasy of the forms. Lianas of the genus *Bauhinia* have wood that exhibits so many regular little plug-holes that it resembles a speleologist's ladder. In the forest, you can often observe a climber that descends to the ground from above, forming a great eyelet, only to rise again onto another tree, forming long festoons that go on to unfold in the canopy. This phenomenon is caused by the fall of the host tree or of one of its branches, from which the climber, having fallen with its host, has climbed anew, taking advantage of other nearby plants. Climbers and adult lianas can also propagate horizontally along the canopy layer, taking advantage of the contacts between branches and leafy fronds. This may, in part, prevent a tree from falling when the wind blows, but it is equally true that if one of these trees falls, it can more easily drag down with itself the others thus connected. Lianas develop, above all, in light gaps and marginal areas such as gallery forests, and some remain quiescent while awaiting for the formation of a light gap.

The Ecology of Climbers. By definition, a climbing plant has to "climb" upwards. To achieve this common objective, the strategies adopted are many. The most simple is the use of brute force by a robust but plastic trunk that tends upward, wrapping itself around, supporting itself upon, and grasping onto the host plants with its hooks and tendrils. This is the case with the climbing rattan palms (*Plectocomia* and *Calamus* spp.), which can develop to 200 m (650 ft) in length.

Other climbers, such as those of the Araceae family, among which are the genera *Philodendron, Monstera, Rhaphidophora,* and *Scindapsus,* have two types of roots. The first type goes out at a right angle from the stalk at many points and develops an adhesive functionality. Others have an alimentary purpose and descend from above, like simple filaments, but these ramify as soon as they reach the soil.

Another technique, employed by lianas such as the *Leea, Cissus,* and *Tetrastigma,* is that of putting out false roots from the stalks or from leaves, which twist around in search of support for their progress upward. Some species wrap around with an astonishing speed: just a few minutes to complete the first turn as soon as contact has been made with the support, demonstrating the tactile stimulus for the development of the appendage.

In addition to the burden they represent for them, climbers compete with trees for light, water, and nutrients. Normally, the trees that are most easily attacked by climbers are the slow-growing species. By rapidly increasing their height and, more importantly, their diameter, trees avoid those climbers that have need of relatively thin trunks in order to be able to climb and begin their development. Other plants are not bothered at all by climbers and live comfortably together with them, suffering only minimally. There are climbers that have the appearance of a normal sapling during their initial growth, exhibiting a particularly straight bearing and with but few leafy fronds. Only when they have arrived at the base of the canopy layer do they begin to twist themselves around (e.g., *Strychnos*). Some members of the Aracaceae and Bignoniaceae families are slender climbers in youth, adhering fast to various trunks, but they radically change appearance and reinforce themselves in structure as soon as they have reached the foliage of the canopy.

About 10% of all the plants of a tropical forest are climbers. Secondary forests are particularly rich in climbers, stimulated by the fact that light can easily enter because of larger open spaces and shorter trees.

Epiphytes are plants that live with their roots attached to the trunk or to branches of other trees, often at the height of the canopy layer, without having need for an actual support structure in contact with the soil.

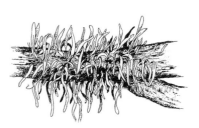

Two species of epiphytes.

Some plants, among which are many stranglers, are called semi-epiphytes, because they begin as true epiphytes, taking root on high, among the branches and foliage, but, at a certain stage of their development, they begin to generate long roots that drop until they reach the ground. Once these have penetrated the soil, they begin to lignify, becoming more robust and propagating; thus the plant is no longer an epiphyte but a direct dependent upon nutrients gathered from the soil.

Epiphytes appear to develop well and without difficulty. In reality, they live in difficult conditions to which they are well adapted. From the time of the germination of the seed within a crack in some bark, a cavity in a trunk, or a bifurcation of some branch, the small plant manufactures its own soil for itself, and this soil is retained by the roots that fix it to the substratum. This "aerial soil" is composed of detritus transported by rain flowing from the crowns along the trunks and branches, or from fallen leaves, decomposing bark, excrement, or small dead animals—or even from the fallen leaves and decayed matter of the epiphyte itself. Under such austere and difficult conditions, some species have surprisingly accentuated vegetative reductions, for example, orchids that have no leaves. This renouncing of appendages and structures diminishes the living volume of the plant, which thus saves energy. Some trees, in turn, take advantage of their guest epiphytes, producing small roots from their own trunks that work their way into the humus retained at the base of the supported plant.

Other trees have evolved, instead, in such a manner as to discourage the survival of epiphytes on their branches and trunks, by means of mechanisms that still are not well understood.

Epiphyllous plants are, in general, the mosses, lichens, algae, and liverworts (Hepaticae) that live on the surfaces of leaves. They require an extremely high degree of shade and humidity. Contrarily to what would be expected based on the rule followed in temperate areas, where mosses and lichens are found primarily growing on mature plants, here the epiphylls occupy the leaves of young trees in the understory, so as to guarantee themselves this special microclimate. One leaf can host up to ten different species of epiphylls. Some are strictly epiphyllous, meaning that they can live only on the leaves, while others are capable of developing on branches and trunks as well. Epiphylls seem to prefer leaves without drip tips, those heart-shaped leaves with apical tips that favor dripping, perhaps because the rainwater runs less easily and so can stagnate upon the surface of the leaf.

Thanks to analogous adaptations and evolutionary convergences, many tree species are extremely similar, and it is often quite difficult to distinguish among various trees from an external examination, or even more so from below. The pygmies of the DRC can recognize dozens of trees, from various signs, such as the color of the bark before and after a cut, or by the flavor or the odor. Even so, the indigenous abilities of recognition underestimate the number of species by many. In Sumatra, for example, the local name *"meranti"* describes the genus *Shorea,* but the particular name *"meranti merah,"* which ought to refer to a species, in reality, includes over twenty different species of trees that have been identified by botanists.

The Great Fauna of the Forests

Notwithstanding the fact that tropical moist forests cover barely 6% of the dry land on the planet, they host from 50% to 80% of all the living forms in the world. Some faunistic categories are enormously well represented and diversified. Probably 70–75% of all arthropods (meaning insects, crustaceans, arachnids, etc.) live in these habitats. Many species, genera, and zoological families live only in forests of the tropical latitudes.

The animals of the rainforest are subject to some general and constant ecological rules, just as are the members of the plant kingdom.

25. Adult male orangutan in the primary forest.

For example, the general rule for tropical plants—providing for a great diversity of species but often a relatively low abundance of individuals—holds true for tropical fauna as well. In the jumbled network of vegetation that is stratified from the soil on up to the canopy, myriad **microhabitats** and **ecological niches** are distributed. These are portions of environments, more or less easily distinguishable in space and through time, to the limitations of which certain species have become adapted to living and not others. The significance of this partitioning is the reduction or avoidance of competition among species by differentiating the vital space—sometimes even with respect to minute details. In the forests of Borneo, for example, where the gibbons live at heights over 30 m (100 ft), orangutans normally move around between 20 and 30 m (65 and 100 ft), and the macaques from the ground on up to 10 m (35 ft).

Some species are super-specialized, for living in micro-environments that are truly unique, such as certain Amazonian tree frogs that confine their living habitats to the pools of water that form between the leaves of epiphytes. Different species of geckos, both in Asia and in Africa, some of which are characterized by their emitting of repetitive, sonorous, and peculiar noises at night, live exclusively on the vertical walls of the buttresses of large trees, where they hunt insects and other arthropods.

Further methods for **avoiding competition** are linked to behavioral or dietary specialization or to the choice of principal period of activity: daytime, nighttime, twilight, etc. Some adaptations are amazing, and they always aim at endowing the species with strategies and means for survival, among which one of the primary is that of knowing how to profit from exclusive alimentary sources, those presenting no competitors. Consider the example of the wasps that know how, while flying, to extract the prey trapped in a spider web before the arrival of the spider, without becoming trapped there themselves. Or animals that are capable of resisting the poisonous or irritating substances present in many fruits and leaves, as with the orangutans in relation to the climbing *Strychnos ingatii,* from which the deadly strychnine is extracted, but which appears to provoke nothing more from these great anthropomorphous monkeys than abundant salivation. These extreme strategies for specialization—sometimes species-specific, sometimes individual—can only be understood by considering the high diversification of species that has occurred through the course of millions of years within these environments.

Predatory Ants

In movement everywhere, on the ground, on trunks, branches, and leaves at all heights, ants represent a visible constant of tropical moist forests. One of the relatively small types of ants you can see, in their endless columns through the forest, are the leaf-cutter ants. As their name would suggest, these can often be observed returning to the nest with fragments of plants between their mandibles. Other species are carnivorous and, indeed, fearsome predators. Army ants (Dorylinae) live a nomadic life and stop only to reproduce. Their cycles of movement and rest are linked to the timing of their procreative phases. For about seventeen days, they lead an erratic life, traveling about with their larvae, which they hold solidly between their mandibles, transporting them under the abdomen. When the larvae turn into pupae, they cease communicating chemically with their bearers, and this is their signal to stop. They "set up camp," usually under a tree trunk, where the workers defend their queen, whose belly has already, in the meantime, become loaded with new eggs that are now ready to be deposited. As soon as the pupae have left their chrysalises and the new larvae have been born from the eggs, the march resumes. Army ants are blind and advance by olfactory signals. If you could succeed in reaching the beginning of their long column, what you would observe would be an unexpected disorder and an uncertain, wide advancing front. Their bite is painful, and during their nomad phase, troops containing thousands of individuals advance. Insects, spiders, crustaceans, and even reptiles and mammals stay clear of the advancing of the hoard, which offers no chance of survival for anything that allows itself to be encountered. Many birds, called "ant-birds," have learned how to take advantage of the advancing of these troops of army ants, by catching insects that are stirred in their attempts to flee.

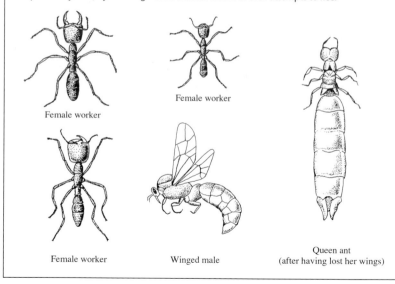

Female worker

Female worker

Female worker

Winged male

Queen ant
(after having lost her wings)

   Interspecific competition—and the related responses of each species for avoiding it—also involves other activities that make up the life of a wild animal. As is seen for the songs of birds, the cries of primates, as well, are partitioned throughout the arc of the day. The orangutans of Sumatra communicate primarily in the dark before dawn, around 4 A.M., and in the late afternoon, around 5 P.M. Gibbons, which in comparison are much more vociferous, communicate at around 8 A.M., and certain langurs, in the early morning, around 6 A.M., and the late evening, about 7 P.M.

A Fervid Aerial and Arboreal Life

The great vertical development of tropical vegetation imposes the requirement of aerial and arboreal adaptations on very many animal species.

   In Borneo, for example, we witness a percentage of arboreal species equivalent to 45% of the total, as opposed to only 5%–15% for temperate forests. Besides the many species of flying squirrels, there are other astonishing animals that live here, such as "flying" serpents, lizards, and even tree frogs. Other than the structural reasons, one motive for the arboreal preference of many species is the fact that a large quantity of the available alimentary resources, such as leaves, flowers, seeds, and fruits, reside and

26. The first glimmerings of
dawn in the primary forest.

27. The green wall of the virgin
forest of Danum Valley.

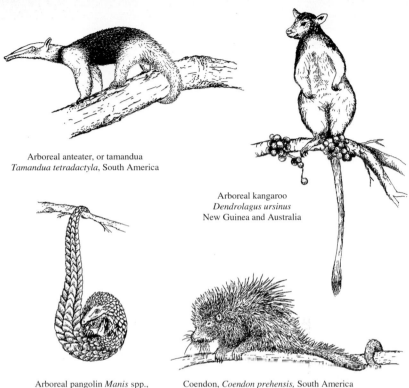

Arboreal anteater, or tamandua
Tamandua tetradactyla, South America

Arboreal kangaroo
Dendrolagus ursinus
New Guinea and Australia

Arboreal pangolin *Manis* spp.,
Asia, Africa

Coendon, *Coendon prehensis,* South America

The great vertical development of the tropical moist forests has induced many animals to provide themselves with mechanisms and patterns of behavior that facilitate their arboreal lives. Prehensile tails, highly developed musculature, nails, and any other stratagem for allowing them to hold onto trunks and branches. Many terrestrial animals have their arboreal cousins.

station themselves in the canopy before falling to the soil to decompose. This, additionally, is the principal cause for the characteristic bimodal distribution of the forest insects: many on the ground, very many in the canopy, and comparatively few in the intermediary strata.

The birds, by contrast, demonstrate adaptations to flight within a close and intricate environment: short, rounded wings, and often with long tails that help steer better. On the level of intraspecific communication, the col-

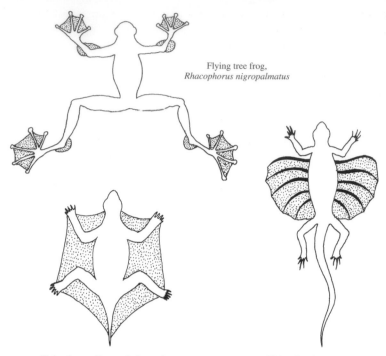

Flying tree frog,
Rhacophorus nigropalmatus

Flying lemur, *Cynocephalus variegatus*

Flying lizard, *Draco volans*

Certain extreme adaptations to arboreal life are represented by various "flying" species of the forests of Borneo. Besides a number of species of flying squirrels (*Petaurista* spp. and others, distributed also in other regions) and the flying lemur or colugo (*Cynocephalus variegatus*), there exist a flying tree frog (*Rhacophorus nigropalmatus*), a flying serpent (*Chrysopelea pelias*), and a flying lizard (*Draco volans*). These animals are all—to varying degrees—endowed with membranes and outgrowths that permit them to glide from the heights of the forest canopy. The distances that can be covered are often considerable: about 50 m (165 ft) for the serpent and over 130 m (430 ft) for flying lemurs.

ors of plumage play an important function that is complementary to the acoustic one. (For the significance of the coloring of tropical birds, see chapter 5, "The Fauna.")

The **transmission of sounds** is very different through the forest than through the open air, in that the vegetation and differences of humidity and temperature muffle and diminish acoustic impulses. Certain structures of the tropical forest cause "sound windows," because of which certain wavelengths will pass and others will not, producing the effect of modifying audibility in an irregular fashion. In general, sounds of short wavelengths are better reflected from obstacles than are those with long wavelengths. The low frequencies are absorbed with greater difficulty by the humidity. The temperature, which increases progressively from the soil towards the canopy and with the advancing of the day, reduces the audibility of sounds. Animals that emit their sounds from the canopy, thereby reducing the absorptive effects of the soil, increase the distance over which they can be heard.

Underground Life. If the arboreal life in the Tropics is highly stimulated, the fossorial and underground life receives little incentive from a terrain that is always humid and compact. The soil of tropical forests is characterized by the scarcity of the small hypogeal fauna that, at other latitudes, represent an important ecological factor and an alimentary source for many predators. In the soils of the forests of the Tropics, earthworms are scarce, and the most abundant subterranean larvae are, perhaps, those of the cicadas and the coleopterans, which feed on the apices of roots and the sap of plants.

One can frequently encounter small mounds of freshly turned earth, from the center of which a small tunnel descends. This is what remains after the emergence of a cicada nymph that, after a long wait—more than ten years for certain species—finally emerges above ground, to complete its metamorphosis by clinging to the base of a tree trunk, and emerging shortly thereafter from its chrysalis. In contrast to its long subterranean life, the winged life rarely lasts more than a year, and often only a few months.

Pollens and Pollinators

The great abundance of vegetation in the forests, in turn, means that there are more animals than in temperate latitudes that feed on the nectars and pollens of flowers.

The abundance and the diversification of nectarivores, in fact, is another characteristic of tropical ecology. Besides the (extremely numerous) insects, there are many species of birds, bats, rodents, and monkeys that feed—some in a more, some in a less, exclusive manner—on the nectar of flowers. American hummingbirds (family Trochilidae), Afro-Asiatic sunbirds (family Nectariniidae), African sugarbirds (family Bromeropidae), Southeast Asian and Australian flowerpeckers (family Dicaeidae), Australasian honeyeaters (family Meliphagidae), and Hawaiian honeycreepers (family Drepanididae) are examples of the convergence of animals that are not related to each other, but that resemble each other in form and behavior because they have adapted, by chance, to take advantage of the same resource: pollen. Hummingbirds are, without doubt, among the most amazingly specialized birds, and their reproductive season coincides with that of the flowering of the plants upon which they depend. Most frequently, they choose flowers having bright red petals, the color best seen and favored by birds (many insects, by contrast, cannot distinguish it), and with tubular shapes that they can easily reach, by means of specialized beaks, which the various species have developed to varying degrees for this purpose. These animals, during their alimentary activities, also perform the important role of pollinators. One characteristic of the Tropics, we see, is that animals are highly involved in plant pollination, and it is not at all rare in tropical latitudes that particular genera or species of plants have their own exclusive pollinators. For example, until the technique was discovered for the artificial pollination of vanilla (Orchidaceae), it was impossible to raise the plant outside of its original area of distribution (South America), which coincides with that of its essential pollinating insect. Three examples of entomophily in Amazonia, all within the same botanical family (Lecythidaceae) are: plants of the genus *Gustavia,* which attract many bees of small and medium size; the *Eschweilera,* which attracts only sufficiently robust bees and wasps, those that know how and are capable of forcing entry into the flowers, the so-called "carpenter bees" of the genus *Xylocopa;* and the *Couratari,* which can be pollinated only by bees having long rostra, capable of reaching the insides of the flowers. Pineapples (Bromeliaceae) are plants originally from Amazonia, with tubular flowers and external stamens, pollinated, for the most part, by birds.

Bats are also important pollinators. The local populations understand these relations well. In Brazil, for example, the Latin name of the trees of the genus *Andira* derives from the term *andirà,* which in the *lingua general* means "bat." The plants pollinated by chiropterans have prominent flowers, with long stalks that extend through the canopy layer (for example, all the *Caryocar,* the "giants" of the Amazonian forest), or hanging below the branch, to facilitate the flying mammals' landing and grasping on, as well as their echolocating them through the dark of the night. These flowers often produce large quantities of nectar, in order to increase their attractiveness, but they never appear in numerous groups, This avoids satisfying the hunger of the bats, thus constraining them to visit other flowers on other trees, which favors cross pollination, In many cases, the trees are

In the majority of cases, animals that feed on pollen also act as pollinators for plants. Sometimes it is more obvious how the plant has drawn an advantage from the action of the pollinator, because it has adopted particular strategies to facilitate the pollination. This is the case with the remarkable South American orchid *Gongora maculata* (above). The upper lip of the flower contains substances that attract bees, but it also contains substances that are slightly toxic, which stun or "intoxicate" the bee shortly after it has landed, causing it to fall backwards onto the underlying part of the flower where the stigma is, which is then fertilized by the pollen that the bee has transported from other flowers. Equally striking is the adaptation of the beak of the Amazonian hummingbird, *Ensifera ensifera,* which has developed great length so as to be able to reach the nectar of the long tubular flowers of certain passion flowers.

sexed, meaning either male or female, and thus the passage from the flowers of one tree to those of another is essential for increasing the possibilities of fertilization.

Some of these cases are good examples of the possible coevolution of animals and plants, while in other cases, it is just the product of a probable successive diversification of the techniques and choices on the part of the animals that reduce competition among themselves. In addition to the arboreal mammals and birds, there are also terrestrial animals that participate in the **dispersion of seeds** as well: they feed on fruits fallen to the ground and disperse them through their excrement.

Specialization devices, fantastic and original adaptations, surprising forms and colors, and an astonishing wealth—these are the ingredients of the most fascinating natural formula that exists on the planet. The tropical rainforest is an environment that unites this grand explosion of life to a structure that renders both visiting and observation quite difficult.

But if it is true, for example, that the fauna is less visible in tropical forests than elsewhere, then it is necessary to be more attentive, more patient, more informed, and more directed toward general aspects of the ecology of the individual protagonists—which are just as fascinating. When compared with the ostentatiousness of the fauna of the savannas or the coral reefs, the forests are environments that reveal themselves best to those who have an "extra" degree of knowledge and passion. Certainly, once having entered into this admirable natural dimension, the satisfaction and involvement will truly be profound and total.

28. Coastal vegetation in a sheltered cove approaching right to the limits of the seawater.

Chapter 8

Coral Reefs

Among the most marvelous and unimaginable spectacles reserved for us by tropical nature are the coral reefs, which, because of their extraordinary harmony of forms, colors, and movements, are also called coral gardens.

Coral gardens are a pantropical phenomenon (generally restricted to the seas between 30° latitude, north and south), meaning they are present throughout the entire tropical area, and they are linked to particular conditions that we will examine in what follows.

Certain climatic and hydrological situations can promote the development of corals, even beyond the strictly defined limits of the Tropics, as happens because of the warm currents moving from the Caribbean towards the Bermudas, or those that go from the China Sea towards Japan. Where cool currents penetrate instead—and this happens on the southwestern coasts of Africa and South America—the coral recedes towards the direction of equator. In general, the true coral formations of madrepore (order Scleractinia) are confined, with little variation, to the area between 30° latitude, north and south.

Reef-Building Corals

When we speak of corals, we refer to small animals belonging to the category of coelenterates, which are therefore relatives of sea anemones. Various types of corals exist in the world, in waters that are warmer or cooler. Those we refer to when speaking of coral reefs, however, are quite particular, and tropical corals are the only ones that develop enormous colonies—thousands upon millions of individuals, constructing gigantic structures that are, in reality, agglomerations of their external, protective "skeletons." They are responsible for the development of coral banks, and because of this, they are defined as reef-building corals.

The principal characteristic of a sea supporting banks of corals is that it has warm waters. The minimum temperature, considered to be the limit for the development of the most cold-resistant reef-building corals is 18°C (64°F). Obviously there is also a maximum temperature, which is found to be about 30°C (86°F). Where the temperature of the superficial strata does not vary beyond these limits, the area is potentially suitable for the development of coral barriers. The temperature of the waters also influences the presence of certain species more than it does for others. Thus, waters between 25–29°C (77–84°F) are optimal for the branched corals, while below 24°C (75°F), it is the smooth, compact forms that grow best. Two other factors intervene, however, the first being the depth of the waters, since the barrier formations develop within about 40 m (130 ft) of the surface (or in exceptional cases, as deep as 60 m, or 200 ft), as they need a considerable quantity of light, and the second, the presence of a suitable substratum upon which the corals can establish their individual structures.

Corals do not tolerate fresh waters (salinity less than 20 ppt), so they are not able to live near the mouths of rivers. The same holds true for turbid waters, which prevent the penetration of light. A large part of the responsibility for the northern interruption of the Great Barrier Reef of Australia is owing to the rivers of New Guinea, just as the mouth of the Amazon

---

Corals in Competition

In the complex and intricate ecosystem of the coral reef, everyone is interested in surviving, including the corals. The competition among the various species is particularly keen and has stimulated some singular solutions. It is not uncommon to observe the broad umbrella of a plate coral *(Acropora)* showing an interruption in coincidence with a brain coral situated immediately below it, which appears to have impeded the action of having itself covered over and obscured, by means of who knows what mechanism.

The fluids involved here are anything but mysterious. Many species of soft corals continually secrete toxic or repellent substances that cause any new settlements or expansions of nearby colonies to keep their distance. Certain hard corals have the ability to extend tentacular stinging filaments, which are ten to a hundred times more painful than normal, until they touch any nearby invaders, irritating them or killing them. Some species even extend outgrowths of their digestive apparatus, with the same purpose.

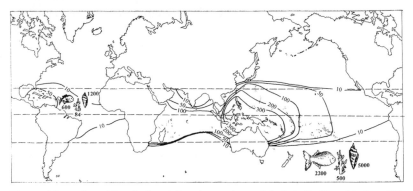

The coral formations richest in faunal diversity are those of the Indo-Pacific, with about 500 species of corals, 2,200 of coral fish, and 5,000 of mollusks. The next most important block of coral reefs forms in the Caribbean area. The coral reefs of the western Indian Ocean, including the waters around eastern Africa and the Red Sea, represent the third most important block in the world. The numbers between the lines indicate the species of reef-building corals that live within the circumscribed area. The diversity generally diminishes toward the eastern versants of the oceans.

River prevents the development of barriers south of the Caribbean. The same effect occurs in many areas of Indonesia, such as Sumatra, Sulawesi, Borneo, and along the Indian and Malaysian coasts. The coastal waters of the northern Persian Gulf host few coral barriers because of their turbidity. Many islands of the Pacific are characterized by the presence of channels that open within the coral barrier, uniting the coast with the open sea, and coinciding with points where waters from the rains stream forth or where small torrents open out to the sea. Here, it is not that the corals are eroded by the torrential currents, which actually are neither abundant nor vehement in these small islands, but rather that they are limited by the fresh waters.

Geography of Coral Formations

The Three Coral Zones of the World. Observing the distribution of coral reefs in oceans across the globe, we can note how these are principally relegated to the western margins of each ocean. The principal motive for this is that these portions have broad, submerged continental platforms, frequent volcanic phenomena, islands, and shallow waters, where the coral can easily develop. The world's three major coral reef blocks are: those areas between the Caribbean and the adjacent islands, as far as the Bermudas (representing 15% of the world's surface covered by coral reef); the islands of the occidental portion of the Indian Ocean and the coasts of eastern Africa (30%); and the multitude of islands around Southeast Asia and the western Pacific Ocean (55%).

In terms of **numbers of species,** the Indo-Pacific is by far the richest area, where the maximum diversification coincides with the Indonesian islands, the Philippines, and the coast of northern Australia. Towards the east, in the Indian Ocean and even more so in the Pacific, this wealth diminishes slightly. The richest region in the Atlantic is the Caribbean, even if this is by far inferior to the Indo-Pacific; however, there is no direct correlation between the number of species of corals (meaning biological wealth or diversity) and the dimensions or impressiveness of the barrier. For example, it might be surprising to know that the majority of the famous Polynesian barriers and atolls are constructed by fewer than fifty species, as opposed to the more than five hundred in Indonesia or the Philippines. Only when there are fewer than fifty species do the barriers tend to become smaller and less complex.

Biogeography of corals. The reasons for this difference in the wealth of species are not well known, and different theories go back to the climatic variations of the last few geological eras, as well as to successive mechanisms for the dispersion of corals within the oceans. In the two principal areas for abundance of corals, the Atlantic and the Indo-Pacific, there are some genera and families in common, but no species. This, together with fossil findings and the knowledge of continental drift, demonstrates distant analogies, as well as the current differences. In the configuration of the planet, the two oceans were united around 200 million years ago, approximately the time when reef-building corals first evolved. With the movement of the continental masses, the Atlantic was divided from the Indian by the interposition of Africa, and from the Pacific by the union of South America with North America. Since then, interoceanic communications were maintained only at the latitudes of the capes of Africa and Patagonia, but in waters that are unsuitably cold for the life of corals. In the new conditions of isolation, those common predecessors differentiated into separate species in the two oceans, though still remaining members of the same genera. The corals of the genus *Acropora* are numerous and exhibit various forms, although they are generally ramified or flat. One-fifth of all the reef-building corals in the world belong to this genus, albeit in various, localized species within the oceans.

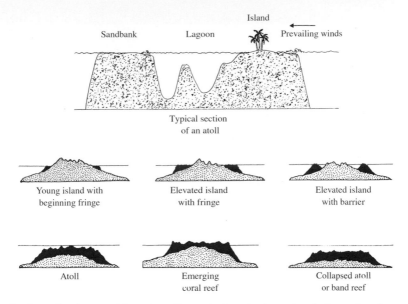

Sections of various coral formations. The rocky base is shown dotted; the coral reefs are highlighted in black.

Barriers, Fringes, and Atolls

Charles Darwin, in his publication on coral reefs in 1842, was the first to propose the theory of reef formation and evolution, building on the discovery of coralline fossils in inland areas or even in mountains. That theory, which is still held as valid, explains the dynamics of the three principal categories of coral formations. When a volcano emerges from tropical seas, it creates conditions favorable for the development of a fringe-like coral reef, or **fringe reef,** about its sloping coasts. Here a coral bank develops that tends upward and outward, increasing in thickness and width. After the phases of eruption and emersion, the volcano slowly sinks. This process can bring about the formation of a **barrier reef** when a channel of deep water forms between the island and the fringe reef. In practice, it is often the old fringe that is found to be detached from the coast because of the sinking. When, later, the volcano submerges definitively, only the ring of coral around the old island remains, and an **atoll** is born. Analogous barrier formations exist along the coasts and derive,

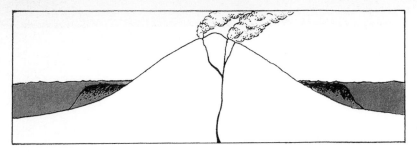

Young island with fringe

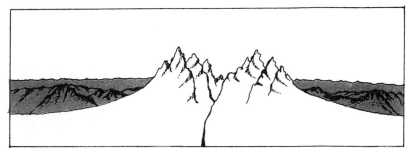

Beginning of the sinking and creation of new fringe and barrier

Advanced phase of sinking and creation of an atoll

again, from the movements of the sinking or the emersion of lands, from the advancement of the submerged continental platform, and from many other variable factors. Normally, the typical coral formations along the coast are of the fringe reef type or, less frequently, of the barrier type, even if the difference between the two is often somewhat vague. **Patch reefs**

form on hillocks of the continental shelf, while **bank reefs** usually develop in deeper waters on seabed irregularities (at 30–40 m, or 100–130 ft). The many atolls of the Indian and Pacific Oceans vary in diameter from 1 to 160 km (0.5 to 100 mi), more frequently varying between 5 and 30 km (3 and 20 mi). The study of sediments in the depths of the existing coral barriers or atolls seems effectively to demonstrate that these rest on ancient volcanic soils, and in certain cases, they have been dated back some thousands or even several millions of years.

Hard Corals, Soft Corals, and Still Others

As has already been said, the reef-building corals are coelenterates, and, in looking at them from close up, we can note that each individual animal is a **polyp.** It closely resembles a sea anemone, to which it is a near relative in the evolutionary sense. It has one or more rings of tentacles, utilized for capturing small prey or organic particles in suspension, which are carried

---

Enormous Edifices Constructed by the Sea

Coralline formations are constituted of the calcium carbonate gathered and used by polyps to fortify their structures of support and shelter. The sea is saturated with this substance that—even though it is not very soluble—is present in enormous quantities in the immense oceanic volumes. Corals absorb the calcium carbonate and fix it within their own "skeletons." Each polyp begins working on this structure from the moment it manages, as a larva, to adhere to a suitable substratum, later dividing itself and eventually originating thousands and millions of identical genetic pairs, forming a colony in which all the polyps are connected among themselves, where they all deposit calcium together. When the colony originated by a single polyp has grown large, it begins to reproduce sexually, producing larvae that can wander about on the currents, transported until they find some suitable substratum where they can begin new colonies. If a coral breaks, it is not necessarily destined to die. Indeed, in certain species, especially those that are ramified, the pieces fractured and transported by the currents can give rise to new colonies or promote colonization in new areas.

The Wealth of the Tropical Seas
(in number of species)

	Indo-Pacific	East Pacific	West Atlantic	East Atlantic
Mollusks	6,000+	2,100	1,200	500
Crustaceans				
Stomatopoda (mantis shrimps)	150+	40	60	10
Brachyura (crabs)	700+	400	400	200
Fish	3,000+	1,300	1,500	300

Sources: Vermeij 1978, in McNeely et al 1990; and WCMC, Global Biodiversity (London: Chapman and Hall, 1992).

---

to the center, where its mouth opens. At the slightest contact, the tentacles and body retract within the protective skeleton. Few species are solitary, but rather, in the majority of reef-building corals, one polyp reproduces to form colonies of vast numbers of individuals, and in this manner they develop the great structures called coral reefs.

In **hard corals,** the calcium is deposited around and under the polyp and between the tissues that separate each individual from the others. The quantity of calcium precipitate produced by the metabolism of the polyp's tissues, therefore, is extremely high, and the structure is hard and heavy. The seawater that bathes the polyps is saturated with calcium carbonate, and particular conditions within the body of the polyp reduce the solubility of this, causing the salt to precipitate in a crystalline form. Once the polyps have died, their skeletons remain, like rocks of pure calcium carbonate, and they are very resistant. Waves and tides erode them only very slowly, and their particles go to form sand and islands. Further, they are excellent substrata for the establishment of new colonies. Each species of reef-building coral deposits the calcium and constructs its skeleton according to characteristic patterns and based on building techniques that are genetically regulated. From this, the many recurrent and fantastic forms for the various species derive, contributing to the stunning scenario of a coral reef; and thus, there are practically as many different types of architecture for the various colonies as there are different species of corals known in the world—nearly a thousand. Round corals as solid as sandstone, such as the *Porites* in the Red Sea or *Siderastrea* in the Atlantic, dotted with tens of thousands of small discoidal openings that appear like fine decorations. Brain corals, such as the *Platygira* in the Indo-Pacific, or the *Colpophyllia* and *Diploria* in the Atlantic, whose ocelli are replaced by the lines and squiggles in which the polyps make their homes. Foliaceous corals, like the *Agaricia* of the Caribbean. Corals ramified like shrubs or the horns of ungulates, or else flat, with broad edges, such as the various species of bush, elk-horn, or plate *Acropora,* found in all the tropical seas. Leafy corals, broad and thin like umbrellas or bowls, such as the *Pachyseris* of the Indo-Pacific. Mushroom corals, like the Atlantic *Montastrea,* or vase corals, like the *Turbinaria,* and the *Seriatopora,* elegant and delicate in appearance, like a closely gathered, densely ramified shrub. Within every category, the individual species or genera differentiate even further, although sometimes the differences are minor.

Soft corals do not deposit calcium in the form of external structures, but instead produce a gelatinous matrix, compacted by dispersed spicules of calcium carbonate. This is why these colonies are flexible and soft to the touch. Some typical soft corals are those of the genus *Scleronaphthya,* which look like colored shrubs. With their abundance of ramifications, they resemble actual plants more than colonies of small animals. After the death of the colony, the structure dissolves rapidly.

Mushroom corals are not attached to rock foundations, but lie on the bottom or on the sand. Normally they are small and discoidal in shape, sometimes oval, flat, or slightly convex. The genera *Fungia* and *Cycloseris* are the most widespread and well-known. These corals, which appear underwater to be pieces of stone abandoned on the bottom, in reality are living animal forms that are actually even capable of small movements, such as righting themselves if accidentally overturned. The living part normally exits from the skeleton during the night, and the coral becomes animated with dozens of tentacles.

The Structure of the Reef

The profile of a coral reef is generally the same throughout the world, and it may extend from just a few meters in width, such as the fringe of a volcanic island, to several hundreds of meters in an atoll.

From the Slope to the Reef Flat. At the outer margin of the reef, we encounter **boulder corals,** which are resistant to the strong movements of the water in this zone. Right where the waves break and the slope begins, towards the deep waters, at the boundary between the ocean and the reef, we often encounter a raised, extruding part, which is extremely resistant because it is constituted of old corals, dead and encrusted with red algae, which are responsible for the characteristic pink color of the these areas. This seaward ridge, even though it projects a half meter beyond the base of the reef, is usually submerged by waves, sometimes even during low tide. The structure of this part of the bank is surprisingly efficient in attenuating the impact of the waves, and often its amplitude and conformation cause the returning wave, after it has crashed against the bank, to knock in opposition against the arriving wave, thereby reducing its power. The seaward slope descends rapidly towards the deep sea, with crags, caverns, precipices, terraces, and wells that can be practically vertical. On

The Largest, the Heaviest, the Lightest Corals

Some corals grow quickly, as much as 10 cm (4 in) in one year, but these have a lower density and are more porous. Those that grow more slowly, by contrast, perhaps just a few millimeters per year, are compact and solid. Two examples of the first case, the *Alveopora* (Indo-Pacific) and the *Colpophyllia* (Atlantic) are so porous that, once dried, they will float on the water. In contrast, the *Leptastrea* corals are so much harder that it is nearly impossible to see with the naked eye the cracks of the tunnels where the polyps lodge.

The largest corals are those of the genus *Acropora* in the Indo-Pacific and the Atlantic, which are ramified so that they closely resemble submerged shrubs, the *Porites* in the Indo-Pacific, and the boulder corals *(Montastrea)* in the Atlantic, which are capable of forming blocks of material as large as 10 m by 100 m (33 ft by 330 ft), starting out from a single polyp and eventually developing colonies with millions of individuals over hundreds of years. Giant clams (*Tridacna* spp.) often end up being incorporated into the blocks of coral that grow around them, as do the tubes of many mollusks, coelenterates, and, even more frequently, annelids, serpulidans, and sabellids. The unified appearance of the whole deceives the observer by making it seem like those retractile appendages and the valves, ornamented with splendid colors, are actually parts of the coral organism.

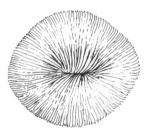

Mushroom coral, *Fungia* spp.

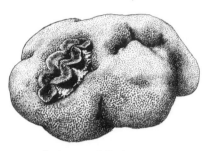

Sandstone coral, *Goniastrea* spp.
(with a *Tridacna maxima* incorporated)

Elkhorn coral, *Acropora* spp.

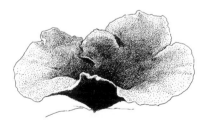

Vase coral, *Turbinaria* spp.

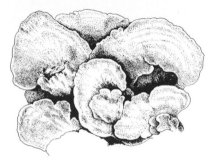
Leafy coral, *Pachyseris* spp.

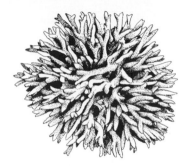
Bush coral, *Seriatopora* spp.

Branched coral, *Acropora* spp.

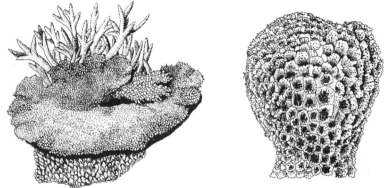
Table coral, *Acropora* spp.

"Light" coral, *Alveopora* spp.

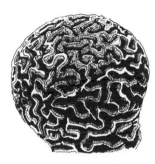
Brain coral, *Platygyra daedulea*

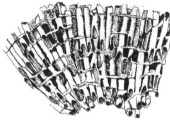
Tubipora or false coral, *Tubipora musica*

this, which is defined as the outer slope, once a certain depth has been reached, beyond the violent action of the waves, the bank increases in size, and a rich variety of corals live. In the more sheltered areas, where there is no turbulent interface between the ocean and the bank, the reefs have no ridges, and the slope towards the open sea is inclined, but not so steep. Beyond the ridge, towards the interior of the coral bank, a slightly deeper zone opens up, called the **moat,** where the water is constantly being churned by the waves. Here, every few seconds, each individual coral colony can undergo pressures of several kilos per square centimeter (many pounds per square inch). The moat is one of the zones of the bank where the greatest wealth and diversity of corals is encountered, but this is usually difficult for snorkelers or divers to explore because of the continual and strong currents coming in and going out. The reasons for such wealth are that the water is always oxygenated and that the ecological conditions are extremely homogeneous. Because they do not experience the effects of the low tides, owing to their continual submergence by the waves, the corals of the moat do not suffer thermal stress or dehydration. Proceeding towards the interior, the **reef flat** begins, which is a sort of plateau running parallel with the surface, with few variations in depth. The biological diversity of this area, usually the most extended part of the reef, can sometimes be amazingly elevated, but in other cases it can be reduced by the effects of the low tides, which often select the species that are less sensitive to dehydration.

In fact, the **tides** do play an extremely important role in the ecology of the reef, but at the same time, their influence is a limiting factor. During the low tide, the conditions can become prohibitive for the life of a coral. Many corals emerge through the surface and suffer dehydration. The low water and pools can be heated to as high as 30°C (86°F) or 40°C (104°F) by the sun and so lose much of their oxygen, whereas, in the meantime, living organisms increase their oxygen demand with the rising of the water temperature. The salinity, as well, can increase dangerously with evaporation. Corals often remain dry, and even if exposure to the atmosphere only lasts two or three hours, when this exposure coincides with the hottest hours of the day, the thermal stress is considerable. In the reef flats, only the corals capable of enduring these difficulties are selected, and this is precisely what occurs in many tracts of the Great Barrier Reef in Australia. With the return of the high tide and favorable conditions, it is common to observe mounds of foam being dragged away by the currents. This is the

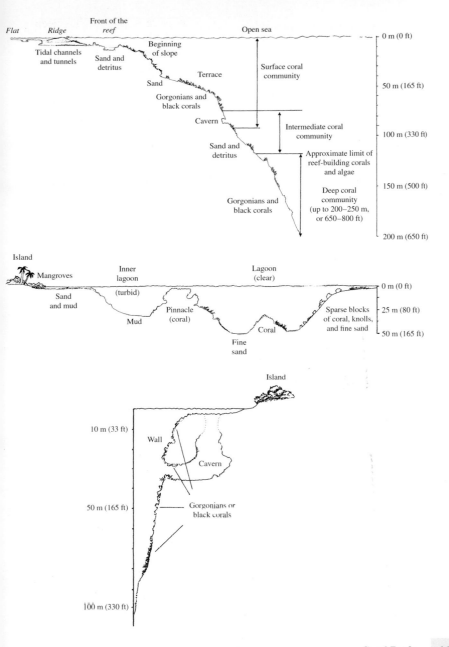

Flat
Ridge
Front of the reef
Open sea
Tidal channels and tunnels
Sand and detritus
Beginning of slope
Sand
Gorgonians and black corals
Terrace
Cavern
Sand and detritus
Gorgonians and black corals

Surface coral community
Intermediate coral community
Approximate limit of reef-building corals and algae
Deep coral community (up to 200–250 m, or 650–800 ft)

0 m (0 ft)
50 m (165 ft)
100 m (330 ft)
150 m (500 ft)
200 m (650 ft)

Island
Mangroves
Sand and mud
Inner lagoon (turbid)
Mud
Pinnacle (coral)
Fine sand
Lagoon (clear)
Coral
Sparse blocks of coral, knolls, and fine sand

0 m (0 ft)
25 m (80 ft)
50 m (165 ft)

Island
10 m (33 ft)
Wall
Cavern
50 m (165 ft)
Gorgonians or black corals
100 m (330 ft)

Different Colors for Different Functions

The bright colors that the fish of coral reefs are famous for correspond to different functions. First of all, in accordance with the previously noted theory regarding the variegated plumage of tropical birds, the same considerations hold true for tropical fish: the energetically favorable conditions of tropical habitats make it possible for animals to invest resources into the production of fantastic colors and appendages. Further, as a consequence of the favorable environmental situation of the Tropics and, again, of the differentiation among species, complex and eccentric colorings function to reduce or eliminate visual competition or confusion among the species. In this sense, easily noticeable colors can often aid recognition by other members of an individual's own species, whether for attraction (sexual) or repulsion (territorial). Some fish have different colors when they first hatch than they do during their adult stage, a phenomenon that happens especially frequently in highly territorial species, so that the young, which have yet to gain experience, can wander about the reef without provoking the wrath of the owners of various territories.

Many colors and forms that are vividly obvious can be understood as warning signals in poisonous or stinging species, as a means of discouraging predators from attacking. And exceptional results in mimetic colorings are achieved by fish and invertebrates (crustaceans especially), whether by prey, to elude predators, or by predators, to avoid detection when laying their traps.

Fish in this multicolored and fantastical panorama have many variegated colorings of bands and stripes, and these have the function of confusing the profile or contours of the animal, rendering it more difficult for predators to distinguish them.

mucus that was secreted by the corals to protect themselves from the sun, being washed away by the fresh, new, vital waters. Fortunately, the low tides have an advancing period, reaching low point at about half an hour later each day, so that they do not always coincide with the hottest hours of the day. Furthermore, the tides of greatest amplitude, those that are capable of causing the corals to emerge into the atmosphere, do not occur throughout the entire year, but only in certain seasons.

Within the bank of an atoll or a barrier, there is another small slope oriented toward the center, where the waters are somewhat deeper. Often, in the lagoon, there are broad sandy or slimy tracts from which rocky or coralline formations can emerge, called **knolls,** and these rise toward the surface, repeating, in miniature form, the structure of the section of the coral reef.

Descending along the outer slope, the violence of the waves diminishes, until we encounter very calm waters, pervaded by a tepid and azure light. With the depth, the luminous rays are filtered more and more, until only the blue wavelengths of the spectrum are left, and the whole scene is painted as a surreal monochrome, typical of the sixth continent. Only the

Shells

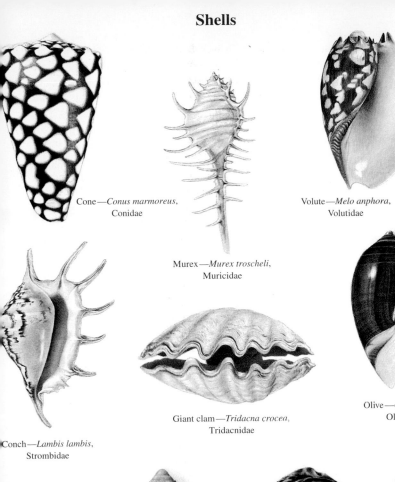

Cone—*Conus marmoreus*,
Conidae

Murex—*Murex troscheli*,
Muricidae

Volute—*Melo anphora*,
Volutidae

Conch—*Lambis lambis*,
Strombidae

Giant clam—*Tridacna crocea*,
Tridacnidae

Olive—*Oliva vidua*,
Olividae

ton—*Autochiton torri*,
Chitonidae

Margin—*Marginella goodalli*,
Marginellidae

Cowry—*Cypraea tigris*,
Cipraeidae

Mitre—*Mitra papalis*,
Mitridae

light of a flashlight or a camera flash will restore the true colors, and we discover, with much surprise, that red is the color that dominates at these depths. The corals become less and less numerous, and as the variety of species diminishes, the abundance increases of those individuals whose species have been successful in colonizing these levels. About 20–30 m (65–100 ft) deep, where the slopes are not too vertical, the **leafy corals** are at their maximum development, because here their thin, flattened forms are ideally suited for gathering the most of the filtering light. Down at this depth, we can observe a continuous, fine rain of sediment, originating from the strata closer to the surface. Leafy corals draw advantage from this important source of nutrition, as they have developed ramifications with slightly inclined edges, representing a judicious compromise between the requirement of being able to intercept light, which would have preferred edges parallel to the surface, and that of being able to gather the sediment without being buried by it. Down deep, we encounter the *Turbinaria,* a coral in the shape of a vase, which, having the same requirements as the leafy coral, has chosen the architectural solution of growing in the form of a funnel, a shape which allows the sediments gathered in its broad upper surfaces to slide all the way down to the bottom of its base.

Even farther down, only few of the reef-building corals can survive, one of which is the very beautiful, ramified *Dendrophylla,* completely black. At around 40 to 50 m (130 to 165 ft), with the increasing obscurity, the true kingdom of the sponges and gorgonians begins (these latter are more abundant in the Caribbean reefs than in the Indo-Pacific, where they maintain more traditional, fan-like forms, if compared to the bizarre tridimensionalities of their Atlantic counterparts), and these occur only in the duskiness of cavities and caverns.

Descending farther, we notice an obvious and abrupt change in the temperature of the waters. Here, we are at the thermocline, meaning the point where two masses of water at different temperatures are in contact but maintain a notable isolation because of the total absence of mixing. The separation is so distinct that it is possible to hold one hand in the warmer layer and the other in the colder one, which is a few degrees lower.

Invisible, but Indispensable, Algae

Even though the primitive reef-building polyps are the principals responsible for the building of the bank structure, which has, in fact, taken the name "coral" from them, botanists will not hesitate in pointing out the irreplaceable role performed by members of the vegetal world.

At first glance, a coral reef confuses us because of its seeming absence of marine algae and plants. Yet the botanists are right that, without plants, these barriers and atolls would not be able to form—indeed, the plant component here is at the very basis of the ecosystem, just as in other environments throughout the world.

An Efficient Symbiosis. The apparent mystery can be solved if we look through the eyepiece of a microscope. The algae (in fact, the enormous quantities of algae) present in the reefs are not to be sought among the masses or the ramifications of the corals, but within the tiny organisms of the individual polyps. These are called *zooxanthellae,* which are unicellular dinoflagellate algae that live in symbiosis with the polyps. The algae produce oxygen and nutritive substances from the energy of the sun, in forms that the polyps are able to absorb, while the polyps, besides protecting the algae from animals that prey upon plankton, provide them with other opportunities for food, such as nutritive substances from the discarded scraps of the small prey or detritus that they have gathered with their tentacles. The waste product of carbon dioxide from the coelenterates (since they are animals) is the basis of the algae's function of photosynthesis. Sea anemones, giant clams, and other reef organisms host *zooxanthellae* as well.

The great majority of dinoflagellate algae that live among the reef-building corals belong to just one species, which is distributed throughout the world, *Gymnodimium microadriaticum.*

When we observe a colony of coral, we are also indirectly observing an immense, carefully guarded community of algae, members of which are held prisoner inside of each individual polyp. Many aspects of the biology and the interrelations between the algae and the polyps are still obscure, however it is evident that the reef-building corals live together with the algae and that they regulate the number of these, liberating excess numbers to the outside when they reproduce too rapidly. It also seems certain that the motive behind reef-building corals' living only in clear, highly illuminated surface waters is connected to their plant guests' need for light, as they live by photosynthesizing.

Besides these microscopic algae, the photosynthetic world around the corals also numbers a few brown algae. There are some green algae as well, like the *Caulerpa,* that resemble small spheres attached to the substratum, and, in greater numbers, red algae, especially of the encrusting sort, like the *Porolithon* in the Indo-Pacific and the *Lithothamnion* in the Caribbean. Some experiments have been conducted in which coral colonies have been enclosed in cages that impede access to fishes or other large animals, and these have demonstrated that the usual absence of algae is due, more than anything else, to **herbivores.** In these experimental areas, in fact, the algae quickly invade the corals, covering them and often suffocating them. If you do happen to observe a rock or a coral formation in natural conditions that is covered with algae, you can be sure that you have entered into the territory of the small sergeant fishes (genus *Abudefduf* of the damselfish family, the same family as the anemone fishes), which are so ferocious in their territorial defense that they effectively prevent any other marine organism from coming near, including herbivorous fishes and curious underwater divers (try it if you don't believe it!). It has been calculated that on a coral reef about 1–5 kg (2–11 lbs) of algae are produced per square meter per year. It is actually the intense alimentary activity of such specialist herbivores as the sea urchins, crustaceans, mollusks, and fish that prevent the proliferation of the algae. Parrot fishes (genus *Scarus,* so called because of their robust mouth in the form of a beak) and surgeonfishes (genus *Acanthurus,* named for the sharp appendage that protrudes from the base of the tail in case of threat) are the most active and specialized herbivores of the reef. Coralline banks attract more herbivores than any other marine ecosystem. Parrot fishes have evolved a specialized mouth for nibbling on the algae that grow upon the surfaces of the corals, and as they graze they leave clear signs of their passage. With every pass, a parrotfish scrapes the surface stratum of the corals' calcareous skeletons, which is then typically expelled from the fish's mouth in the form of a delicate cloud of small fragments. Parrot fishes damage many of the polyps as they eat, but, on the other hand, they favor them by impeding the development of algae.

A Universe of Life among the Corals

Nobody can say how many animals and plants there are among the coral reefs of the world. If the number of animal species is disproportionately higher than the number of plant species, the biomass, or quantity of living mass, of the photosynthesizers far exceeds that of the animal kingdom.

In analyzing the ecology of the reef, we discover that a relatively small proportion of the animals actually eat coral. The starfish *Acanthaster,* with its thorny coating and exaggerated bumpiness, is a great devourer of coral and can cause serious damage to the barrier when many such individuals are concentrated in one area. The sea worm *Hermodice carunculata,* which lives in the Caribbean, can devour one square centimeter of coral in an hour. Butterfly fishes as well, such as the pantropical *Chaetodon* and the Indo-Pacific *Heniochus,* feed preferentially on corals and other small animals that they capture among the fissures and in their dens, taking advantage of their small, characteristic mouths that protrude like pincers. This type of mouth is a morphological peculiarity that is widespread among many of the fishes that prey upon small invertebrates, such as the angel fishes (e.g., *Centropyge,* of the Indo-Pacific), or the stupendous Moorish idol *(Zanclus),* or certain file fishes and leatherjacket fishes of the Monocanthidae family, among others. Triggerfishes (Balistidae), puffers (Tetraodontidae), and porcupine fishes (Diodontidae), on the other hand, bite the coral with their extremely robust mouths.

A very large number of animal species feed on suspensions, plankton, or detritus. Many others are predators. Notwithstanding the very high percentage of herbivores, the **predators** are still the dominant category of animal species, and such an elevated occurrence of predation has resulted in the evolutionary pressure responsible for the prodigious differentiation of the various strategies of defense and attack. This is why many animals live in cavities, whether natural or of their own construction. For the most part, they feed by waiting patiently in their refuges for material in suspension to be transported to them by the ocean currents. Some species are strictly nocturnal, while others yet are astoundingly mimic, or endowed with poisonous or stinging substances, or thorns, or shells. In keeping pace, predators have evolved their own techniques of response, sharpened their nocturnal vision, developed resistance to poisons and repellents, and, beyond these, developed their own techniques of sabotage and aggression, such as the powerful chelae of certain crabs that are capable of breaking apart carapaces, or the siphons of certain mollusks that are capable of drilling into the shells of bivalves. The numerous seashells that are found on the beach showing a small, mysterious hole through one side are testimony to these fearsome attacks.

There are some remarkable cases of defense and predation. The anemone fish, or clown fish, *Amphitrion* finds refuge in the heart of the thick, stinging tentacles of several reef anemones, which the majority of the small animals of the reef avoid as the dangerous death trap that it is. The advantage is hypothesized to be reciprocal, but, without doubt, it is greater for the fish that, in this manner, secures for itself a refuge of exceptional safety. The advantage for the anemone is less clear, but it would appear

The Trumpetfish

The trumpetfishes (*Aulostomus* spp.) are extraordinary species of fishes that often are associated with porcupine fishes or parrot fishes. Their long, thin form recalls a large pipefish, and they can measure up to 60 cm (24 in). Its exceptional specialization consists in flanking or often even adhering to the back of these coral-eating or herbivorous fish and waiting until they begin to feed. (In the figure, the trumpetfish has teamed up with a puffer). As the puffer bites the coral into pieces or scrapes the surface of it, many tiny calcareous and organic particles rise from the surface, attracting small fish from the surrounding area. The trumpetfish takes advantage of this fact, preying upon them with its rapid darts. The pairing of the contrasting shapes of an inflated puffer (or a disk-shaped triggerfish) and its assiduous escort, the long *Aulostomus,* provides one of the most hilarious and curious spectacles of the entire coral reef.

Clown Fish and Their Anemones

The anemone fish (genera *Premnas* and *Amphiprion,* also known as the clown fish) astonish us by the nonchalance with which they swim unscathed—now disappearing, now reappearing—among the dangerous tentacles of tropical sea anemones. These coelenterates possess stinging cells that are extremely dangerous for other fish and often painful for humans as well.

No matter how carefully you look when exploring a coral barrier, you will almost never encounter an anemone fish without its anemone. Only rarely do certain species or certain adult individuals—those of larger size—abandon the anemone's tentacles, if insistently disturbed, to take shelter in a nearby fissure among the coral. The function of taking refuge within the anemone is obvious: there is no safer place in the whole barrier. During the night, when the anemone closes, the fish retires inside. The coelenterate takes a certain benefit, as well, because its fish guest is very intolerant of any approaches that might represent a menace to its living shelter, especially those few surgeonfish that are capable of feeding on these stinging anthozoans. The "jealousy" is so exaggerated that even inoffensive and harmless commensals, such as small crustaceans, are often accosted and chased away.

How the anemone fish succeeds in tolerating such contact that for others is mortal is not yet completely clear, but it is believed that the fish is covered by a secretion protecting against the stinging cells of the anemone, probably obtained from the same mucous produced by the coelenterate. The tentacles of the anemone, in fact, are covered with this substance to prevent the stinging effect when their tentacles touch one another. This is demonstrated by the fact that if an anemone fish is kept away from its anemone for some time (for example, in an aquarium), it cannot return immediately to swim among the anemone's tentacles. A period of cautious contacts is necessary, the purpose of which is probably to "immunize" its skin anew, by covering it over with protective mucous. Perhaps as a consequence of the specificity of this mechanism, some clown fishes choose and tolerate but a few sea anemone species, and some anemone species do not host any anemone fish. Others, like the Indo-Pacific bubble anemone *Entacmaea quadricolor,* host more than ten different clown fish species, while *Cryptodendrum adhaesivum* and *Heteractis malu* are known to host only Clark's anemone fish.

that it takes advantage from the leftovers from any especially abundant meals consumed by the fish.

The baroquely ornate and colorfully fringed lionfish *(Pterois volitans)*, a member of the same family as scorpion fishes, uses slow, steady movements to conceal its habit of attacking and killing prey with its nasty sting, mortal even for humans, which it uses for defense as well as for offense. Or, the deceiving technique of the false cleaner wrasse *(Aspidontus taeniatus),* which, by imitating the appearance and movements of the true cleaner wrasse *(Labroides dimidiatus),* is able to take small bites out of its unwitting victims, who were expecting—instead of these surreptitious attacks—the welcome service of being liberated of external parasites. And the long and painful spines of the *Diadema* urchins that are capable of directing themselves upward, by means of special sensors of light and dark, or those rarer *Heterocentrotus* urchins, with their robust, triangular bases. These long needles provide the *Diadema* with a safe shelter from such small fish as the cardinalfish (*Siphamia* spp.) or the more sensational razor fish *(Aeoliscus strigatus),* distributed between the Indian Ocean and Hawaii. These latter have the habit of camouflaging themselves by orienting themselves vertically, snout downward, among the ribbon-like *Thalassodendron* plants, or else by taking refuge among the long needles of sea urchins. Some of the swellings that appear on the surfaces of corals are nothing other than the refuges of certain crustaceans that stimulate the polyps to develop over them, even to the point that they create a type of cavern for the crustacean, which it accesses by means of an opportunely maintained entry hole.

There are thousands of surprising examples such as these, and there are many other yet-undiscovered types of interactions, patterns of behavior, strategies, and specialized devices among the protagonists who live in the coral bank.

Among the vertebrates, the **fishes** are the most striking and diversified of protagonists. Sensational, fantastical forms and spectacularly brilliant colors. No one who dives around a coral bank will ever forget the impact of the colors and shapes of its fishes. Even today, we have no convincing or exhaustive explanation for such vivacious colorings, and the most plausible hypotheses are connected to what has been said, in an earlier chapter, regarding the colors of tropical fauna. Besides the differences of shapes and colors among various species, even within a given species there can be marked differences between the males and females or between the young and the adults.

Certain species are highly characteristic and unusual, and these especially attract the curiosity and interest of those who take pleasure in snorkeling. The puffers and porcupine fishes, for example, are characterized by the fact that they can swell themselves up with water when frightened, thus greatly augmenting their own bodily dimensions and reducing their possibilities of being swallowed by a would-be predator. Out of water, they swell themselves up with air, and once thrown back into the sea, they float like balloons for several minutes, until they can resume their original dimensions by expelling the air they were storing. Coral formations are, without a doubt, the most exciting of all places for practicing **fish watching.**

Another well-represented category is that of the worms. Smooth and elastic roundworms (nematodes) are especially abundant, and these normally live in the sand and feed on detritus. Sipunculids dig tunnels under the corals and are stockier and more leathery. The annelid polychetes, or bristleworms (Polychaeta), have lateral appendages with which they dig and move, and there are some very colorful species of these, some of which feed on coral. Many have evolved the habit of constructing for themselves a calcareous tube within which they can live and take shelter while remaining permanently fixed to the substratum; from there they extend showy fan-shaped outgrowths to intercept the detritus in suspension.

Change of Scene from Day to Night

At nighttime in the coral garden, just like at nighttime in the forest, there are new activities and new protagonists that become animated. There are two periods of about half an hour each, during the phases of changing luminosity around twilight and dawn, when life seems to interrupt itself and an uncustomary calm pervades. After that, each one adopts his own strategy.

Some of the corals recede into their skeletons, especially those that rely principally on the nutriment supplied by the *zooxanthellae* contained in their interior. The disappearance of the light interrupts the photosynthesis of the algae, and this perhaps is the signal that induces many polyps to retract, rather than the sensation of darkness. Other corals choose this time to extend their polyps, thus changing the color and appearance of those rocks that appeared during the day to have been unarmed and lifeless. During the night, in fact, there are an infinity of small crustaceans and other zooplankton that emerge from their cavities or labyrinths and rise toward the surface, offering an exceptional opportunity for the polyps to capture them. Many fish abandon their holes or dens, taking advantage of the darkness that so confuses the attention of many prey. Sharks, morays, groupers, and other predators are primarily nocturnal, as are many mollusks and crustaceans, whether predators or herbivores.

The large and elegant tropical morays live in caverns and among the labyrinthine coral formations during the day. As they move their mouths rhythmically to pump water through their gills, we can observe the small cleaner shrimps that challenge those fearsome predators' fangs to try to gather up a few shreds of their latest prey—a truly extraordinary case of specialization, and a no less remarkable ecological niche.

The fish that are preyed upon, for their part, often prefer to unite themselves into shoals or schools when it is dark, and those that were so visible and showy during the day hide for their safety by night in cavities and caverns. Still others, those that are well adapted to the nocturnal life, leave their diurnal refuges at this time, and so, each protagonist puts into practice his own personal strategy, or, more appropriately, his own "specific" strategy. At night, parrot fishes assume a most original behavior before retiring: they secrete a spherical, gelatinous covering constituted of mucous and wrap themselves inside of this as though in a sleeping bag. They sleep this way every night, and every morning they emerge. It is possible to observe the empty "balloons" moving among the currents for a time before they break apart. Prey and predators, of course, do not rely on vision alone, but also on sounds, other vibrations, and chemical signals. It is also necessary to take into account the full moon that occurs each month, whose brightness, even though weak, can reach 20 m depth in the clear waters of coral gardens.

Some corals leave their polyps extended all the time, both day and night (e. g., *Euphyllia* and *Goniopora,* which also have the largest colonial polyps, as long as 10 cm, about 4 inches). Others can be stimulated to do this, for example, by the presence of nutritive material in contact with or near their surfaces (the corals are capable of detecting a few parts per million of organic substances, such as amino acids dissolved in the water).

Sands and Beaches

The sands at the bases and vicinities of coral reefs are white because they are constituted primarily of the calcium carbonate from eroded corals. The death of a coral can occur naturally, as a result of mechanical, physical, or climatic agents, such as waves, light, heat, depth, or the chemical composition of the waters, or alternatively, through the predation of fish, mollusks, echinoderms, or other organisms that feed on corals. After its death, it disintegrates into smaller and smaller particles, until these reach the dimensions of the grains of sand that accumulate on the beaches. Other plants and animals also contribute significantly to the formation of sand, such as annelids, shelled mollusks, and single-cell or multiple-cell

Coral Fishes

Triggerfishes (family Balistidae)
Intelligent, curious, and tremendously given to exploration, triggerfishes often live in areas rich with currents or about the coral reef platform towards the open sea. They eat crustaceans, urchins, and coral as well, and attack and devour fish that are sick or dying. During combat, they emit sounds by striking their teeth together or by raising and lowering their dorsal prickle. The majority of species, the most colorful ones, live solitary or in pairs, ferociously defending their territories; the gregarious species have dull colors. About thirty species exist.

Puffers (family Tetraodontidae)
Puffers do not have actual scales, but their skin is scattered with small plates and thorns. They do not have pectoral fins, and all species in the family can ingest water to inflate the body, which has no ribs. Out of water, they inflate with air, which they often have difficulty in expelling. They swim by waving their dorsal and anal fins, and are capable of turning in circles or swimming backwards. They use quick flicks of the tail to accelerate when fleeing from danger. Their food consists of shrimps, mollusks, and crustaceans, which they break apart with their powerful teeth and jaws. Some species also feed on coral. All puffers have the habit of driving their prey out of their dens by blowing on the sand. There are about a hundred species in the family.

Moorish idols (family Zanclidae)
Certain authors include this family with that of the Acanthuridae (surgeonfishes). They do not have stings or bony plates as the surgeonfishes do, but like them, they move using their pectoral fins primarily. These fish are flattened laterally, with very elegant shapes, colors, and movements.

Porcupine fishes (family Diodontidae)
These fish have cutaneous spikes that can either be mobile or always "bristling" erect. They have powerful teeth that often protrude from the mouth. They are capable of crushing shells, sea urchins, and the carapaces of crustaceans. Their body is round, their eyes, large. They swim by waving the dorsal and anal fins, aided by their pectoral fins. They use flicks of the tail only for fleeing. They are capable of inflating themselves by swallowing water. Out of water, they inflate with air, which, however, often proves harmful to them because of the difficulty they have in expelling it completely. They allow themselves to be approached easily, fleeing only if touched. There are about fifteen species.

Angelfishes, butterfly fishes (family Chaetodontidae)
The family is divided into two principal subfamilies, that of the angelfishes (Pomacanthinae) and that of the butterfly fishes (Chaetodonthinae). The butterfly fishes have forms that are laterally compressed, with a small, protruding mouths for feeding on small invertebrates. The angelfishes, by contrast, are primarily herbivorous, feeding on algae and, to a lesser extent, sponges and bryozoans. This is a numerous family, with about two hundred angelfishes and forty butterfly fishes. The adults live alone, for the most part, or in pairs. Near all butterfly fishes are distinguished by a black band running over the eye and many species exhibit two dark spots around the caudal area or on the dorsal fin, which confuses the true position of the eye and the orientation of the fish.

Surgeonfishes (family Acanthuridae)

The principal characteristic of this family is that they possess two sharp, cutting spines positioned at either side of the caudal peduncle. These spines are transformed scales that can protrude and be oriented to function as offensive blades capable of inflicting painful wounds. Some genera, such as *Acanthurus* and *Parachanthurus* swim quickly and deftly, while others, such as the *Zebrasoma* prefer to move slowly among the corals. Over a hundred species have been described, mainly in the Indian and Pacific Oceans.

Soldierfishes, squirrelfishes (family Holocentridae)

This is a family that includes a number of primitive species. The subfamily Holocentrinae is made up of squirrelfishes (so named for the striped coloring of many species), while the subfamily Myripristinae is constituted of soldierfishes (for their habit of swimming in compact, ordered formations). They have a characteristic habit of turning their head upward or downward to enter into cavities and grottoes. They are active during the night and not very visible during the day. Their greatly developed eyes favor nocturnal vision. About seventy species have been described.

Boxfishes (family Ostraciontidae)

These fish owe their name to the polygonal, bony plates that cover their bodies and heads. Their mouth, eyes, and fins protrude from the "box" of the body. Some genera are also endowed with spines. Like the puffers and porcupine fishes, they swim by moving the dorsal and anal fins, and the tail fin is used for more powerful propulsion only in case of flight. They feed on invertebrates and algae. There are about thirty species.

Damselfishes, demoiselles, sergeants, anemone fishes (family Pomacentridae)

The family of pomacentrids is a large family, numbering over two hundred species (according to the still-confused systematics). Among the most characteristic species are the sergeant fishes (genus *Abudefduf*), anemone fishes (genera *Premnas* and *Amphiprion*), and damselfishes (genera *Dascyllus* and *Pomacentrus*). Many pomacentrids care for their eggs until hatched. The genera *Amphiprion* and *Premnas* are noted for their capacity of dexterously taking refuge among the stinging tentacles of anemones.

Parrot fishes (Scaridae family)

Related to the wrasses (Labridae), this family includes fishes with vividly brilliant colors and a dentition that recalls the beak of a parrot, which is well-adapted for the herbivorous diet of this species that grazes on algae on the surfaces of rocks and corals. Some species also feed on corals. Many parrot fishes wrap themselves up every night in a covering of mucous, from which they emerge in the morning. It is not easy to identify the various species, because there are notable differences in coloring even between the males and the females, among other things. For some authors, there are over two hundred species, for others, no more than a hundred.

Scorpion fishes, rouge fishes, lionfishes, turkey fishes, stonefishes (Scorpenidae family)

This family is well represented, in temperate seas as well in cold seas. There are some strikingly spectacular and poisonous species in the Tropics. Some examples of these worth noting are the scorpion fishes (subfamilies Scorpeninae and Tetraroginae), the very poisonous and elegant lionfishes (genera *Pterois*, subfamily Pteroinae, and *Nemapterois*, subfamily Pteroinae), the Napoleon fishes (genus *Amblyapistus*, subfamily Tetraroginae), and the stonefishes (subfamily Synanceinae).

Fish

Damselfish
Microspathodon chrysurus
Pomacentridae, subfamily Pomacentrini

Moorish idol
Zanclus cornutus
Zanclidae

Surgeonfish
Acanthurus olivaceus
Acanthuridae

Boxfish
Ostracion meleagris
Ostraciontidae

Angelfish
Pomacanthus imperator
Balistidae

Triggerfish
Balistoides conspicillum
Chaetodontidae, subfamily Pomacanthinae

Parrotfish
Scarus sorididus
Scaridae

Cardinalfish
Apogon compressus
Apogonidae

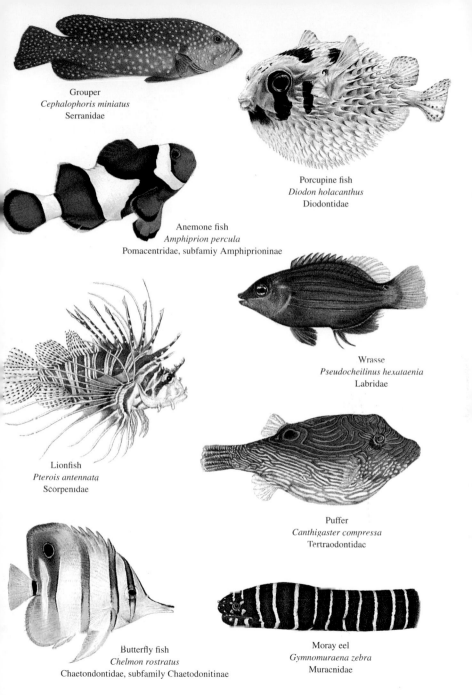

Grouper
Cephalophoris miniatus
Serranidae

Porcupine fish
Diodon holacanthus
Diodontidae

Anemone fish
Amphiprion percula
Pomacentridae, subfamiy Amphiprioninae

Wrasse
Pseudocheilinus hexataenia
Labridae

Lionfish
Pterois antennata
Scorpenidae

Puffer
Canthigaster compressa
Tertraodontidae

Butterfly fish
Chelmon rostratus
Chaetondontidae, subfamily Chaetodonitinae

Moray eel
Gymnomuraena zebra
Muracnidae

foraminifers. Further, there are coelenterates that are defined as **false corals,** such as the blue corals *(Heliopora)* or the *Tubipora,* which construct a sheltering structure in the shape of an organ pipe, hence their name, the **organ pipe corals.** The red color of their skeleton is evidence that these do not belong to the true reef-building corals, whose colors result from the living tissues, and not from the calcareous skeleton. Fragments of *Tubipora* stand out easily in the white, coralline sand.

Some of the green algae can produce large quantities of sandy detritus locally, because of their rapid decomposition. These are the species of the genus *Halimeda,* which somewhat recall the terrestrial maidenhair fern, as they are formed of chains of disks having varying sizes according to the species, the nature of the seas, and the ecological conditions. Normally, one disk is developed each day, and these die frequently, liberating the calcifications that they contain.

Many characteristic species live in the sandy clearings that frequently open out among the reefs or, in the more extended ones, within their interior margins. There on the bottom, perhaps between a coral and some sand or among the branches of an *Acropora,* the large and common *Linkia esatentacolari* may be seen standing out: sea stars of a beautiful, brilliant blue color. In lagoons or sheltered areas having sandy bottoms, green algae of various species will often develop, as do various aquatic plants that form submerged prairies, such as the *Thalassodendron,* one that sea turtles find highly delectable. The holothurians (sea cucumbers) are very abundant, with some species as long as a meter, or even longer—others are stockier—and often highly colorful. There are many species of filtering mollusks and detritus-eating animals. There are some characteristic, irregular echinoids, such as the heart urchins *(Lovenia),* near relatives of the sand dollars, belonging to the same class as the more common sea urchins, but with a flattened, rather than a spherical, skeleton, and with needles that resemble more a type of fur than rigid and radiate spines. Movements of life on the sandy bottom can usually be appreciated more easily and more frequently from observations of their traces than from trying to observe the living protagonists. Lines, tracks, fin marks, small mounds and holes, volcanoes of sand spewing out grains of filtered detritus from whatever-that-is living at the bottom of that tunnel. There are even some mushroom corals living in this substratum, which begin their development on the fragment of a shell, detaching later in their growth.

Sea Turtles

The tropical seas are the most famous seas for observing sea turtles, those large, curious, marine reptiles. When we see how clumsily they swim with their flippers along the surface of the open sea, snout protruding beyond the water (as reptiles, they can breathe atmospheric oxygen only), we almost have the desire to try to rescue them.

In reality, sea turtles are extremely resistant and extraordinarily well-adapted to life in the sea, where they lead the greater part of their existence. That slow crawl used in relaxed conditions can transmute unexpectedly into a rapid sprint, especially in younger specimens.

It is possible to encounter specimens of all the living species of turtles in the Tropics, even though some are more abundant than others in certain areas. Some species, such as the *Caretta caretta,* also frequent subtropical waters, although they do not appear in the colder seas (there are accidental exceptions). Turtles choose tranquil and isolated beaches, those of atolls and islands for the most part, for laying their eggs and then burying them under the sand.

The seven existing species of sea turtles are divided into two families: those covered with horny scutes (Cheloniidae) and those having leathery backs (Dermochelyidae). These are: the green turtle *(Chelonia mydas);* the loggerhead *(Caretta caretta);* the olive ridley *(Lepidochelis olivacea);* Kemp's ridley *(Lepidochelys kempi);* the flatback *(Chelonia depressa);* the hawksbill *(Eretmochelys imbricata);* and the leatherback *(Dermochelys coriacea).*

Hawksbill turtle, *Eretmochelys imbricata*

Green turtle, *Chelonia mydas*

Loggerhead turtle, *Caretta caretta*

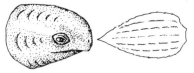

Leatherback, *Dermochelys coriacea*

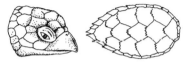

Olive ridley turtle, *Lepidochelis olivacea*

The Tropical Intertidal. Where the crystalline waters of the reef bathe the beach, there is an interesting transitional environment between the sea and the land. In that band subjected to the oscillations of the tide or the waves of the undertow, the sand is spotless and inviolate, scattered only with the remains of shells and the beached carcasses of small animals and tiny algae. Extremely rapid and ever suspicious are the fleeting crabs of the genus *Ocypode,* also called ghost crabs, because of their habit of emerging during the night from their dens dug in the sand. The largest specimens are more strictly nocturnal and reside in deep galleries that are dug with the descent oriented towards the interior of the beach. The large entry holes of these dens actually seem more suitable for lodging rodents than crabs. The ghost crabs are fearsome predators and significantly responsible for major losses to the turtle hatchlings, which must aim for the sea, just after emerging from their shells, in a laborious and desperate flight over the sand.

From the open waters of the vast ocean, beyond the ridge and across the reef, back on up to the fine, white sands of the beach, our long voyage comes to an end, the voyage through that special cross section of tropical life, the coral garden. Through places where the beauty is in enjoying the hot sun and the warm, clear waters, but where it can also be sufficient just to look around, to notice that one is surrounded by a wondrous ecosystem that unites aesthetic beauty and naturalistic interest, and in so doing, forges what many find to be the most enrapturing and exciting of all tropical habitats.

Chapter 9

The Savanna

G reat spaces dominated by grasslands yellowed from the sun and dotted sparsely with umbrella-canopied trees. This is the most classical vision of the African savannas, the one to which novels and documentaries have inured most of the world's population.

One fourth of the entire dry surface of the planet is occupied by savanna vegetation, and even though these exist as well in Asia, South America, and Australia, those of Africa are the most extensive and the most famous. In southern Asia, where the climate is closely linked to the monsoons, what actually develops are deciduous woods, rather than true savannas. In central Africa, by contrast, savannas border directly with tropical moist forests, generating a mosaic of grass patches and evergreen woodlands. In this regard, there has also been influence over the millennia from the indigenous populations, who have "managed" the vegetation using fire, thus promoting the development of grasslands for livestock breeding, to the detriment of the forest cover.

Fire and Rain

Rain and fire are the principal determining factors in the ecology of the savanna. Fires are frequent there, and sometimes these are due to natural causes, such as the intense heat of the sun beating down on the dehydrated expanses of grass during the dry season. It has been man, however, who from time immemorial has promoted fires to produce grazing lands, for his livestock or to attract the antelopes, in order to hunt them. After the

fire, the subterranean roots of gramineous plants are stimulated to new germination, producing young green shoots and suckers even during times of drought, which irresistibly attract a large number of herbivores.

The effect of these fires is principally that of containing the development of trees and shrubs, favoring the broad grassy expanses. The so-called bush fires are slow and produce limited amounts of heat, involving primarily the herbaceous stratum. Even at just a few centimeters (a couple of inches) below the soil, there is no change in the temperature, so that the fire damages neither the roots nor the hypogeal fauna. Only low bushes and young trees and sprouts are destroyed, but the mature trees remain unscathed. The small fire that burns the grasses does not develop flames that are capable of reaching the canopies. For this reason, we find trees in certain areas that are partitioned into classes of the same age, coming from seeds that germinated and were able to grow for sufficiently long periods without fires to permit them to grow to a fireproof height.

Halfway between Desert and Forest

Savannas are almost exclusively tropical environments, where xeromorphic plants (those adapted to dryness) dominate. The principal family represented among these is that of the grasses; bushes and trees, varying in density and diversity, are also included.

Among the plants, the adaptations to prolonged dryness vary from species to species, but there are some devices that are practically constants. One of these is the periodic loss of leaves during the dry season, an effect that reduces transpiration. Others are the reduction of the surface area of leaves, the presence of deep taproots that search for moisture, and the development of a sclerophyllous nature, meaning that the leaves are protected by leathery coverings.

Savannas appear where the climate and rainfall are inconstant throughout the course of the year and there exist actual **dry** and **rainy seasons.** In order for a savanna to develop (or in order to prevent a real forest from evolving), it is necessary to have a dry season that varies from at least three and a half months to about seven and a half. In eastern Africa, we can distinguish a season of "great rains," generally from March to May, and one of "little rains," from November to December. The culmination of the dry period is frequently between late summer and early autumn, however, this pattern is often shattered in practice. Delays or anticipations in the start or the end of the rains, in fact, are extremely common, and the indigenous populations know this well, such as the Masai of Kenya and Tanzania, who are constrained to moving their herds about in order to avoid disasters due to prolonged dryness or other caprices of the rains. The wildlife know it as well, particularly the migratory herbivores, which are able to locate the patchy patterns of rains in these regions.

Savannas, where trees occupy from 10 to 40% of the ground area, are habitats whose characteristics are halfway between those of forests and those of deserts. A confirming piece of evidence of this intermediary position, ecologically speaking, can be seen by examining the values of their primary production. The quantity of plant matter produced averages about 1,200 g/m^2 (2.6 lb/yd^2) per year in the savanna, as compared with 2,500 g/m^2 (5.5 lb/yd^2) in tropical moist forests and 200 g/m^2 (0.4 lb/yd^2) in deserts. Even from a strictly geographical point of view, the location of savannas is in the intertropical band, between the rainy equatorial areas and the subtropical desert areas.

In Africa, savannas are classified on the basis of the types and densities of arboreal and shrub species. Trees in the savanna are sparse and not very tall, from 6 to 12 m (20 to 40 ft), except for the colossi of these habitats, the **African baobabs.** Mature individuals usually do not even reach a height of 30 m (100 ft), but at the base, their trunk circumference can exceed 40 m (130 ft), meaning a diameter of about 10 m (33 ft). All of Africa is dominated by one single species of baobab, the African baobab *(Adansonia digitata),* while in Madagascar, fully seven different species have been described throughout the island, some with reduced dimensions but having fantastical forms, others, such as the *Adansonia grandidieri,* capable of competing with the African baobab for majesty.

A large part of the African savanna is dominated by **acacias** (*Acacia* spp.), as the approximately forty species frequently make up about half of all the trees growing. Acacia trees are often associated with *Commiphora,* particularly in semiarid scrublands and wooded savannas. One of the most typical pan-African species is the *Acacia tortilis,* with its characteristic canopy, flattened and dilated like an umbrella. Other species have a wide distribution as well, like the paperbark acacia or the white thorn acacia *(Acacia plyacantha),* which reach as far as the Indian subcontinent. In some areas, trees such as the *Brachystegia* dominate, in association with

Dwarf baobab, *Adansonia fony*
(height 5 m, or 5.5 yd)

Grandidier's baobab, *Adansonia grandidieri*
(height 20 m , or 22 yd)

African baobab, *Adansonia digitata*
(height 25 m, or 27 yd)

In all of tropical Africa, there is only one species of baobab, the gigantic *Adansonia digitata,* and in Australia, there are a couple of other species, but the island of Madagascar possesses seven different species, most endemic. Some, such as the *Adansonia fony,* have bizarre forms and reduced dimensions, others, such as the *Adansonia grandidieri* or *Adansonia za,* are no less impressive or spectacular than the *A. digitata.*

isoberlina or combretum, and these give rise to the so-called **miombo** woods or savannas, where the arboreal density is notably superior, so that the impression is often that of an actual woods, even though sparse and rich with open spaces.

In Central America, there are savannas dotted with palms or conifers *(Pinus caribaea),* while in Australia it is the eucalypti that dominate the arboreal component.

The Savannas and Forests of Madagascar. In virtue of its isolation, which has lasted over a hundred million years, the island of Madagascar hosts a great number of endemic animals and plants.

From the point of view of climate, the northern mountain chain and the central highlands function as barriers to the moisture-bearing winds and the Asiatic monsoons, producing, as a result, an extremely varied distribution of vegetation. To the north, on the mountains and on the eastern versant, a luxuriant tropical forest dominates. Immediately behind the mountains of the north, in the plain that opens out to the northwest, a dense and low deciduous forest extends.

Even farther to the south, still on the western versant, an exciting baobab savanna opens up, which then gives way to the unusual "spiny forest," an impenetrable tangle of fantastical and exclusive trees and shrubs, such as bottle trees, octopus trees, dwarf baobabs, and bushes with thousands of thorns and just as many shapes. The arid, subdesert soil has induced these plants to transform their leaves into thorns, and the endemic family of Didcreaceae, especially, numbers dozens of species that recall the succulents typical of the desert, such as the cactus or euphorbia. The thorny forest and the tracts dominated by the Didereaceae in the south-southeast of the island make up one of the most bizarre and fascinating vegetation systems on the planet.

The *Bushveld* of Southern Africa. A good part of southern Africa is occupied by a savanna vegetation defined as the *bushveld,* which is dominated by *Acacia* (spp.), miombo woodland (*Brachystegia* with *Combretum* and *Julbernardia*), and mopane woodland *(Colophospermum mopane).* Baobabs grow there as well, in the northernmost part of the region. Some acacia species, such as the *Acacia karroo,* are limited to southern Africa, while in the southwest it is often the trees of the species *Acacia erioloba,* or giraffe acacia, that dot the landscape with their dilated canopies and dark bark.

Often, in the more arid areas, the *bushveld* transforms into a *thornveld,* which is characterized by fewer trees and an abundance of thorny shrubs.

American Savannas. The South American savannas have a substantially different ecology than those of Africa. A savanna type of vegetation ranging from open grasslands to savanna woodland forms in some areas of central Brazil, where it takes the name of *cerrado.* This is the largest savanna area in the Western Hemisphere, with over one hundred million hectares (385,000 square miles), although this figure is decreasing quickly because of agricultural expansion. In these savannas, the vegetative structure involves a series of adaptations that are typical of the other savannas around the globe, even if the rainfall and humidity during the South American dry season are generally greater than in Africa. Small savannas are scattered all around the area of Amazonia, resulting in mosaic habitats with patches of woodlands or rainforests, though the largest expanses of these are found to the north of the Amazon River. The *vàrzea* savannas, like the *llanos* of Colombia and Venezuela, are open areas that flood during the rainy seasons, particularly abundantly between the Rio Negro and the Xingu and around the Orinoco, while *caatinga* savannas form in northeastern Brazil. In the dry season, much of the terrain dries out and is rapidly colonized by the growth of grasses in and among the shrubs (such as the very common *Artemisia*), palms (like the *Mauritia flexuosa*), and mature trees that easily tolerate either flooding or long periods of dryness. Often these groups of trees and shrubs, called *matas,* assume the appearance of an island within a sea of grass, whether dry or half-submerged by flooding.

One of the most characteristic and broad expanses of land in tropical South America that can be compared to a savanna forms where Argentina, Bolivia, and Paraguay meet, under the Mato Grosso. This is the region of the **Chaco,** where the rains are abundant but irregular. The vegetation is constituted of great, grassy plains dotted with sparse woods, among which *Copernicia* palms can frequently be seen, as these are also resistant to a prolonged aridity.

Asian Savannas. The areas of tropical Asia, also, exhibit actual savannas, although these are subjected to the effects of monsoons, which bring rains and humidity for a good number of months during the year, but more often the vegetation is woods and seasonal forests, with trees that lose their leaves, and a less intricate, less luxuriant vegetation than that of the rain-

Klipspringer
(*Oreotragus oreotragus*)

Impala (male)
(*Aepyceros melampus*)

Springbok
(*Antidorcas marsupialis*)

Gerenuk (male)
(*Litocranius walleri*)

Common reedbuck (male)
(*Redunca arundinum*)

Above and following pages: Some examples of species of wild African bovids (antelopes) belonging to the most typical genera.

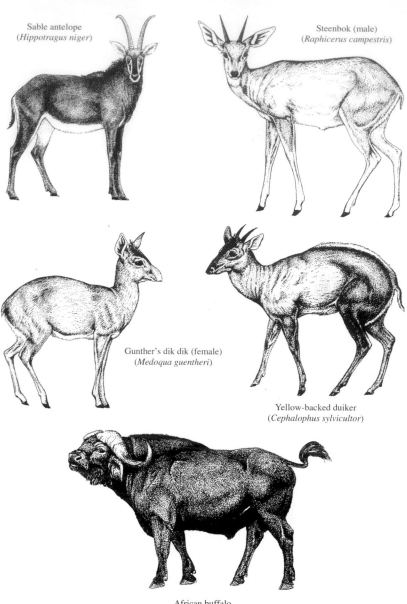

Sable antelope
(*Hippotragus niger*)

Steenbok (male)
(*Raphicerus campestris*)

Gunther's dik dik (female)
(*Medoqua guentheri*)

Yellow-backed duiker
(*Cephalophus sylvicultor*)

African buffalo
(*Syncerus caffer*)

Waterbuck (male)
(*Kobus ellipsyprimnus*)

Gemsbok
(*Oryx gazella*)

Gnu, or blue wildebeest
(*Connochaetes taurinus*)

Red hartebeest
(*Alcelaphus buselephus*)

Kudu (male)
(*Tragelophus strepsiceros*)

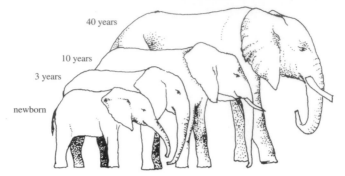

40 years

10 years

3 years

newborn

Comparison of the African elephant's dimensions at various ages.

forest jungles. In India and Southeast Asia, just as in Africa, these environments are populated by numerous large herbivores, such as deer, elephants, gaurs, and bantengs (the latter two being wild cattle), which attract the great Asian predators, such as tigers, leopards, cuons (wolf-like canids), and wolves.

In India there are arid zones that are more properly referred to as savannas, one to the northwest, including part of the Indus River basin, and a second in the Deccan highlands. These subdesert areas are characterized by an abundance of sand, in which acacia trees and *Zizyphus* bushes grow. Thus, their appearance is generally less desolate than that of an actual desert, such as the nearby Sahara and its Middle Eastern continuation into Asia, but they do not exhibit as much vegetation as an African or South American savanna.

The Kingdom of Grasses and Herbivores

A constant and characteristic element of all savannas is the great abundance of grasses, which can often be very tall, such as the *Ponicum maximum* in Africa, which can exceed 3 m (10 ft). Savannas have evolved a correspondingly great abundance and diversity of herbivores that are bound to this ready availability of forage. The African savannas continue to hold the world record. Indeed, there are 99 different species of wild bovids living in tropical Africa, primarily in savanna environments, of

Getting to Know the Camp Visitors

At first sight all buffaloes appear to be equal to each other, and the same holds true for zebras, giraffes, elephants, and many other animals. In reality, though, with a bit of attention, it is possible to recognize every single animal individually. The celebrated naturalist Ian Douglas-Hamilton, during his studies at Lake Manyara in Tanzania, was able to recognize dozens of elephants individually. Something simple, and quite pleasant indeed, is learning to recognize the individuals that have developed the habit of approaching the camps and lodges of tourists, or the specimens that we meet during our safaris. The characteristic signs that relate most importantly to each species are various, and it is necessary to pay attention to these, in particular, in order to be able to recognize each specimen.

Here is a brief, schematic list:

- Elephants: shape of the tusks (large or small, curved or straight, symmetrical or not, broken, etc.); cuts or patterns of indentation along the margins of the ears; wounds and scars on the body; dimensions.
- Rhinoceroses: dimensions and shape of the horns; scars and wounds on the body; indentations along the margins of the ears.
- Giraffes: dimensions and shape of the horns; indentations along the ears.
- Zebras: width and combination of the stripes, especially on the posterior part of the thighs; the tail.
- Buffaloes: dimensions and curvature of the horns; markings along the margins of the ears; dimensions.
- Lions: size and shape of the mane; scars along the muzzle, ears, or body; color of the coat.

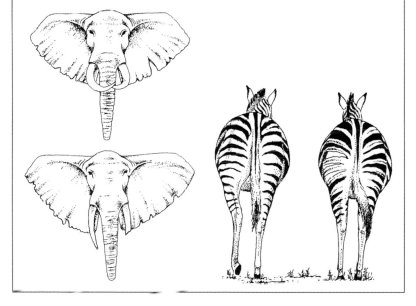

which 72 are exclusive to the region. The subfamily of antelopes (Antilopinae) finds its maximum diversification here, with 55 different species. The obvious complement to this wealth of grasses and herbivores is a notable diversity of great carnivores. One-third of the world's felines live in the African savanna environment, including some species with strikingly large dimensions, such as the lion *(Panthera leo),* the only strictly social feline, the leopard *(Panthera pardus),* the cheetah *(Acinonyx jubatus),* the serval *(Felis serval),* and the caracal *(Felis caracal).* There are, moreover, three species of hyenas, three of jackals, and the wild dog *(Lycaon pictus).*

As in any predator-prey relationship in nature, the grasses and the ungulates of the savanna have evolved **techniques of "hunt" and defense,** which are linked to one another.

Many Poaceae of the grasslands have developed hardened tissues by concentrating silica or lignin within; or they have become dangerous or unpleasant, containing poisonous, irritating, or nauseating substances; or they have transformed their leaves into needle-like or hooked thorns or have learned to grow in the midst of poisonous plants, so as to take advantage of those defenses. Some attract ants that have painful bites. On their side,

the herbivores have developed an exceptional grinding dentition, prehensile lips and tongues for ripping off grasses and leaves, necks of lengths suitable for reaching the various strata of vegetation, and refined systems for digesting the coriaceous vegetable fibers, including the technique of rumination used by bovids (buffaloes, antelopes, and gazelles) and other even-toed ungulates (chevrotains, giraffes, deer). Some are endowed with important counterdefenses, such as insensitivity to certain poisons and other chemical defenses; the black rhinoceroses of certain areas, for

Lion
(*Panthera leo*)
about 15 cm (5.9 in)

Cheetah
(*Acinonyx jubatus*)
about 10 cm (3.9 in)

Spotted hyena
(*Crocuta crocuta*)
about 12 cm (4.7 in)

Black-backed jackal
(*Canis mesomelas*)
about 6 cm (2.4 in)

Wildebeest
(*Connochaetes taurinus*)
about 8 cm (3.1 in)

African buffalo
(*Syncerus caffer*)
about 15 cm (5.9 in)

Impala
(*Aepyceros melampus*)
about 6 cm (2.4 in)

Zebra
(*Equus burchelli*)
about 10 cm (3.9 in)

African elephant
(*Loxodonta africana*)
about 50 cm (20 in)

Hippopotamus
(*Hippopotamus amphibius*)
about 25 cm (10 in)

The swellings found on the acacia branches at the bases of thorns are reactions to the presence of ants, or better, they are probably reactions to being inoculated by the ants with phytohormones that are irritating for the tissues. The ants build nests within these galls, and the acacia derives advantage from this, because the ants will actively defend the plant against browsing herbivores of whatever class. As an indicator of the efficacy of this defense mechanism, the acacias housing ants are known to have a greater leaf biomass than "undefended" plants.

example, base their diet largely on euphorbia plants, which have latex that is irritating for the majority of animals, including humans. Others have lined the mucous membranes of their mouths with a horny covering that permits them to chew the thorns and prickers of plants without difficulty.

Acacias and Ants. Many—but not all—acacias have large, abnormal swellings at the bases of their long, sharp, leaf-protecting thorns. With a bit of attention we can easily notice how those galls are linked to the presence of ants. This is not the result of a casual coincidence; it is a specific reaction of the plant to the presence of ants; rather than a defense, this is the trees' form of hospitality. The ants find refuge in the galls and are thus induced to remain, and during their stay, they travel far and wide, all over the entire plant, protecting it with their bites from the tongues or lips of the many savanna herbivores in search of food. These myrmecophilous plants (literally "friends to ants") demonstrate another example of the frequent cooperation among ants and plants, which is very common in the tropical latitudes.

Characteristic, Specialized Fauna

Great accumulations of earthen matter molded into grotesque and fantastical forms, whose irregular intentionality seems to reflect some quite precise purpose: another visible indicator that we are in the savanna landscape. These **termite mounds** are the residences of immense colonies of termites, those small isopterans that are so very abundant in the tropical latitudes. In South America there are many different species of the genus

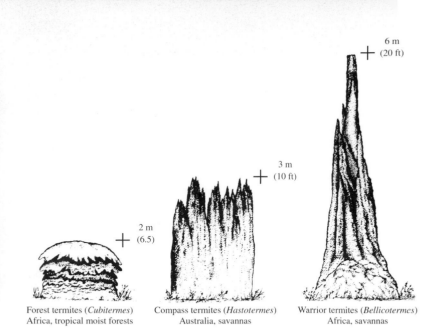

6 m
(20 ft)

3 m
(10 ft)

2 m
(6.5)

Forest termites (*Cubitermes*)
Africa, tropical moist forests

Compass termites (*Hastotermes*)
Australia, savannas

Warrior termites (*Bellicotermes*)
Africa, savannas

Termite mounds are structures of a compact, cement-like substance made from a paste of saliva and sand or earth. The shapes vary according to the species (about 2,000 exist) and they may be external or subterranean, lodging from a few hundred to millions of individuals. The great termitaries that are visible above the ground are generally spire-shaped or sloping, a form that reduces the erosive effect of the rains.

Nasutitermes, while in Africa, it is the genera *Bellicositermes* and *Cubitermes* that are responsible for the largest and most monumental structures, which can easily reach 5 m (16 ft) in height. Termitaries normally begin with a broad base and continue upward, terminating in one or more pinnacles, recalling the spires of a medieval castle. Some species of *Cubitermes,* by contrast, construct termitaries that are smaller, resembling more the shape of a mushroom, or still others with peaks like canopies that can more easily withstand the erosion of the rains. This latter is the most frequent morphology of the termitaries of the species living in tropical moist forests or in forests subject to heavy rainy seasons

The termites of the savanna, just like those of the forest, can feed upon the wood of trees and plants, or on organic material in decomposition, whether of animal or plant origin, often already partially humified. Some species *(Bellicositermes)* have the singular habit of promoting the growth of underground fungus gardens inside their termitaries and of feeding upon them.

Inside those great, patiently constructed edifices of mud, resides the colony of thousands or millions of individuals, all distributed into rigid castes according to their various social functions, just as are bees and ants. Such an abundant availability has pushed some animals, the **myrmeco-phages,** to a specialized diet based almost exclusively on termites. This is the case for the African aardwolf *(Proteles cristatus),* a close relative of the hyena, for the aardvark *(Orycteropus afer),* the world's only living representative of the primitive family Tubulidentata, and for the three Afro-Asiatic species of terrestrial or arboreal pangolins *(Manis* spp.). In South America, there are other myrmecophages, such as the anteaters *(Mirmecophyla tridactyla)* and armadillos *(Priodontes* spp.), which prefer savanna habitats to the forest.

Birds: Flying and Otherwise

Another typical faunistic category of the savannas is represented by the terrestrial birds. Among these, the **ostrich** *(Struthio camelus)* is the largest, reaching up to 2.5 m (8.2 ft) in height, and is completely incapable of flight. The reproductive organization of this species is fascinating. The

Spectacled weaver
(Ploceus ocularis)

Masked weaver
(Ploceus intermedius)

The Kori bustard, a typical representative of the terrestrial birds of the African savannas, is among the heaviest flying birds, with males reaching up to 10 kg (22 lbs).

male frequents a harem of females, three or four generally, but he couples first and most often with his favorite, then later, also with the others. The females all lay their eggs in a single nest, which is usually just a simple depression in the ground. Only the favorite female and the male hatch the eggs and raise the young. Predators can most easily reach those that are on the outside, which are those of the "secondary" females, laid after those of the "first lady," whose eggs occupy the central part of the nest and are well guarded by the hatching adults.

The **bustards** (Otididae) are another category of terrestrial birds. Even though they can fly, they prefer to hide among the high grasses of the savanna. Some species have small dimensions, while others, such as the Kori bustard *(Otis kori)*, can reach weights of up to 10 kg (22 lbs). The wild fowl (Galliformes) are also terrestrial, among which we note especially the francolins (*Francolinus* spp.) and guinea fowl (Numididae), frequently observable in dense groups. There are six species of guinea fowl, all African, and these are the progenitors of the current domestic forms.

Oxpeckers

In Africa, the large herbivores—from the rhinoceroses to the giraffes, from the buffaloes to the antelopes, and even to the smaller impalas and gazelles—are often seen being visited by birds flying about, very actively, birds that grasp onto the back, the flanks, or even the muzzle, pecking here and there, and obtaining, oddly, nearly absolute tolerance. These are the oxpeckers, of which two species exist, the yellow-billed oxpecker *(Buphagus africanus)* and the red-billed oxpecker *(B. erythrorynchus),* belonging to the same family as the common European starlings.

Their sharp, cutting beak is a well-adapted instrument for tearing away ticks and for striking parasitic insects that hide between the fur and the skin of pachyderms. Their claws are hooked, and, in a curious convergence with woodpeckers, the tail is robust and serves as balancing support for the bird as it clings vertically to the flank of a hippopotamus, the neck of a giraffe, or the thigh of a rhinoceros.

The relationship between oxpeckers and the large fauna of the savanna goes much farther than just the simple removal of parasites. The oxpeckers regularly function as alarm signals, especially on behalf of rhinoceroses and buffaloes, which are animals having poor eyesight. With their excited chattering, they warn that something, possibly downwind, moves among the high grasses or bushes. Pay attention while on foot on a safari if you hear the alarmed cry of a number of oxpeckers from behind a shrub, because it is almost certainly the announcement of the presence of a large animal.

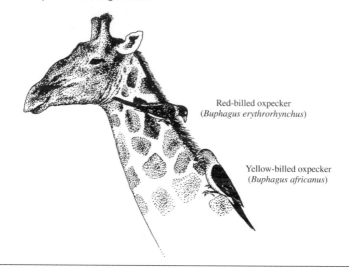

Red-billed oxpecker
(*Buphagus erythrorhynchus*)

Yellow-billed oxpecker
(*Buphagus africanus*)

Also interesting among the African savannas are the passerine weavers (Ploceidae), often with yellow coloring and various embellishments of black on the head and body. These are the birds responsible for the hanging nests seen frequently in the branches of acacia or baobab trees.

In the sky is a continuous, sparse circling of **vultures,** distinguishable from eagles and the other raptors by their rectangular silhouette and their enormous and broad, fringe-tipped wings (up to 3 m span, about 10 ft). The **African marabou storks** (*Leptoptilos crumeniferus*) are also gigantic, and in their elegant flight, the long legs extend backward, the great beaks, forward. Vultures and marabous represent the principal category of winged necrophages, birds that are specialized in detecting the carcasses of dead animals. Considering the abundance of ungulates and the elevated presence of predators, it is easy to understand how, in just the savanna park of the Serengeti-Masai Mara in Tanzania and Kenya, vultures consume something like 33,000 kg (72,600 lbs) of meat each year. The great, circling flight afforded by their broad wings and the ascensional currents of hot air rising from the soil allow them to soar very efficiently and to survey vast expanses of land with only a minimal expenditure of energy—equivalent to about one-thirtieth of that used in actively beating flight.

Vultures remain in visual contact with one another, even at great distances, and as soon as one makes a move to land, demonstrating the presence of a food source, all the others hasten over, and the message is propagated for many miles, quickly mustering dozens of vultures around the same carcass.

Hospitality for the European Migrants. From the ornithological point of view, the savannas play another key role. More so than the tropical moist forests, where the conditions are homogeneous and the alimentary sources do not fluctuate, the savannas are extremely important areas for the wintering of many migratory birds coming from the farther northern and southern latitudes. In the Northern and Southern winters, many species, especially the insectivorous ones, leave the rigorous climates of their homelands and engage in migratory movements, some longer, some shorter, and some of which are absolutely spectacular.

Billions of birds migrate from Europe and western Asia to Africa, to benefit from the climate and the availability of insects. The European swallows and swifts arrive in Africa during the Northern winter, along with many other migrants, so that we find there the same birds, mixed among

Red-billed wood hoopoe
Phoeniculus purpureus
Africa
Phoeniculidae—Africa

Birds of the
African Savannas

Black-headed weaver
Ploceus cucullatus
Africa
Ploceidae—Europe, Asia, Africa

Carmine bee-eater
Merops nubicus
Africa
Meropidae—southern Europe,
Africa, Asia, Australia

Lilac-breasted roller
Coracias caudata
Africa
Coraciidae—Europe, Asia, Africa, Australia

Yellow-billed hornbill
Tockus flavirostris
Africa
Bucerotidae—Africa, Asia

Helmeted guinea fowl
Numida meleagris
Africa
Numididae—Africa

Crested francolin
Francolinus sephaena
Africa
Phasianidae—worldwide

the resident African species, that come back to Europe to nest in the countrysides in April. Less dramatic, but still significant, are the northward movements of birds from the southern regions of Africa, towards the more tropical savannas.

With their structural characteristic of such open environments, the savannas lend themselves optimally to the observation of animals. Because of the abundance of herbivores and their predators, which generally typify all the savannas on the globe—and most especially those of Africa—these habitats unite the fascination of a special landscape with the irresistible attractiveness of their fauna. It is in this combination of elements—the immense spaces, the distant horizons, the gentle, golden prairies dotted with acacia canopies, the great wild herds and the large predators in their pursuit—that we find the basis of the famous *mal d'Africa* ("Africa sickness"), linked indissolubly with its savannas and megafauna.

Chapter 10

Deserts

When we think about the deserts of our planet, it is, once again, a common and widespread stereotype that dominates our image: visions of immense expanses of sand, populated only by sinuous and gentle, golden dunes.

Deserts are not actually typical environments of the tropical regions. Indeed, they are more characteristic of the subtropical latitudes (see chapter 2, "The Climate") that happen to be affected by high pressures, which result in extremely scarce precipitation. Still, deserts can often extend from the subtropics into areas that are within the intertropical zone, while remaining close to the borders between the two regions.

There are five great desert blocks in the world, all relegated to the margins of the Tropics. These are: the Sahara Desert and the deserts of the Middle East, which are connected, in turn, to the Gobi in central Asia; the complex of deserts in southern Africa, including the Namib, the Karoo, and the Kalahari; the South American deserts, including the western, coastal Atacama Desert and Patagonia in the east; the North American deserts in Mexico and California, including the Mojave and the Sonora; and the Australian desert.

Hot and Cold Deserts, Arid and Semiarid Deserts

For a rough starting definition, we can divide deserts into hot or cold, the latter of which are often at high altitudes, where temperatures below freezing can be frequent during the winter. Further, some deserts are coastal deserts, such as the Atacama and the Namib, in marked contrast to the others, which are primarily continental.

A **coastal desert** is strongly influenced and benefited by the atmospheric humidity that derives from the fogs and mists coming in from the sea, which can penetrate inland for more than 100 km (60 mi). This humidity not only attenuates the temperatures, reducing the daily and seasonal excursions to about 5°C (9°F) throughout the course of the year, or 10°C (18°F) throughout the course of the day, but it also contributes to increasing the precipitation reaching the soil as it condenses during the night. Thus, in the Namib, fog is responsible for depositing between 30 and 40 mm (1.2 and 1.6 inches) of water per year, as contrasted with the contribution owing to rains, between 10 and 15 mm (0.4 and 0.6 in). Fog occurs on about two hundred days out of the year, invading the desert in the early hours of the morning, disappearing with the emergence of the sun, and then reappearing in the evening.

Deserts are also famous for their **elevated maximum temperatures.** In the inner areas of deserts, temperatures of 50°C (122°F) are easily reached or even exceeded, especially at the end of the summer period. The clear skies, however, mitigate the average values, because the soil and air rapidly lose their heat at night because of the absence of clouds or humidity, cooling with excursions of over 20°C (68°F).

Deserts cover about one-third of all the earth's surface, and the various categories of deserts are evaluated on the basis of the intensity of the local precipitation. Four percent of the dry land on the planet falls into the category of extremely arid desert, 15% into that of arid desert, and 14.6% into that of semiarid desert.

The Hydric Deficit

The desert is a habitat characterized primarily by its **scarce rainfall.** Some deserts receive less than 50 mm (2 in) of rain per year, while about 800 mm (31 in) fall per year in Rome. It is not at all uncommon for there to be entire years with absolutely no rainfall. Port Etienne, in Mauritania (coastal Sahara), has averages around 35 mm (1.4 in) annually; Callao, in Peru, 30 mm (1.2 in); Swakopmund, in Namibia, 15 mm (0.6 in); in Egypt, many stations measure only 0.5 mm (0.02 in). Another important characteristic, encountered previously in the semiarid environments of the savannas, but even more accentuated in deserts, is the annual variability of the rains, which can be highly marked. In Europe, the value of precipitation varies annually by no more than about 20%, while in the Sahara, this variation can reach 80% or even 150%. This results from the possibility of occasional but violent downpours, during which more rain falls in one storm than in a number of succeeding years combined. In many deserts, the dried beds of great rivers are readily visible, because floods easily occur as a consequence of these torrential rains, whose periodicity can vary between a few years and ten or fifteen years, or even more.

About 50% of the water that falls on these occasions runs away rather than penetrating. These sudden and powerful flows of water are capable of transporting enormous quantities of sand, over 100 t of sediment per hectare (45 tons per acre), which has the effect of newly cleaning the river bottom of any dunes that have begun to invade the river course.

Origins of the Desert. A desert originates from a repeated dearth of precipitation. An important contribution to an explanation of how deserts are formed comes from paleontology and paleogeography. During the glaciations that occurred during the Pleistocene epoch (1 million years ago), the world was much different than now (see chapter 1, "Tropical Geography and Biogeography"). In the areas that are deserts today, rainy or pluvial periods, which coincide with glaciations, have alternated with arid or interpluvial periods, which coincide with the warmer, or interglacial, climatic periods. A good demonstration of this can be obtained by examining the levels of water for certain still existing lakes. Lake Chad, for example, at the edge of the Sahara, was once at least 120 m (400 ft) deeper and covered a much greater expanse than now. Many internal basins that today are salty were once brimful of fresh waters and enormously broader in expanse, during the pluvial periods. In much remoter epochs, the environmental situations were different still. It is the most recent climate, however, that has most influenced the current distribution of deserts, which are localized where there are descending air currents, producing high pressures.

Many deserts are formed as a consequence of local factors, such as mountainous barriers that block the moist air currents, so that the leeward versants exhibit extremely low rainfalls. This is the mechanism in the case of the Andes and the semidesert of Patagonia that it blocks. Furthermore, cold oceanic currents often originate cool and constant winds that bring

41. The great, red sandy dunes of Sossusvlei, in the Namib Desert.

little humidity or, at best, fogs. This is the case for the Atacama, the coastal desert of Peru and northern Chile, which is affected by the cold Hudson current, and the Namib Desert, which is affected by the Benguela current. Both of these currents are Antarctic in origin.

Arid and Sandy Soils. The desert soils are called *aridosols*. They are characterized by the fact that they are leached very little, because of the reduced precipitation, and enriched very little by organic material, because of the scarce vegetation. They are mineral soils, not very mature, and have a total absence of ground litter or humus. They have an incoherent superficial stratum that is often crumbly and sandy. Another characteristic of desert soils is that they tend to have high levels of salinity, which is caused by the rapid evaporation of water and the consequent concentration of salts, especially sodium and magnesium chlorides, sodium and calcium carbonates, magnesium and calcium sulfates, and sodium nitrate (especially in the Atacama Desert). The low rainfall produces the effect that the salts become concentrated in basins, wells, or depressions, rather than being leached out, as happens in moist climates.

Among the sands and pebbles, strange and compact formations sometimes break unexpectedly through the surface. These are called **crusts,** which are frequently composed of calcium carbonate (in which case they

---

The Ancient Sahara

The history of the Sahara began about 600 million years ago, when the foundations of granite and schist first started to be eroded. The seas invaded these regions several times, depositing their sediments, and the climate varied many times, alternating between luxuriant forests and steppes, between marshes and savannas. The dinosaur fossils, the rock paintings depicting the hunting of ungulates and the grazing of domestic herbivores, and the great underground petroliferous deposits are unequivocal indicators of this past history.

For the last 60 million years or so, the Sahara has been dry land, definitively emerged, with no further marine ingressions. During this period, the colonization of animal and plant life began, developing—while keeping pace with the climatic changes—into the current ecology of the largest desert in the world. The valleys, hills, and depressions and the bare, still riverbeds that appear today are the results of these ages of erosion and morphological modifications. They are also indicators—within the landscape of the most immense sand and rock reservoir in the world—of the ancient presence of lakes, rivers, slopes, and wooded plains.

In the Paleolithic period, the Sahara was still dominated by savannas (as demonstrated by the numerous rock paintings depicting the typical fauna of these habitats), the stage preceding the actual process of desertification.

Deserts of the World

If we wanted to design a map of the deserts of the world, it would be possible to subdivide them, with a good degree of precision, into two large categories based on their degree of dryness. The extremely arid deserts suffer a total absence of precipitation for periods of more than twelve months. The climatic stability is extremely low, with annual or biennial variations in rainfall of more than 30%. These are the most typical climatological characteristics of the true deserts, such as the Sahara and part of the Arabian Desert, the Mojave Desert of North America, the Namib and parts of the Kalahari, the Atacama of South America, the Gobi in Asia, and part of the desert of Australia.

Arid or semiarid deserts, by contrast, have relatively higher total average precipitation, less prolonged periods of dryness, and less than 30% variability in the tenor of precipitation. Examples of these are parts of the Kalahari and the Karoo deserts of southern Africa, the Saudi Arabian and Middle Eastern deserts, the Iranian Touran, the deserts of India, Tibet, and Mongolia in Asia, the Chihuahua Desert of Mexico, the desert of Patagonia in South America, and a large part of the Australian desert.

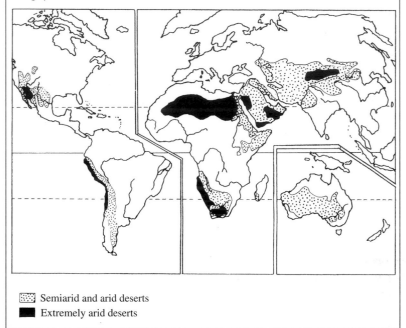

:::: Semiarid and arid deserts
■ Extremely arid deserts

are called **calcrates**), reaching several meters (or yards) in depth and appearing where the precipitation averages from 200 mm to 500 mm (8 to 20 in) annually. Crusts of silica **(silcrates)** are often organized into opal and quartz, and these appear frequently in southern Africa and Australia. In more arid areas, with only 50 to 200 mm (2 to 8 in) of precipitation annually, crusts of calcium sulfate form **(gypcrates),** while in the Atacama, with even lower levels of rainfall, sodium nitrate formations appear. The composition of the various crusts is evidently linked to the solubility of the compounds that are selected in relation to the abundance of rains, which are accordingly more or less capable of dissolving them and concentrating them.

Sun, Heat, and Wind

The high temperatures and solar energy are the principal forces of the desert capable of producing chemical or physical modifications. Frequently, for example, desert rocks are dark because they are covered with **desert varnish,** a thin patina of magnesium and ferrous oxides.

Deserts can experience some notable daily thermal excursions, which can even succeed in splitting rocks apart, for example, when the highest temperatures reached during insolation (about 80°C, or 176°F) can drop by more than 60°C (108°F) during the course of the night. Recent research has indicated how the penetration of humidity into rocks favors their breaking and crumbling under the action of the sun, as it augments the volume of the water through heating. Furthermore, salinity, combined, again, with humidity, creates erosion from the inside out. With heat and evaporation, the mineral salts tend to crystallize and increase in volume, as they do also by means of **hydration,** the insertion of water molecules into their crystalline structure.

As a consequence of this process, the rock undergoes **exfoliation,** a flaking process giving rise to the many pointed, rocky laminae that seem to have been driven mysteriously into the soil, where the mother rock resided before the shattering. The greater impact of the combined erosive effects of temperature, water, and salts is also evidenced by the accelerated deterioration of ancient monuments located in humid, salty desert areas. The desert landscape—because it is so stark and so visible, so utterly

42. Gemsbok, a desert antelope.

43. Irregular dunes of the Skeleton Coast.

barren of any of the vegetation that elsewhere covers plains and slopes—is dramatic in appearance, and the distances seem greater, the horizons, infinite. We find lone **inselbergs,** great rocky hills—sometimes rounded, sometimes jagged and steep—emerging as though by enchantment from the expanses of a sandy or rocky plain. This is a landscape formed largely during the past rainy climates of the glacial epochs and modeled today by the successive mechanisms of erosion that are typical of the desert, with effects that differ according to the quality of the rocks. Hills of impermeable rocks, polished by water and wind alone, appear with pointed peaks and vertical walls. The rocks that are most permeable to the water are also the same ones that are most subject to the crumbling caused by the sun, and around hills of this sort of rock, much coarse detritus deposits, in the form of an escarpment. Characteristic conical accumulations of detritus can also be encountered at the mouth of a river that emerges from a canyon, as it thrusts itself out onto a level tract.

The winds are important in the modeling of the landscape through their slow erosion of rocks. Their impact is notable because the absence of vegetation leaves the soil, dunes, and mountains completely exposed. The erosive action is especially linked to the presence of sand, which functions as an abrasive agent. Dunes are given their shape and orientation by the nature of the winds, and large or small depressions are excavated, but the most spectacular results of this eolian action appear in the rocks that are eroded and polished, sometimes into dramatic and fantastical forms.

The soil is often paved with stones of various dimensions that appear to have been placed carefully into the sand. These are the so-called stone pavements that originate, primarily, from the mechanical action of the winds, as they displace the lighter material, leaving the heavier intact.

The desert **sandstorms** that are so often dramatized in adventure literature can, in certain places, occupy as many as thirty days out of the year and involve a radius of 200 km (120 mi) or more, transporting enormous quantities of sand and dust for great distances. The sands of the Sahara have been found to come back down in rains as far away as England and Finland. A volume of air of 9 m^3 can contain up to 30 g of sand and dust (or nearly an ounce of sand in 9 yd^3 of air). A one hundred-meter-high storm stretching 500 km by 600 km (or a hundred-yard high storm stretching 300 miles by 400 miles) can thus transport up to 100 million tons of sand!

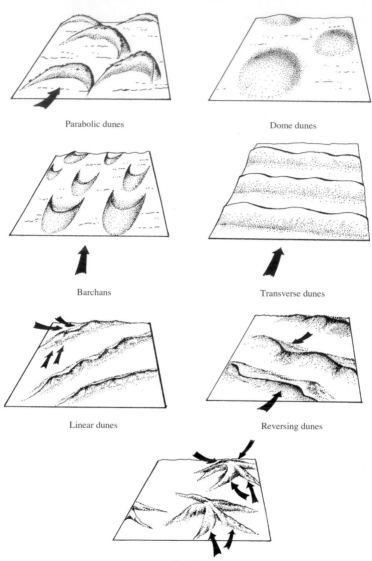

Parabolic dunes

Dome dunes

Barchans

Transverse dunes

Linear dunes

Reversing dunes

Star dunes

There are many types of sand dunes, shaped principally by the direction and force of the prevailing winds (indicated by arrows).

Seas and Waves of Sand

Only one-third of the world's deserts possess soils with eolian sands, and in America, only 1% have sandy dunes. The most spectacular and boundless *ergs* (literally "seas of sand") are in the Sahara and in Arabia. The grains originate, for the most part, from alluvial or lacustrine (lake) deposits of past eras, from marine beaches, and from the erosion of rocks such as sandstone and granite. Sand particles begin to rise with winds greater than 20 km/h (13 mph). The smallest grains (those < 0.15 mm in diameter, about 6 thousandths of an inch) rise from the soil, and they enter into suspension as dust, rising to great heights. The intermediary granules (0.15 to .25 mm, or 6 to 10 thousandths of an inch) are lifted across brief tracts and then fall again, shaking and lifting other granules. The largest particles (those > 0.25 mm, or larger than ten thousandths of an inch) roll along the ground.

Dunes form because granules begin to rest on other sand, where the friction is higher or where an obstacle—a bush, a rock, or the carcass of a large animal—facilitates the accumulation of sand, behind the barrier initially, as the eddies of wind interrupt the transportation of the grains. The form of the dunes is influenced by various factors, the most important of which are the direction and constancy of the wind.

African Deserts and Their Dunes

Since the different varieties of dunes are formed in relation to the wind patterns, the morphology, and the climate, it is logical that certain deserts, more than others, are characterized by different typologies of sandy dunes.

	Namib	Kalahari	South Sahara	North Sahara	East Sahara	West Sahara
Linear Dunes	***	****	**	**	**	***
Barchans	**	*	**	***	**	**
Star Dunes	**	—	—	*	**	—
Circular Dunes	*	—	—	—	*	—

Modified from A. Goudie, 1989.

Legend, indicating relative abundance of certain principal types of dunes.

—	none
*	up to 10%
**	10–30%
***	30–60%
****	over 60%

44. Detail of a kokerboom, a tree typical of the Namib Desert.

The most typical dunes, the **barchans,** are those that originate with constant winds and are oriented perpendicularly to the direction of the wind. These are moving, crescent-shaped sand dunes. **Dome dunes** often originate from particularly violent gusts of wind, which level the peaks and cause the walls to collapse. *Seifs,* or **linear dunes,** by contrast, are parallel to the direction of the air flow, and appear in constant wind patterns, sometimes stretching many kilometers in length. With variable winds, **star dunes** often form, where each arm is oriented towards one of the directions of the prevailing winds and remains partially sheltered by the other points. The same occurs in the case of contrary winds, which originate **reversing dunes.**

Rising and Falling Dunes

Dunes are dynamic heaps of sand, subject to changes that can either be sudden or constant. In many deserts, great sand dunes advance with the winds, sometimes alarmingly fast, sometimes invisibly slow, swallowing up the landscapes that precede them.

In certain cases, the presence of a ford or a riverbed can be sufficient to interrupt this advance. Each periodic flood—every five, ten, maybe twenty years—sweeps away the invading sand and impedes it from exceeding the shores of the river.

This is what happens in Namibia, where the city of Swakopmund, at the mouth of the Swakop river, has been saved again and again for decades, thanks to the rare but periodic and powerful floods of the river, which stem the movements of the dunes from south to north. Beyond the river, every attempt to construct a railway has failed because of the continuous and unstoppable movements of the immense quantities of sand.

When a highland plateau or a chain of rocky hills emerges before these mobile masses, the sand gives rise to ascending (**climbing**) dunes on the windward versant and descending (**falling**) dunes to the leeward. In front of a high rocky wall, at some distance that varies based on the force of the winds and the dimensions of the obstacle, mounds of sand will form parallel to the barrier, where the sand is transported by the reflected wind. These dunes take the name of **echo dunes.**

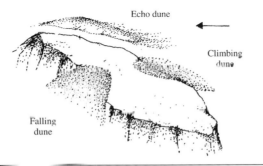

Echo dune

Climbing dune

Falling dune

In nearly all the dunes there is a windward slope, which is compact, rounded, and typically undulating in appearance, and a leeward slope, which is steep and yielding and where the sand accumulates after the wind moves it beyond the crest to fall in this sheltered space.

The Difficult Contest for Those Living in the Desert

In such an austere and inhospitable environment, each inhabitant must be highly specialized in order to survive. In spite of the common notion that a desert is deserted of life, there are actually many living protagonists. The principal limiting factor for successful animal and plant species is, obviously, the dearth of water, and some of the most significant adaptations have evolved in solution to this basic problem.

In the desert, many of the plants are **annuals,** or even **ephemerals.** These arise only after the rare rains and rapidly conclude their cycle before the new drought begins. They have no need of any particular specialization, other than opportunism and rapid growth.

The perennial plants, in contrast, must be much more tempered. Normally they are **xerophytes,** meaning that they have coriaceous leaves, covered with waxy films and closed stomata, in order to reduce the transpiration and evaporation of internal liquids. Many plants have reduced leaf surfaces, or they have transmuted them into thorns, uniting the functionality of resistance to the sun's heat and that of defense against herbivores. Some species curl their leaves during the dry periods, just as mosses and lichens do. All you need do is wet them with a bit of water from your canteen in order to be able to see them extend and swell up again—this happens in just a few seconds. Other plants have fleshy tissues where they are able to concentrate and conserve great quantities of reserve water. This is the case for all the so-called **succulents,** of which the most typical representatives are the American cacti (Cactaceae) and the Afro-Asian euphorbia (Euphorbiaceae), the two being ecologically homologous. In these species, which often are summarily confused with one another—the analogies are the result of evolutionary convergence: the two species have adapted to similar habitats on different continents—the leaves are nearly all transformed into thorns, and the photosynthetic function has been transferred into the tissue of the stem, which is, in fact, green.

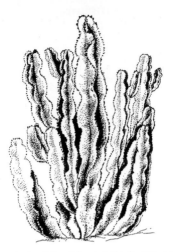

Euphorbias are typical succulents of the Afro-Asiatic deserts, ecologically homologous to the American cactus.

Still other plants grow only in the proximity of sources or basins of water dispersed in the desert (in oases), or around riverbeds where underground water flows (these could be considered as linear oases). These plants, which are **phreatophytes,** have extremely long roots, which reach down to the moisture coming from the permanent water table. This is the case for the well-known date palm *(Phoenix dactylifera)* of the oases in the Sahara and the Middle East. These are species that have deep roots for successfully seeking out the subterranean moisture, but when the stratum is too distant, there are other species that live by spreading their roots out along the surface, in order to enjoy the moisture that condenses during the night, but which is insufficient to penetrate deeply into the soil.

Normally perennial desert plants have a very slow development, because of the unfavorable environmental conditions, and a very long life, which obviates difficulties involved with regeneration. The most exaggerated example of this is the *Welwitschia mirabilis*, a primitive plant related to the conifers and endemic to the Namib Desert, which grows at an extremely slow pace. It bears two leaves only, which extrude from a flattened

Saurians

Whiptail
Cnemidophorous sp.
Ecuador
Teiidae—America

Flat lizard
Platysaurus spp.
Africa
Cordylidae—Africa

Day gecko
Phelsuma laticauda
Islands of the Indian Ocean
Gekkonidae—pantropical and subtropical

African agama
Agama agama
Africa
Agamidae—Africa (excepting Madagascar), Asia, Australia

Skink
Mabuya sp.
Malaysia
Scincidae—worldwide, especially Africa, Asia, Austral[...]

Common iguana
Iguana iguana
Iguanidae—North, Central, and South America,
Madagascar, Galapagos Islands, Fiji, and Tonga

Nile monitor
Varanus niloticus
Africa
Varanidae—Africa, Asia, Australia

Common chameleon
Chameleo chamaleo, southern Europe, Africa
Chamaeleontidae—Africa, Asia, southern Europe

Snakes

Boa constrictor
(*Boa constrictor*)
Central and South America

Egyptian cobra
(*Naja haje*)
Africa

Green tree python
(*Chondropython viridis*)
Asia, Australia

Black mamba
(*Dendroaspis polylepis*)
Africa

Bamboo viper
(*Trimeresurus albolabris*)
India, Indochina

False coral
(*Lampropeltis triangulum*)
Central and South America

Sea serpent
(*Laticauda semifasciata*)
Philippines, Indonesia

Gabon viper
(*Bitis gabonica*)
Africa

Anaconda
(*Eunectes murinus*)
South America

stalk that increases slowly in width, and these measure just a few centimeters at ten years of life. We know of one example that has been dated at 1,500 years of age, the oldest currently known, which would have first sprouted at the time Attila and his Huns crossed the Alps.

Animals of the Desert. Adaptations that are equally remarkable are encountered among the animals, which, in order to survive, have no fewer problems to resolve than do the plants.

Male cones

Female cones

Welwitschia mirabilis (millenary specimen)

Sand and Obstacles

The presence of obstacles to the wind in sandy deserts produces particular and characteristic mounds of sand. If the obstacle is solid, such as a rock, for example, and in a position to oppose a portion of the wind flow, an area immediately behind the obstacle will experience various whirling eddies, which will vary in size in accordance with the size of the obstacle. In this area, which is relatively protected from the wind and where wind forces converge from around the two sides of the obstacle, sand accumulates (a).

The larger and more impenetrable the obstacle is for the wind, the broader and more extended the heap of sand will be (b).

When the obstacle is an enormous rocky mass or an isolated hill, with a broad base at one end and a vertex that is somewhat narrowed at the other end, it is possible for mounds of sand to form before the windward wall, in a typically arched conformation (c). The concave of this arch is not caused because the sand grazes the rock, but rather because the reflecting wind causes a depression just at the point of contact. This is the same mechanism by which echo dunes are formed.

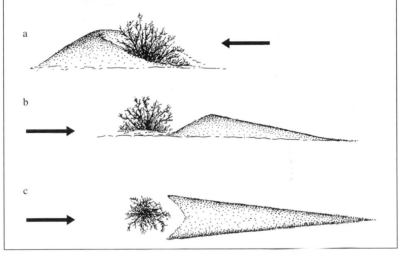

a

b

c

Heat and lack of water are again the principal factors limiting the possibilities of life, the factors that must be addressed by the choices and strategies of each individual organism.

To these factors is often also added the scarcity of food, which is partially resolved by the low density of animals in the desert. Similarly to what happens during the winters of the temperate latitudes, when many species hibernate, desert animals reduce their metabolism during the summer by means of estivation, when they become less active, often in the shelter of rocks or underground. The same can occur in the case of a marked or prolonged drought. This seasonal behavior recalls what also happens on the scale of a single day: activities are stopped during the hottest hours, and everyone seeks shelter in the shade. Large-dimensioned species, such as the ungulate or carnivore mammals, which are endowed with a relative facility of movement, as flying insects and birds are also, often undertake **nomadic movements** or actual **migrations,** to find more hospitable areas during periods that are particularly unfavorable because of high temperatures or drought.

There are many morphological and physiological adaptations to the torrid climate of the desert. According to **Allen's Law,** animals in hot desert regions have smaller bodily dimensions than their homologous species living in colder areas, with the purpose of more easily dispersing the heat. The opposite is true for the appendages, which are more developed and sometimes moist in animals living in hot areas, in order to cool off more easily. This is the case for the enormous ears of the jack rabbit *(Lepus alleni),* the hare of the Sonora Desert in America.

Many desert animals are capable of tolerating long periods without drinking. They aid themselves in this regard by eliminating a urine that is highly concentrated, thus reducing their loss of water, or, in some cases, they eliminate just the crystallized uric acid, as happens with many birds and reptiles. The feces, as well, are extremely dry. Some American desert iguanas use a salt gland positioned near the eye socket to eliminate salt through excretion. The liquid of the excretion falls into a small channel of the nasal duct before flowing out, which allows much of the water contained in it to evaporate and be reabsorbed as vapor during inhalation. Some desert mice, such as the jerboas (family Dipodidae), alternatively, conserve the water that would be lost in respiration by making it pass through a series of intricate ducts that open into the nasal sinuses, where the air loses moisture as it cools.

Together with the limpid landscapes and the grand horizons, the greatest marvel that the desert holds for those who visit it is, doubtlessly, the encounter with life in such an inhospitable environment. Plants and animals of the desert do not seem to be noticeably concerned by the possibility of hostilities lurking in the surroundings, and they demonstrate that they have mastered the art of overcoming difficulties. Admiring an oryx with its long, straight horns as it crosses slowly over the sand dunes, or discovering a young *Welwitschia* that "just" germinated a few years ago, out in the arid middle of a sun-parched expanse of sand and pebbles, is an experience that induces us once again to reflect upon the vital resources of our planet, on the unimaginable diversity of forms and adaptations, and on how strong they are, but also how fragile, these obstinate living beings of the deserts.

45. Ecotourism is not always . . . "eco"!

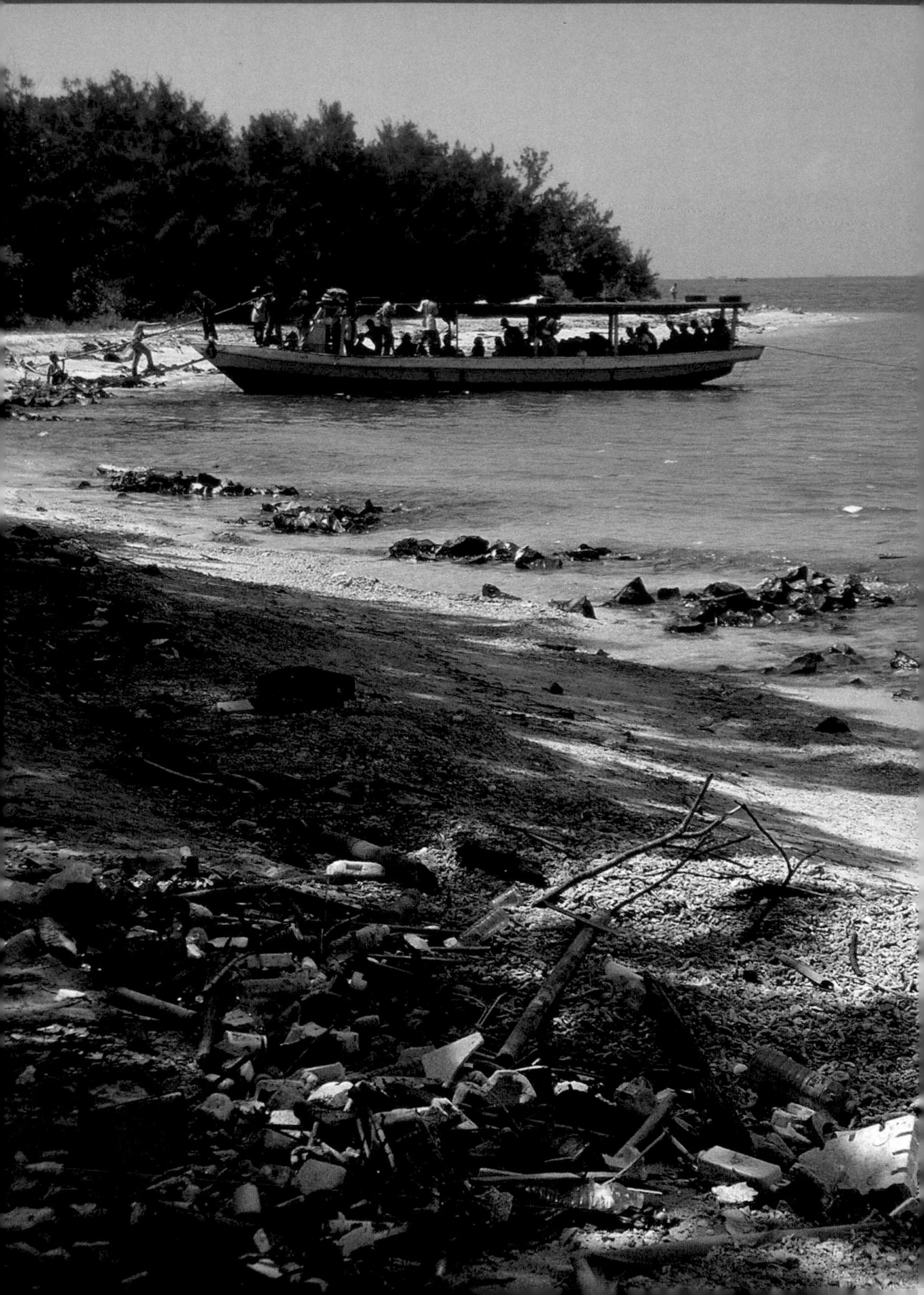

Chapter 11

The Tropics in Peril

The natural paradise contained between those two imaginary but "significant" lines, the tropics of Cancer and Capricorn, is facing new issues and unprecedented challenges. The rhythms marking those natural laws that were responsible for producing—over the millions of years—such a wealth of living forms, such a complex ecology, are today being threatened by unexpected, fast-developing, deep disturbances. Along with our planet's biodiversity, man also has evolved, and in the last few hundred years, he has developed a cultural and technological growth that today enables him to manipulate profoundly the very world that has been his progenitor.

Among the forms of impact that man has on what is today defined as the "natural world," the most disastrous for the Tropics are those that involve the **destruction of habitats** and the **extinction of species.**

The Tropics are obviously not immune from the serious problems that have been distressing the temperate and more industrialized areas of the planet for decades now, such as pollution, the generation of waste material, energy abuse, and use of technologies that are highly dangerous. Indeed, in certain cases, it is the Tropics that are specifically involved, as in the case of the exportation of toxic waste from industrialized countries to developing nations, where they end up being dispersed into the environment owing to the lack of adequate structures for their storage or disposal. Other examples are: the underpriced sale of insecticides that are nowadays illegal in nations of the first world; the development of toxic or harmful industries without adequate purifying or security equipment; and the exploitation of

Some Local and Global Negative Effects of Tropical Deforestation	
Local	*Global*
Loss of fertile soil (cover removal, alteration of chemical properties)	Soil erosion, desertification
Lower agricultural productivity, crop failure	Retarded forest regeneration
Decrease of water retention	Reduction of primary production, diminished recycling of nutrients
Change of local climate patterns	Alteration of water cycles, climate
Loss of trees and renewable timber resources	Impact on global climate patterns
Diminishment of usable wildlife (fish, game, plants that are sources of fruits, vegetables, bases for medicinal drugs, fibers, and more)	Increase of atmospheric CO_2 (from fires)
	Decrease of CO_2 fixing capacity
	Loss of natural habitats
	Loss of biodiversity
	Loss of natural components of support for man's emotional and physical life
Loss of recreational, inspirational landscapes	Impact on evolutionary processes of life on earth

natural resources without proper environmental impact assessments, mitigative techniques, or environmentally friendly approaches.

At any rate, probably the most serious of all the social and ecological problems of the tropical areas is the **increase in the human population.** Even if many tropical nations currently have quite low population densities in comparison with the Northern or Western countries, their rate of increase is extremely high. Among the tropical countries, the Asian nations are those with the most elevated populations, followed by the countries in Central and South America, then those of Africa and Oceania.

Today the world population numbers 6 billion and increases at an accelerating pace, currently about 100 million per year or 250,000 each day. By about the year 2100 it is calculated that the population will have doubled or tripled, depending upon the population-control measures adopted by various governments, and that 90% of this increase will originate in the tropical regions of the third world. In a more positive scenario hypothesizing that governments of the world adopt sufficient programs and policies promoting ecological and sustainable development, the forecast would have the world population reaching 8 billion by the year 2050 and potentially declining to 6 billion by 2100. At present, though, the population of India is forecast to exceed that of China by the year 2050. A particularly emblematic example of this demographic increment and its environmental impact can be seen in Ethiopia, which had 5 million

The Greenhouse Effect, the Albedo Effect, and Others

When solar rays strike the surface of the earth, they are partially reflected, dispersing back out into space. The emission and buildup of waste gases from human activities, such as carbon dioxide (CO_2), reduces the reflection of the rays, and their heat is retained in the atmosphere.

This process is called the "greenhouse effect," because the gas buildup acts just like the glass panes of a greenhouse, which make it more difficult for heat that has penetrated with insolation to disperse to the exterior.

Tropical deforestation plays a fundamental role in the production of carbon dioxide, via the common practice of starting fires to obtain pastureland and fields for cultivation. Whereas 64.3% of the emissions of CO_2 can be imputed to industrial origin (which would be difficult to reduce in the short term), approximately 30% can be imputed to the combustion of tropical forests, and, here, the ability to intervene, possibly even immediately, would seem more likely.

Deforestation, furthermore, reduces the plant cover, producing bare or nearly bare ground. This causes a greater reflection of solar rays and lesser transpiration. A great jungle tree can liberate something like 760 liters (200 gallons) of water, as vapor, into the atmosphere in one day, meaning that one-half hectare of primary jungle can liberate about 75,000 liters (about 20,000 gallons), twenty times more than an equivalent surface area of the sea, and immensely more than a portion of bare ground. Logic tells us that, by deforesting, we reduce the release of water into the atmosphere, with the result of a marked reduction of rains. The consequence of the albedo effect on a world scale, produced or aggravated by the destruction of tropical forests, will involve a diminution of rainfall in the equatorial zone, an increase of rainfall in the tropical band, and a noticeable aridity in the Northern Hemisphere (not in the Southern Hemisphere, which is dominated by oceans) between 40° and 85° latitude. This is part of the global climatic change that is currently predicted.

Deforestation also has the serious effect of a reduction of the production of oxygen, essential for life on the planet. A virgin tropical forest produces 28 t of oxygen per hectare (12.5 t per acre) per year, for a world total of 15,300 million tons (16,900 million avoirdupois tons) per year.

inhabitants in 1920 and 46 million in 1987, and where, currently, 97% of the original forests have been destroyed. Another example is Haiti, which had a population of 2 million inhabitants and 60% of its original forests in 1920, but in 1987, the population had already risen to over 6 million, and only 2% of the original forests had been preserved. In 2040, it is forecast that Nigeria will have more inhabitants than there are today on the entire continent of Africa.

Several nations are already constrained to practice programs of **transmigration** in order to alleviate the excessive overcrowding in certain regions. The Indonesian government is transferring tens of thousands of people each year from the island of Java, which is one of the most densely populated areas in the world, into the unpopulated territories of Irian Jaya (on New Guinea), Kalimantan, and Sumatra. The impact of the new settlements on the ecology of these areas, as well as on the indigenous populations, is tremendous; and the living standards of the colonists, blinded by the mirage of a promising future, are miserable.

The Brazilian government, as well, has conducted and is still projecting numerous colonization programs. One such project that has been, disastrously, underway since the sixties, is the POLONOROESTE project (Programma integrado de Desenvolvimento da Regiao Noroeste do Brazil) in the region of Rondonia.

The new 1,500 km (1,000 mi) state highway, BR 364, which united Cuiba in Mato Grosso to Port Velho in Rondonia, gave access for the first time to 24 million hectares (60 million acres) of virgin Amazonian forest. Thirty-five thousand colonists' families were transferred into the area, with the result that about 6 million hectares (15 million acres) of jungle were destroyed in less than seven years, under the blows of the machete and from the fires of these settlers, who were desperate from the distresses and fevers of malaria. Today more than half of Rondonia is considered deforested area, an incomplete statistic that does not even consider the social drama of those colonists who have been decimated by malaria and impoverished by the progressive sterility of the soil, and who, in many cases, have fled back to the cities in a vicious circle of increasing poverty and

---

The "Cocaine Connection"

An increasingly frequent motive for Amazonian deforestation is connected with the production of cocaine. The coca plant (*Erythroxylum coca*) is cultivated illegally and often in remote areas of the virgin jungle, in order to elude the legal authorities. In Colombia, proceeds from the commercial traffic of cocaine exceed by more than double those from the traditional sales of coffee. About 270,000 ha (670,000 acres) of forest in the great Huallaga Valley have already been converted into coca plantations, which, because of the problem of the progressive sterility of the soils, are moved every two to four years into new spaces. For reasons related to the deforestation of areas to be occupied by plantations, landing fields, and laboratories for processing, over 750,000 ha (1.85 million acres) of Amazonian and Andean forest have already been destroyed in the country of Peru alone, and the situation is equally serious in Colombia. Further, incredible quantities of the toxic substances used in the processing of coca to obtain the narcotic cocaine hydrochloride are dumped into the ecosystem, for example, 15 million liters (4 million gallons) of sulfuric acid per year, 6 million liters (1.6 million gallons) of acetone per year, and 6 million liters of toluene per year, in addition to the 50 million liters (13 million gallons) of kerosene burned and 3,200 cubic meters (4,200 cubic yards) of carbon dioxide emitted each year. In 1989, a study revealed that fully 150 Peruvian watercourses have been contaminated quite seriously by these pollutants.

The Most Important Endangered Tropical Areas

There are fragile areas whose conservation is considered an environmental and naturalistic priority on a world level because of their great biological wealth, their numerous examples of endemic or rare and endangered species, and for the broadness and variety of the habitats represented.

The following list, compiled by the field's greatest experts and by international organizations such as UNEP (United Nations Environmental Program), WWF (World Wildlife Fund), IUCN (World Conservation Union), and Birdlife International, includes the areas of the world that merit maximum attention, because they are of great naturalistic importance and have already been subjected to serious destruction. For the most part, these are forest habitats. Only 5% of the tropical forests existing in the world are protected: 6% of those in Asia, 4% of those in Africa, and 2% of those in the Americas.

Tropical America	The coastal forests of Ecuador
	The Atlantic forests of Brazil
	Eastern and southern Brazilian Amazonia
	The mountains of western Amazonia
	The Colombian Chocò
Tropical Africa	The forests of Cameroon
	The mountains of eastern Africa
	Madagascar
	Western equatorial Africa
	The Sudanese savannas
Tropical Asia	Sri Lanka
	Kalimantan (Indonesian Borneo)
	Sarawak (Malaysian Borneo)
	Sulawesi (Indonesia)
	The eastern Himalayas
	Peninsular Malaysia
	The Philippines
	Indochina
	Bangladesh, Bhutan, and eastern Nepal
	Vietnam, coastal Kampuchea, and Thailand
	Southeastern China
Oceania	New Caledonia
	Hawaii

tribulation. The trans–Irian Jaya road, already underway, and its related transmigration program present exactly the same scenario, the same catastrophic results, both for man and for nature.

An elevated population faces many problems, related to the need for alimentary production (and therefore subsistence); communal infrastructures, such as roads and means of communication; an economy that can absorb the demand for work places; sanitary and scholastic structures; etc. All this is scarce in most of the tropical nations, so that they thus face situations that are extremely difficult from a socioeconomic point of view. Malnutrition and famine, with decimation through starvation, are still frequent today in the poorest African countries and in certain areas of the Indian subcontinent, as are the spread of diseases and epidemics.

Because of the climate and the type of soil, many tropical countries cannot develop a flourishing and productive agriculture. Further, because

---

Protected Areas of the Tropics

In the last few decades, the attention of the scientific world and public opinion have been turning ever more toward the conservation of tropical wildlife and their habitats. The results are encouraging, even if insufficient. Hundreds of reserves and natural parks have been instituted for the protection of habitats and species.

Often, however, the management is poorly administered, the means are inadequate, and the personnel, limited. The consequence is that in many tropical parks of the third world, illegal activities continue, such as the cutting of wood, hunting, and poaching. Often the economic revenues that the parks promote through tourism aid neither the park (insignificant funds are reinvested) nor the local populations, who often become hostile about the restraints imposed upon them by regulations.

It seems that the fundamental rules for the proper functioning of a park and the actual achievement of its own aims for the conservation of nature are:

- to have a well-organized system of management, administration, and surveillance;
- to involve the local populations directly, in order that they may receive tangible economic advantages from the existence of the park;
- to provide for a partial, but adequate, reinvestment of the sums obtained from collateral activities (tourism, for example) into the direct management of the park.

	Number of Areas *	Protected Area
Tropical Africa	444	86,090,000 ha (212,600,000) acres
Tropical America	458	76,810,000 ha (189,700,000) acres
Tropical Asia	676	32,280,000 ha (79,700,000) acres
Oceania	52	4,890,000 ha (12,074,000) acres
Australia **	623	35,690,000 ha (88,100,000) acres

*Only those parks or reserves larger than 1000 hectares (2500 acres) are counted.
**Includes portions that are not tropical.
Source: WCMC, 1989.

of the scarcity of means for technological autonomy, they must rely on the intervention of advanced countries to be able to take advantage of their own natural resources, whether from mines or forests, with the consequent reduction of profit for the mother nation. Often there is high pressure for exploitative rather than sustainable use.

Inappropriate Models of Development and Sociopolitical Degradation. The adoption by third world countries of Western models for development and organization and their immature experience in political management makes possible the rampant spread of phenomena that are extremely harmful to the economy of a nation, such as corruption, authoritarianism, and fanaticism, whether political, religious, or ethnic.

Encounters and skirmishes based on deep-seated and historical animosities are very frequent among the various ethnic groups who have been constrained to live together within a nation whose borders have been designated, in many cases, by the European conquerors of the **colonial era** and later institutionalized with the advent of independence. Many of the capitals and large cities that are developed today were founded to satisfy concerns of traffic or defense for the *conquistadores,* rather than for the logical management of a country, so that capital cities, for instance, are often decentralized with respect to the nation's geography.

Bordering populations speak different languages and have absorbed different cultures, only because they were occupied by colonizing nations of different origins. This is the case of anglophone and francophone Africa, or of Spanish and Portuguese South America, or, again, of the Boer South Africa bordering with Portuguese Mozambique and English Zimbabwe. Poverty, dictatorship, wars, massive migrations of refugees, and social inequity are issues that no longer remain disconnected from environmental conservation. It is clear that poverty generates patterns of environmental degradation and ecological crisis generates poverty, in a vicious cycle.

The Well-Being of Man and the Protection of the Environment. The analysis of the problems that concern the people of a nation is essential for understanding the risks facing its wildlife and their habitats. It is generally evident by now how a nation's degree of environmental awareness, its legislative system for the protection of the environment, and the state of conservation of the nation's natural resources are all reflections of the nation's political stability and social and economic well-being. On the other hand, it is also true that in order to achieve these objectives of stability and well-being, many nations have dominated or destroyed large portions of their natural areas and most of the wildlife of their territories. This is the most common situation for the industrialized countries of the Northern and Western Hemispheres, where natural life is better protected and respected today, but where very little of the original wealth and wilderness remains.

Tropical countries today face the necessity of imposing programs for sustainable development that unite progress in well-being for the human population and sustainable use of natural resources, in such a manner that they can be managed and utilized, not destroyed or depleted. As difficult as such programs are to implement, with every day that passes, the Tropics are victims of new aggressions. In many recent cases, the claim of the "wise use" of resources has proved to be just a euphemism, a new cover for implementing forms of exploitation that are far from sustainable.

Impact of the Local Populations. A first level of impact comes directly from the resident populations. The great majority of tropical peoples have a serious impact on the wildlife and natural resources of their own nations, excepting the few cases of native populations still living in a state of total integration with the natural environments (for example, some communities of Amazonian Indios, some indigenous peoples of New Guinea, Australian Aborigines, African bushmen and pygmies, and the Punam of northwestern Borneo). Often it is a case of a low degree of sensitivity to the issues, which, in turn, is linked to lack of education, awareness, and communication. Frequently it is also a problem of subsistence. The natives of Madagascar, for example, are the first who are responsible for the deforestation of their nation, which in the last fifty years has lost 80% of its forests, because wood is the only source of energy available for heating and cooking. In an industrialized country, less than 5% of the energy consumed per capita is consumed for these uses. It has been estimated that 96 million persons have no energy available (firewood) for heating or cooking and can count on only one hot meal per day, on the average, while another billion persons have, at best, a shortage of wood for common uses, consuming about 0.45 cubic meters (0.6 cubic yards) of wood per year, the same amount an inhabitant of the first world consumes in waste paper products alone. It is estimated that by the turn of the millennium, 2,400 million persons of the third world will suffer from an energy shortage of about 960 million cubic meters (1,250 million cubic yards) of firewood

46. Plantations encroaching upon the primary forest.

47. Exploitation roads penetrate the forest.

A large number of the coral formations in tropical seas suffer from problems related to co-habitation with man. In many tropical countries, the practice of fishing with explosives is widespread, even if it is illegal. This type of fishing not only kills in an absolutely nonselective manner a great number of organisms that are not even edible, but, if used in coral reefs, it seriously damages the structure of the reefs.

Another widespread, and even more serious, threat around coastal areas hosting coral formations derives from the use of the calcium carbonate from coral skeletons for producing cement for construction. Many touristically developed areas have built hotels or swimming pools at the expense of the reefs, which are often pulverized using dynamite charges.

The deterioration of portions of the reef produces serious general effects, such as altering the circulation of the waters and, thereby, the impact of the ocean waves upon the shores. A consequence of this is the great reduction or disappearance of many species of marine organisms that are linked to coral reefs, the erosion of the unprotected coast, and the reduction of the supply of sand, owing to the crumbling of the coral and of certain algae.

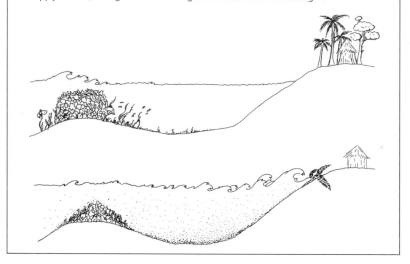

per year, which is equivalent to the energy of about 240 million tons (265 million avoirdupois tons) of petroleum—a problem that can only be resolved with control of demographic growth and an equilibrated management of forest resources. The "sustainability" concept seems to be logical and beneficial, but difficult to implement under the driving force of **modern economy,** which promotes human activities that consume and undermine, rather than conserve, the environmental and natural resources. No monetary value is openly acknowledged for vitally important natural resources or ecological functions whose impairment would provoke vast financial losses, as well as a reduction of the quality of our lives.

The destruction of habitats is, therefore, a direct consequence of this chaotic and sadly unwise socioeconomic organization. Certain naturally available resources are exploited without rationality, as in the case of forests. The **responsibility** lies not only with the local governments who shortsightedly make unlimited use of their countries' resources, but also with the richer nations that support or promote this consumption, in order to satisfy a demand for tropical products by their populations. Many of the countries of Indochina and western Africa have already cut and sold over 90% of their own available wood, destroying vast areas of previously forested land. Other countries located in the tropical forest areas of Central or South America or in the African savannas have destroyed their forests to raise livestock or to establish extensive plantations, which, in many cases, have failed.

High-impact constructions, such as dams, reclamations, or canals, built for increasing the availability of water for agriculture, livestock breeding, or industry, have produced significant climatic and hydrological changes, in addition to profound alterations of the ecosystems. Many of the shortages that have killed or displaced entire indigenous villages in various arid regions of Africa are to be imputed to the altering of courses of rivers by means of large-scale artificial reservoirs and damming. In spite of disastrous failures in the recent past, many more such projects are currently planned.

Loss or Fragmentation of Habitats. The continuity of many forests has been interrupted by roads, settlements, industrial complexes, or artificial basins, and even more by plantations, the raising of livestock, and deforestation. This fragmentation of habitats enormously impoverishes the resident fauna and flora, and alters local climatic conditions, often provoking the extinction of many species. For over half of all endangered species, the cause of their peril is, quite simply, the loss of their natural habitat.

In tropical Asia and Africa, the majority of nations have lost over 50% of their original forests. Of the overall tropical forested area, counting from historical times, 30% has already been destroyed and another 15% is currently being exploited for the extraction of the wood. Each year, at least 7.4 million hectares (or 18.3 million acres, equivalent to more than double

Loss of Closed Tropical Forest Land in the 1980's

Cause	Loss per year	
Commercial timber	45,000km^2 (17,375mi^2)	18%
Wood for fuel	25,000km^2 (9,650mi^2)	10%
Land clearing for cattle	20,000km^2 (7,700mi^2)	8%
Land clearing for agriculture	160,000 km^2 (61,800 mi^2)	64%
Total	250,000 km^2 (96,500 mi^2)	100%

Source: Myers 1984.

Annual Loss of Tropical Rainforests by Region in the 1980's

	Loss per year	
Americas	74,000 km^2 (28,600 mi^2)	0.75%
Africa	41,000 km^2 (15,800 mi^2)	1.10%
Asia	39,000 km^2 (15,000 mi^2)	0.72%
Global	154,000 km^2 (59,500 mi^2)	0.80%

Source: Whitmore 1997.

the surface of the UK) are deforested or penetrated to cut wood. The Atlantic forest of Brazil has been reduced to just 5% of its original million square kilometers (386,000 square miles). The Pacific coast of Central America hosted 550,000 km^2 (212,000 mi^2) of deciduous tropical forest at the time of the arrival of the Europeans. Today less than 2% of these remain intact.

Tropical Forests and Deforestation. One of the most dramatic forms of impact man has on tropical ecology is the destruction of tropical forests. These are the principal motives for such destruction:

- *Substitution by plantations and livestock pasture.* In most cases, this means entirely destroying the whole forest mantle. The most-prized trees are removed first, and then the forest is burnt, to be transformed into pastures and fields. With such killing and slaughter of plants and animals, the loss in biodiversity is incalculable. The conquest of forest land for agriculture and pasture is often undertaken by the simplest and most expeditious of means: fire. A single NASA satellite image shot over Amazonia during the dry season can reveal as many as 2,500 fires in one day. In a single fire during 1988, more than

32,000 km² (12,400 mi²) of Amazonian forest (an expanse as large as Belgium) went up in flames. In just the month of September of 1991, the most disastrous year recorded to date for the Amazonian forest, more than 50,000 fires were counted via air and satellite. One fire in 1989 destroyed 20,000 km² (7,700 mi²) of forest; another in 1990 destroyed 18,000 km² (7,000 mi²). In Borneo, 33,000 km² (12,700 mi²) of forested land, equal in size to the Netherlands, were burnt between 1982 and 1983, and the extensive fires in Sumatra, Borneo, and northern Brazil during 1997 and 1998 have shown that the trend is not changing.

- *Extraction of wood.* There are various methods for extracting wood from a tropical forest, but all represent a serious impact on the ecology, because of the frequent use of scrapers or other enormous mechanical devices. For each large tree that is felled, dozens of smaller and "less valued" trees are unnecessarily uprooted or damaged. A certain level of sustainable harvesting of timber can be achieved, generally either by highly selective logging or through carefully planned routine techniques.

- *Gathering of firewood.* Indigenous populations have always made such use of the forest. The poor peoples of many tropical countries today are numerically advanced, but still lacking in sources of energy for subsistence. The pressure on the forests, therefore, increases enormously, producing results in some limited forest blocks surrounded by dense populations that are sometimes analogous to those of industrial-scale deforestation.

Other causes of tropical deforestation having an extremely serious impact, even if not on as vast a scale as the preceding categories, can be imputed to the construction of roads, the exploitation of mines, or the construction of dams. The "Plan 2010" project in Brazil plans for over 100 large new dams, of which 20 would be in Amazonia. Together these dams would flood a forest area equivalent to Great Britain. For the construction and management of the aerospace platform "Eurospace" in French Guyana, a large dam has been planned that would cause the flooding and deforestation of more than 4,000 km² (1,500 mi²) of virgin forest. In contrast, the plan for the conservation of Brazilian Amazonia remains at a standstill in the face of such an immense economic investment in French Guyana, although it was approved (and publicized) in 1990 by the G7, the seven most industrialized nations of the world. Financial investments for the conservation of the environment are not yet considered to be remunerative, almost as though the oxygen produced in Amazonia had no value for us. An important positive signal, however, comes from the World Bank, the principal financial backer for past operations that have been the most destructive to tropical ecology: the Brazilian dams, the trans-Amazonian roads, the trans-Kalimantan highway, and many others. In a document signed in July of 1991, the Bank committed itself to blocking the financing of any projects involving tropical deforestation, instead

Loss of Habitats for the Wild Fauna of Africa

	Original Habitat	Residual Habitat	Loss
Angola	124,670,000 ha (307,800,000 acres)	76,085,000 ha (187,900,000 acres)	39%
Botswana	58,540,000 ha (144,500,000 acres)	25,758,000 ha (63,600,000 acres)	56%
Burkina Faso	27,380,000 ha (67,600,000 acres)	5,476,000 ha (13,520,000 acres)	80%
Chad	72,080,000 ha (178,000,000 acres)	17,299,000 ha (42,710,000 acres)	76%
DRC	233,590,000 ha (577,000,000 acres)	105,116,000 ha (259,500,000 acres)	55%
Gabon	26,700,000 ha (65,900,000 acres)	17,355,000 ha (42,850,000 acres)	35%
Gambia	1,130,000 ha (2,790,000 acres)	124,000 ha (306,000 acres)	89%
Ivory Cost	31,800,000 ha (78,500,000 acres)	6,678,000 ha (16,490,000 acres)	79%
Kenya	56,950,000 ha (141,000,000 acres)	29,614,000 ha (73,120,000 acres)	48%
Madagascar	59,521,000 ha (147,000,000 acres)	14,880,000 ha (36,740,000 acres)	75%
Namibia	82,320,000 ha (203,000,000 acres)	44,453,000 ha (109,800,000 acres)	46%
Somalia	63,770,000 ha (157,000,000 acres)	37,624,000 ha (92,900,000 acres)	41%
South Africa	123,650,000 ha (305,000,000 acres)	53,170,000 ha (131,300,000 acres)	57%
Sudan	170,300,000 ha (420,500,000 acres)	51,090,000 ha (126,100,000 acres)	70%
Tanzania	88,620,000 ha (219,000,000 acres)	50,513,000 ha (124,700,000 acres)	43%
Zambia	75,260,000 ha (185,800,000 acres)	53,435,000 ha (131,900,000 acres)	29%
TOTAL	2,079,641,000 ha (5,135,000,000 acres)	773,774,000 ha (1,910,600,000 acres)	65%

Source: IUCN/UNEP, 1986.

favoring projects for reforestation, development of secondary forests, and conservation of primary forests. Nevertheless, signed agreements are often ignored, and an environmental impact assessment of "good" can easily prompt the go-ahead for further unsustainable destruction. Despite the much-criticized trans-Amazonian and trans-Kalimantan highways and the transmigration programs executed in the past, an almost identical program

Loss of Habitats for the Wild Fauna of Asia

	Original Habitat	Residual Habitat	Loss
Bangladesh	14,278,000 ha	857,000 ha	94%
	(35,280,000 acres)	(2,118,000 acres)	
China (tropical)	42,307,000 ha	16,500,000 ha	61%
	(104,540,000 acres)	(40,771,000 acres)	
India	301,701,000 ha	61,509,000 ha	80%
	(745,500,000 acres)	(152,000,000 acres)	
Indonesia	144,643,000 ha	74,686,000 ha	49%
	(357,410,000 acres)	(184,500,000 acres)	
Malaysia	35,625,000 ha	21,019,000 ha	41%
	(88,000,000 acres)	(51,940,000 acres)	
Myanmar	77,482,000 ha	22,598,000 ha	71%
	(191,500,000 acres)	(55,840,000 acres)	
Nepal	11,707,000 ha	5,385,000 ha	54%
	(28,900,000 acres)	(13,310,000 acres)	
Pakistan	16,590,000 ha	3,982,000 ha	76%
	(41,000,000 acres)	(9,840,000 acres)	
Philippine Islands	30,821,000 ha	6,472,000 ha	79%
	(76,200,000 acres)	(15,990,000 acres)	
Sri Lanka	6,470,000 ha	1,100,000 ha	83%
	(15,990,000 acres)	(2,718,000 acres)	
Taiwan	3,696,000 ha	1,072,000 ha	71%
	(9,132,000 acres)	(2,649,000 acres)	
Thailand	50,727,000 ha	13,004,000 ha	74%
	(125,300,000 acres)	(32,132,000 acres)	
Vietnam	33,212,000 ha	6,642,000 ha	80%
	(82,065,000 acres)	(16,400,000 acres)	
TOTAL	815,186,000 ha	248,765,000 ha	67%
	(2,014,300,000 acres)	(614,690,000 acres)	

Source: IUCN/UNEP, 1986.

has just been started in Irian Jaya, affecting one of the last extensive blocks of virgin forest, one which is also the stronghold of a diversified indigenous population.

Deforestation of tropical rainforests has accelerated dramatically since the beginning of the century, with the greatest damage concentrated after 1945, in coincidence with the economic boom involving many Northern

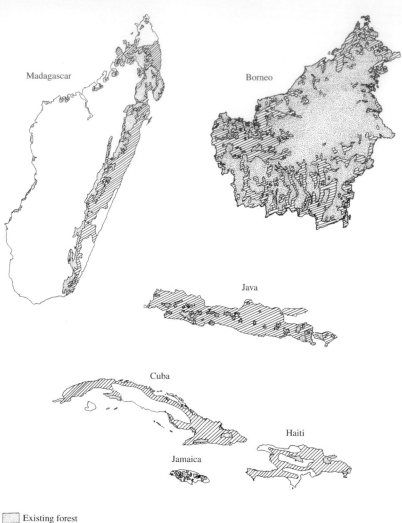

Madagascar

Borneo

Java

Cuba

Haiti

Jamaica

▢ Existing forest

▨ Original forest

Some examples of the serious destruction of tropical forests. The indication of the remaining forest on the islands of Cuba, Haiti, Madagascar, and Java gives an account of the terrible deforestation that has been perpetrated. Borneo still shows broad forested tracts, but deforestation and uncontrolled fires are proceeding at alarming rates.

Nations with the Highest Rates of Deforestation

	Annual Rate of Deforestation		Area Deforested Annually
Tropical Africa			
Ivory Coast	6.5%	Nigeria	297,500 ha (735,000 acres)
Nigeria	5.0%	Ivory Coast	289,770 ha (716,000 acres)
Rwanda	2.7%	DRC	211,500 ha (522,600 acres)
Burundi	2.7%	Madagascar	154,500 ha (381,800 acres)
Benin	2.6%	Cameroon	71,680 ha (177,100 acres)
Guinea-Bissau	2.6%	Liberia	46,000 ha (113,700 acres)
Liberia	2.3%	Angola	43,500 ha (107,500 acres)
Tropical Asia			
Nepal	4.3%	Indonesia	569,475 ha (1,407,000 acres)
Sri Lanka	3.5%	Malaysia	251,940 ha (622,500 acres)
Thailand	2.7%	Thailand	249,345 ha (616,100 acres)
Brunei	1.5%	India	155,523 ha (384,300 acres)
Malaysia	1.2%	Laos	100,920 ha (249,300 acres)
Laos	1.2%	Myanmar	95,823 ha (236,800 acres)
Philippine Islands	1.0%	Philippine Islands	95,100 ha (235,000 acres)
Tropical America			
Paraguay	4.7%	Brazil	1,429,920 ha (3,533,300 acres)
Costa Rica	4.0%	Colombia	835,200 ha (2,063,800 acres)
Haiti	3.8%	Mexico	601,250 ha (1,486,000 acres)
El Salvador	3.2%	Ecuador	342,000 ha (845,000 acres)
Jamaica	3.0%	Peru	278,420 ha (688,000 acres)
Nicaragua	2.7%	Paraguay	191,290 ha (473,000 acres)
Ecuador	2.4%	Venezuela	127,480 ha (315,000 acres)
Honduras	2.4%	Honduras	91,128 ha (225,000 acres)
Guatemala	2.0%	Guatemala	88,840 ha (219,500 acres)

Source: FAO, 1981.

48. Forest burnt by locals to make way for planting.

49. Dams and reservoirs destroy vast areas of forest.

and Western countries. Of the original 24 million square kilometers (9.2 million square miles) in historical times, the closed tropical forests (that is, virgin forests or forests where the trees are dense enough to generate a continuous canopy layer) of the beginning of this century were already reduced to 15 million (5.8 million square miles); today, they number between 8 and 11 million square kilometers (3 and 4 million

Recent Deforestation Rates in the Most Important Tropical Forest Areas

REGION	TOTAL FOREST COVER (in millions)		ANNUAL DEFORESTATION 1981 to 1990	
	1980	1990	(in millions)	(in percent)
AFRICA	568.6 ha (1,405 acres)	527.6 ha (1,304 acres)	4.1 ha (10.1 acres)	0.7%
West Africa	61.5 ha (152 acres)	55.6 ha (137 acres)	0.6 ha (1.5 acres)	1.0%
Central Africa	215.5 ha (532 acres)	204.1 ha (504 acres)	1.1 ha (2.7 acres)	0.5%
Southern Africa (tropical)	159.3 ha (394 acres)	145.9 ha (360 acres)	1.3 ha (3.2 acres)	0.9%
Insular Africa	17.1 ha (42.3 acres)	15.8 ha (39 acres)	0.1 ha (0.2 acres)	0.8%
ASIA and the PACIFIC	349.6 ha (863.8 acres)	310.6 ha (767.5 acres)	3.9 ha (9.6 acres)	1.2%
Southern Asia	69.4 ha (171.5 acres)	63.9 ha (157.9 acres)	0.6 ha (1.5 acres)	0.8%
Southeast Asia (continental)	88.4 ha (218 acres)	75.2 ha (185.8 acres)	1.3 ha (3.2 acres)	1.6%
Southeast Asia (insular)	154.7 ha (382 acres)	135.4 ha (334.6 acres)	1.9 ha (4.7 acres)	1.3%
Pacific Basin	37.1 ha (91.7 acres)	36.0 ha (89.0 acres)	0.1 ha (0.2 acres)	0.3%
LATIN AMERICA and the CARIBBEAN	992.2 ha (2,452 acres)	918.1 ha (2,269 acres)	7.4 ha (18.2 acres)	0.8%
Central America and Mexico	79.2 ha (196 acres)	68.1 ha (168.3 acres)	1.1 ha (2.7 acres)	1.5%
The Caribbean	48.3 ha (119 acres)	47.1 ha (116.4 acres)	0.1 ha (0.2 acres)	0.3%
South America (tropical)	864.6 ha (2,136 acres)	802.9 ha (1,983 acres)	6.2 ha (15.3 acres)	0.7%
WORLD TOTAL	1,910.4 ha (4,721 acres)	1,756.3 ha (4,340 acres)	15.4 ha (38.0 acres)	0.8%

Source : recent FAO estimates. From E. B. Barbier, in F. B. Goldsmith, *Tropical Rainforest: A Wider Perspective,* 1998.*

*Unfortunately, the available figures regarding closed forest cover and deforestation are still unreliable. Companies are reluctant to give data or have an interest in underestimating their actual impact. Data collection is also difficult on an objective scale, because current satellite imagery cannot distinguish between primary, secondary, or heavily logged forests, for which reason various authors and institutions provide slightly, or even remarkably, different figures for a given process. In this text, we have primarily been using figures provided by the FAO.

Top Ten Countries Hosting the Largest Numbers of Endangered Bird and Mammal Species

Nation	Endangered Mammal Species	% Endangered
Indonesia	128	29%
China	75	19%
India	75	24%
Brazil	71	18%
Mexico	64	14%
Australia	58	23%
Papua New Guinea	57	27%
Philippines	49	32%
Madagascar	46	44%
Peru	46	13%
	Endangered Bird Species	% Endangered
Indonesia	104	7%
Brazil	103	6%
China	90	7%
Philippines	86	15%
India	73	6%
Colombia	64	4%
Peru	64	4%
Ecuador	53	3%
USA	50	7%
Vietnam	47	6%

Source: IUCN Red List of Threatened Animals, 1996.

square miles). According to this rhythm of deforestation, something like 150,000–250,000 km²/year (60,000–100,000 mi²/year), we can estimate that between 2050 and 2100, the closed tropical forests of the planet will have completely disappeared.

The Destruction of Habitats and the Extinction of Species. It is logical to think that one of the fundamental requisites for the life of an animal or plant species is the conservation of its habitat. All species show ecological requirements, and very many have, in fact, adapted to particular environmental conditions, habitats without which it is impossible for them to survive.

Biologists involved with conservation retain that the destruction of tropical forests will be the principal cause for the extinction of thousands of species in the next decades, most of which will be small animals that are linked to particular microhabitats of the forest, although many large and charismatic species will also be at risk. Based on fossil records dating back two thousand years, the estimated rate of bird species extinction is currently around one thousand times higher than it was then, and this extinction is mainly a consequence of habitat loss, trade, and hunting. In general, the biodiversity on Earth is being reduced by a rate which is probably 1,000 to 10,000 times higher than it was in pre-agricultural times, when humans started to alter the natural landscape for agriculture and animal husbandry. Humans have been hunters and gatherers for 99% of their history. It is only the last 1% of human history that has seen the advent of agriculture, the domestication of animals, and the vertiginous increase of technological development, with its resulting impact on the natural environment—figures which should give an idea of the urgency required for conservation measures.

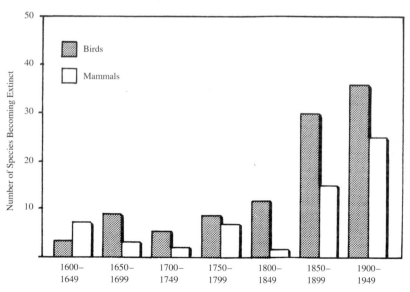

Source: Nilsson, 1983; IUCN, 1988.

Some authors maintain that before the year 2020, from 5 to 15% of all species living today will disappear. Others estimate, based on current deforestation statistics, that each year more than 50,000 species are being extinguished in the tropical forests alone. These statistics often refer to species that are yet unknown to science and use the assumption that only 1.7 million species of living animals and plants are known of the estimated 10 million existing on earth. These data refer only to the most rapid type of extinction, that linked to the destruction of habitats, and do not consider those of the longer term type, which are due to the reduction of habitats or to their fragmentation. The scenario appears almost apocalyptic, and 98% of these species destined for extinction are tropical forest species. In other words, our planet is experiencing one of the most drastic events of mass extinction ever, unprecedented in terms of number of species per unit of time, and it is entirely the result of a single species: man.

Many animal or plant species are so specialized for living in limited and specific geographical areas that they are threatened by complete extinction when their habitat is compromised. For instance, a study conducted on four different forest typologies of Amazonia, in the environs of Manaus, reveals that 83% of the coleopterans lived in one forest, 14% in two, and only 1% was more broadly distributed throughout the four types of forest.

The golden toad *(Bufo periglamus)*, discovered by science in 1964, lives only at the summit of Monte Verde in Costa Rica. A few hours of modern logging would be sufficient to compromise its sole habitat and to extinguish a species that has required millions of years to evolve to its current stage.

The species that are most sensitive to extinction can be characterized as follows:

- predatory species, or those at the highest levels of the food chain of an ecosystem, which often present populations composed of few individuals distributed over wide areas;
- animals of large size with low reproductive rates;
- species with limited distribution, such as insular or isolated mountain endemics, which are easily subject to disturbance or the rapid destruction of their habitat;
- many specialized species that are characterized by a low capacity for dispersion, colonization, or adaptability.

Migratory species, including many birds, are sensitive to the destruction of the environments where they reproduce, or to those where they winter,

The Menace of Introduced Species

Man has introduced animal and plant species into many tropical areas (on islands, especially) that did not exist naturally in the local ecosystems, the effect of which is often disastrous for the species with which they enter into competition or that can become prey for them.

Dogs, cats, rats, mongooses, and pigs are the principal animals that have arrived with man and that are at least partially domesticated on many islands. Many of the local animals have found themselves defenseless against these unexpected predators. Birds incapable of flight or that lay their eggs on the ground and great harmless reptiles, such as tortoises or iguanas, have suffered an elevated predation, and on many islands they have become extinct.

The same holds true for plants. Many imported plants have won in competition against the local plants, destroying the original vegetation and causing the disappearance of many species.

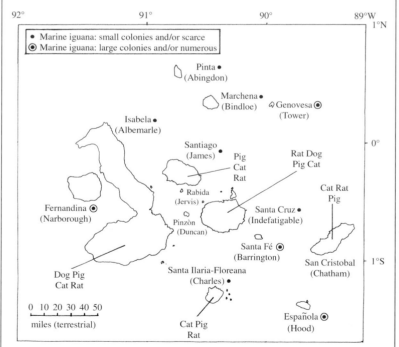

In the Galapagos, the presence of domesticated pigs, stray dogs and cats, and rats, has limited the number of iguanas (see figure) and the marine birds on many islands.

Trade of Tropical Animals. Nearly half the world's endangered vertebrate animal species owe their decline to the direct killing practiced by man. The causes for these persecutions are often of an economic nature, since those who kill the animal sell the body or a part of it.

Many animals having furs, such as the chinchilla, the vicuña, the giant otter, many spotted felines, seals, or other animals from which a prized fur is taken, or those with durable skins, such as crocodiles, monitor lizards, and snakes, are mercilessly hunted for the commercial value they have in the huge and bottomless markets existing in the wealthy countries of the planet.

Nearly all sea turtles are globally or locally endangered, not only because their natural habitats are being destroyed, but also because their eggs

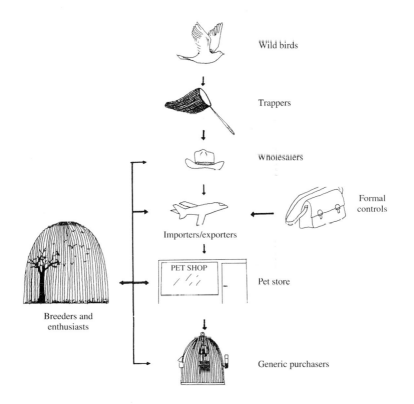

Wild birds

Trappers

Wholesalers

Formal controls

Importers/exporters

PET SHOP

Pet store

Breeders and enthusiasts

Generic purchasers

are being gathered and the adults are being killed, either to serve their meat in restaurants or to fashion souvenirs from their shells.

In Africa and Asia, elephants are killed for their ivory and rhinoceroses for their horns, which are falsely believed in Asian countries to have aphrodisiac properties or are used as handles for the *jamba* daggers that provide symbols of status in certain Arab nations. These are examples of accelerated cases of the destruction of fascinating and ecologically irreplaceable species, for commercial greed or for eccentric beliefs and vanities. Additionally, many animals that are aesthetically attractive, such as certain butterflies and insects, mollusks, and fresh- or saltwater fishes, are endangered because they are indiscriminately gathered for the markets by which they end up in fashionable homes in Europe, Asia, or America. Similar things also happen to young monkeys, especially South American monkeys of small size, which are sold as pets in the West and whose capture often involves killing the mother or both parents. Extravagant fashions also stimulate the trade of spotted felines or large reptiles, such as pythons, boas, and crocodiles. Less obvious, but just as disastrous, is the trade of tropical birds, especially parrots, which are imported by the tens of thousands each year and are victims of an extremely high mortality rate, just during the period of transport, which is often furtive and illegal. It is estimated that for each wild parrot on sale in a pet shop, at least four others died during the process of capture and shipping.

These acquisitions are often made without reflection. If one would only think that before realizing that ivory knick-knack, it was necessary to fell a mountain of flesh and intelligence—the African elephant—a process that often includes destroying its family, killing all of the adult females of the herd, and leaving the calves terrified and defenseless prey to spotted hyenas and lions, then perhaps that useless object of ivory would be seen with rage rather than with aesthetic admiration. The pride of displaying it in the dining room would perhaps be transmuted into shame.

There is an international convention known as CITES, with many countries of the world as members, that regulates the exportation and importation of plants and animals, or parts and products from them. Europe, North America, and the wealthy people of Asian nations are the principal importers of tropical animals, and it is with these that the responsibility lies for the reduction of some of the most fascinating faunistic and botanical categories in the world. It is true that, in some cases, a wise exploitation

50. Flying fox captured for its meat using nets.

51. Wildlife products for sale.

The Hamburger Connection and "Aid" Grants

It is not easy, at first glance, to see a relation between the hamburgers sold in fast-food restaurants and the deforestation of the Tropics or the extinction of thousands of animal and plant species.

And yet, the so-called "hamburger connection" is a classical example of how any ordinary Western or Northern citizen can order, from a distance, the destruction of a piece of the Tropics. North Americans and Europeans are ravenous devourers of hamburgers who, together, import nearly half of all the beef on the world's market. A large part of the "low cost" meat from Panama, Costa Rica, Guatemala, and other countries of Central and South America and Africa crosses American or European borders to end up between buns and covered with ketchup. In those tropical countries, forest land is cleared and burnt in order to raise livestock. In 1980, it was estimated that 72% of the Amazonian deforestation in Brazil took place to obtain pastureland for livestock.

The EU has been subsidizing cattle grazing in Botswana for many years, leading to the degradation of large areas of land and causing profound ecological alterations. Unfortunately, programs that may be considered good financial deals or effective ways of supporting developing economies often, in fact, have a huge environmental cost.

For the USA and the European Union, the monetary costs are extremely low, but the energetic, environmental, and social costs on a planetary scale are immense, and the ecological disaster is irreparable.

In order to produce the meat for one hamburger in a wet tropical area, it is necessary to have a grazing space equivalent to the size of an average living room, about 12 m^2 (or 14 yd^2). In such an area—destroyed to produce about 100 g ($\frac{1}{4}$ lb) of ground meat—there were previously housed an average of more than 500 kilos of biota: plants, flowers, butterflies, birds, monkeys. An immense waste of living energy, whose growth anew would require very, very long stretches of time—it is calculated that a primary tropical forest requires between six hundred and one thousand years to be reconstituted!

and trade of wildlife products can highlight the value of the biodiversity of habitats requiring attention for their conservation, but we know of just a few successful examples out of the many unsustainable cases. Appreciation of the concept of sustainability (that is, the use of a renewable natural resource in such a manner that the resource is not depleted), as well as of the intrinsic value of wildlife and their natural habitats, is our only chance to reverse trends promoted by disruptive and unwisely consumptive approaches to the world's resources.

In these next decades, we are faced with a **life or death struggle** for the **conservation of tropical wildlife and their habitats,** that is, the protection of the ecology of the planet. Destroying or seriously undermining our natural resources of the Tropics equates to depriving the earth of its most important genetic bank, its largest oxygen reserve, its most impressive

In one sense, the consumer can do much by abstaining from or limiting his own consumption of tropical meat, but Western and Northern governments could do even more by inaugurating economic policies and incentives that are more environmentally friendly for tropical ecology and also beneficial in the long term for the recipient country. In more recent years, meat consumption has increased in the tropical countries as well, as a consequence of growing individual financial health.

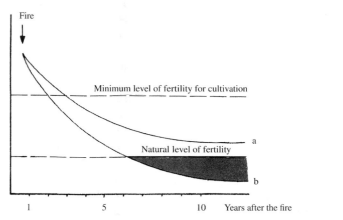

The burning or destruction of a tropical forest in order to establish pastureland or agriculture results in the sterilization of the soil after a few years, as a consequence of the leaching by rainwater of the scarce nutrients naturally available in tropical terrain. [(a) pastureland with rational criteria; (b) pastureland with traditional criteria. The shaded area indicates effects of serious degradation of the soil.]

concentration of natural substances useful to industry, medicine, and human alimentation, and, not least importantly, some of the most beautiful natural life that we could ever enjoy.

It is easy to feel assailed or frustrated by this long list of catastrophic issues and perspectives, but it is important to realize how seriously our human activities threaten the natural environment. There is still much that can be done to reduce the threats, to reverse the trend. Doubtlessly we are already experiencing a dramatic loss of biodiversity and wilderness, and much more will be inevitably lost in the forthcoming decades, but it's up to us to act in such a way as to minimize these effects. Much can be done as individuals, as consumers, in our day-to-day living, when we purchase a product or consume resources, when we talk to other people or vote to elect our government. Much also can be done by joining organizations or

Some Daily Rules for Helping to Protect the Tropics

Many of the human activities that have destructive effects on tropical wildlife and their habitats are related to the behavior of the inhabitants of the wealthy nations of the planet. It is, in fact, from the wealthy nations of Europe, Asia, and North America that a large part of the demand comes for natural products from the Tropics.

A few guidelines or indications for avoiding the consumption or acquisition of materials whose obtainment damages environments or flora and fauna can have an important influence, upstream, in the countries of origin, thus reducing destructive removals, exploitation, and destruction. These guidelines regard personal choices that can aid greatly in curbing the galloping destruction now underway. It is evident that the global solution to the problem of the conservation of tropical wildlife and their habitats, many of which are in nations of the third world, will need to be based on a planned conversion of the individual national economies of the host countries—a conversion that will have to be based on taking advantage of natural resources in a compatible way, rather than on their irremediable erosion.

- Abstain from purchasing materials (such as parquets, game boards, musical instruments, furniture, picture frames, nautical trimmings, coffins, etc.) made from tropical woods. Many shavings and chips, as well, contain tropical wood.
- Abstain from consuming meat of tropical origin. Be especially wary of cafeterias, fast-food establishments, and the like.
- Do not consume frozen fish or crustaceans from the Tropics.
- Do not purchase goods manufactured of leather, skins, tegmina, or other materials of tropical animal origin (ivory, spotted feline furs, snake or lizard skins, objects from the "bones" of tortoises, etc.).
- Do not purchase live animals, such as monkeys, felines, tortoises, parrots, fishes from the sea, etc., nor dead ones, such as butterflies, insects, spiders, dried fish, shells, stuffed crocodiles, snakes, monitor lizards, hunting trophies, etc., unless it is certain that they come from the few existing sustainable, integrated conservation development projects.
- Do not visit exhibits of living reptiles, fish, or insects. The mortality of these animals is often extremely high and they are usually replaced with examples captured in nature.
- Purchase tropical plants only if they come from nurseries.
- Support associations or foundations that are nationally and internationally recognized as assisting in the safeguarding of tropical wildlife and their habitats.

Equally as important as knowing how to make the right choices in the West is adopting a **code of behavior** for use when traveling or living in tropical areas.

- Do not purchase skins, hunting trophies, ivory, or dead, live, or stuffed animals. Few tropical countries have controlled, legal organizations for the sale of these products.
- Don't lose the opportunity to communicate to the locals your interest in tropical nature and its conservation.
- Respect the rules of the parks, and, in particular, do not try to persuade the guides to leave the trails in order to approach wild animals.
- Respect the local cultures. Do not inure them to receiving gifts or tips, unless within the context of friendly exchange in an interpersonal relationship.

NGOs that promote practical conservation action, education and awareness programs, lobbying and advocacy campaigns. The natural world currently faces huge problems, but the effect of individual action can make an increasing difference.

Face the reality, reject frustration, don't give up, and do whatever you can to help. The world's ecological crisis has to be taken as a Great Chance: the great opportunity for one human generation to save our planet, to conserve what makes this world so special and beautiful, so complex and diverse, to build a secure future for humankind and for the plants and animals traveling with us in this fascinating, evolutionary journey of life on earth. Isn't this a worthwhile cause?

Chapter 12

Tropical Dangers and Precautions

W herever you go in the Tropics, you will soon understand how exaggerated are many of the risks and dangers we imagine to be hidden within forests or savanna grasslands. It is often sufficient to get acquainted with the environment in order to dispel many unjustified fears.

On the other hand, neither should one believe it possible to move as freely about in the Tropics as we do in our temperate woods, marshes, or seas. There are risks—even serious ones—and we must learn to become extremely cautious, in every choice, every action. Prudence, not panic; safety, not thoughtlessness.

Caution without Obsession

Many will be surprised at not encountering a single serpent during a visit to a forest or savanna park, or at having to be content with just the traces of the great predators. In the Tropics, there are not unexpected dangers or poisonous or ferocious animals lurking behind every rock, tree, or tuft of grass.

As nearly always, thus, the middle path is best, and moving about in the great tropical wilderness requires us to abstain from either an excessive lightness or an obsessive fear. Pause for a moment to think about your safari guide's outfit in an African park. He wears shorts and maybe even tennis shoes, without socks—not boots or heavy ankle-high shoes for protecting himself from insects or serpents. He does, however, have an extremely attentive regard, and he observes much, both at close vicinity to himself and at a distance. He observes and his pace is sure, but carefully considered. We cannot expect, of course, to acquire the experience of a ranger or a game tracker, but it is important to know that it is mandatory in these environments to arm oneself with caution, self-control, determination, and attention.

Disturbed and Frightened Animals. It is very important not to engage yourself in situations where you have no understanding or with protagonists with which you have no experience.

Never attempt to approach wild animals. Do not snoop about among the bushes, high grasses, winding ravines, or hollow trunks; do not frighten animals in any manner.

In wild game parks, where the fauna are more concentrated and abundant, there are some specific rules that must be respected for your own safety and for that of the animals themselves.

Often it is the animals we underestimate that end up being more dangerous than those that are proud "by reputation." Even though, in Africa, it is the lions and leopards that are the classical large predators (and, effectively, they are very dangerous, even for humans), the majority of incidents occur with buffaloes, hippopotamuses, or elephants, which give the appearance of being distracted or "fat and easy-going"—which is not true: they will make violent use of their own bulk if disturbed.

The most serious incidents with large animals are nearly always provoked by overconfidence and lack of proper caution. Tourists too easily forget that they are dealing with animals that are truly wild and that in this environment, humans may assume the unaccustomed role of prey.

The situation is different for settlers or farmers who work in the fields and who are exposed daily to physical contact with the soil, bushes, and vegetation while concentrating on their work activities. In India, there are about 10,000 snake bite victims each year—a statistic that obviously invites caution, in any case.

Elementary Precautions. Even poisonous and aggressive serpents, such as the Asian cobras, the African mambas, or the American *Bootrops,* will naturally seek to avoid anything that is not prey for them, particularly when it is so much larger than they, as are humans.

A bit of circumspection is sufficient to avoid awkward close-up encounters. One of the first rules, in fact, is to make sure to allow an animal the

Precautions with Africa's Big Ones

When you find yourself walking about in an African savanna, you'll understand how many exaggerations are rooted in our Western imaginations, and how often it is sufficient "to get to know your environment" in order to dispel many unjustified fears. During the daytime, especially, the most common situation encountered by a traveler is silence moved by the wind. Only grasses, bushes, the many spoors and signs on the soil, and, although less noticeable to our human senses, odors and tracks. This is because the great majority of wild animals retreat upon our arrival and tend, of their own choice, to avoid contact with humans. Animals of the wild do pose risks, though, and it is the unexpected or sudden encounters that are the most dangerous. What is important, however, is not to engage in situations or with protagonists of which you have no knowledge or experience.

The primary rules are:
- do not approach wild animals whose reactions you do not know;
- do not snoop about among bushes, twisting gorges, kopjes, or other possible refuges for animals; and
- do not frighten or startle animals.

In wild animal parks, where the concentration of animals is at a peak, there are already rules regarding interactions with animals, and respecting these rules will eliminate many possibilities of incidents. The majority of incidents in Africa occur with hippopotamuses, elephants, buffaloes, and lions. When such animals get involved with tourists, it is usually a consequence of careless or overconfident behavior on the part of the tourists, who forget that they are dealing with powerful animals that are actually wild, endowed with the potential to kill us.

Hippopotamuses are as dangerous in the water as they are on the land. In the water, if they are approached in a boat, they will snort and stage false aggressions, displaying gestures of menace, and usually it all finishes there, unless they are cornered, but it is extremely dangerous to go into the water in the vicinity of a hippopotamus, because they do not tolerate invasions of their aquatic territory. They do appear awkward on land, especially at night, but they are capable of rapid charges and can deal fearsome blows with their enormous tusks.

Buffaloes, in turn, have the "defect" of seeing very poorly and will charge immediately if they suddenly notice you in close proximity.

Elephants, especially solitary males in must (sexual excitation), can easily be irascible. Unintentionally blocking their path in order better to be able to observe or photograph them could be sufficient to provoke a charge from them.

Lions rest in the shade of shrubs and bushes during a large part of the day, nearly immobile and invisible. It is extremely dangerous to venture about on foot without an escort, even just a short way beyond the camp boundaries.

opportunity and enough time to get away from you. There is nothing worse than a cornered animal that is startled, because then attack remains the only alternative. The less you interfere with the vital activities of an animal, the better it is for him and the better for you, because in this manner you will also be able to observe it longer and better, in its natural behavior.

There are some areas that are particularly liable to certain risks. Indian parks and tiger reserves, for example, have elevated concentrations of tigers, and it is absolutely unadvisable to adventure beyond the camp—even for a few hundred meters (or a few hundred yards)—into the undergrowth. The same holds true for African camps that are close to waterholes, where lions and game tend to concentrate, especially during the dry seasons.

There are some elementary precautions to take, such as that of making yourself noticeable, since the great majority of wild animals, even the predators, attempt on their own to avoid humans and react aggressively when taken by surprise. Another simple observation is to make sure that you carefully close the windows and door of your tent or bungalow at night, because that is the time when many spiders and scorpions go hunting about. Even they do not wander about in search of humans, obviously, but when contact with them is accidental, their reaction with a sting may be inevitable.

Dangers with "Small" Beginnings

The greatest worry derives, however, from small animals. A traveler in the Tropics is often submitted to a number of physical stresses, such as any combination of changes in time, season, temperature, humidity, and the like, and these stresses make one more sensitive to contracting sicknesses or infections of various types. Inhaling the dust on the trails can be enough to provoke respiratory problems in subjects who are predisposed, just as the heat may stimulate intestinal or cutaneous disorders.

The **water** can be a vector of numerous risks, which can come from drinking it, if it contains pathogenic microorganisms, such as amoebas, vibrios, or the more familiar salmonella, or even just from getting wet with it, because there exist waterborne larvae that can penetrate into the skin and cause schistosomiasis or other diseases. In fact, it is recommended not to bathe in slow or stagnant fresh waters, which are known to host schistosomiasis, not to drink water that has not been boiled or treated, and not to eat anything—mollusks, crustaceans, fruits or vegetables without peels, or virtually any other aliment—that is raw or partially cooked or that has been washed with uncertain water. Be sure that your ice in hotels or camps has been produced using water that has been sterilized or boiled.

Ciguatera

Ciguatera is the name of the sickness deriving from the ingestion of a toxin produced by tiny dinoflagellate algae living in coral reef habitats. The term comes from Cuba, where intoxication from mollusks, referred to locally as *cigua,* is frequent, but the phenomenon is well-known in all tropical seas. The algae develop within the reefs, and their toxins concentrate in herbivore organisms, reaching dangerous levels farther along in the food chain, particularly in the larger predatory fishes like moray eels, barracudas, snappers, groupers, and the like. Open sea fishes such as tunas or mackerels are usually not affected. The ingestion of ciguatoxic fish can produce symptoms including disorientation, weakness, vomiting, diarrhoa, alteration of breathing rhythm, or even cardiac arrest. People have died from ciguatera, and there is no known cure.

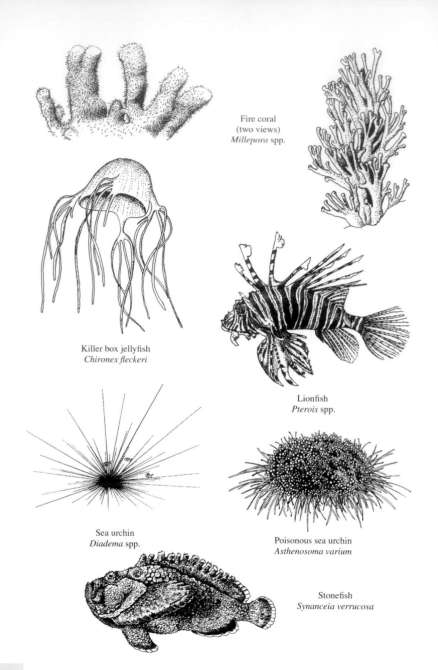

Fire coral
(two views)
Millepora spp.

Killer box jellyfish
Chironex fleckeri

Lionfish
Pterois spp.

Sea urchin
Diadema spp.

Poisonous sea urchin
Asthenosoma varium

Stonefish
Synanceia verrucosa

Sea Snakes

There are about fifty species of sea snakes grouped into the family Hydrophiidae. These can be differentiated from their terrestrial cousins because their head and anterior sections are smaller, their abdominal section is larger, and they have a compressed tail, simulating a flipper, which is used for propulsion. The nostrils can be moved upward and have valvular closings. The Laticaudinae, the most primitive subfamily, have large ventral scales, as do terrestrial snakes, which they use for locomotion. The Hydrophinae, on the other hand, are members of the second, more highly evolved subfamily, and these present better adaptations to marine life.

Sea snakes are distributed in the Indian and Pacific Oceans, with ranges reaching all the way to the coasts of South Africa and Pacific Central America (only the yellow-bellied sea snake, *Pelamis platurus*). The zones richest in species are the coasts of India, Indonesia, northern and northwestern Australia, and some tropical islands of the Pacific. Nearly all the species prefer shallow waters, whether in coral formations or, even better, deltas and estuaries of rivers. The *Pelamis platurus* is the only truly pelagic species, and this is capable of notable movements, while the others appear to be almost entirely stationary.

Other species can reach sizable dimensions, such as the *Laticauda semifasciata,* abundant in the Philippines, which comes close to 2 m (6.5 ft) in length, or those belonging to the genus *Hydrophis,* which have an abdomen three to five times wider than the neck.

Sea snakes are not aggressive towards humans unless disturbed. Their bite, which they utilize for hunting and defense, can be very dangerous and even deadly, depending upon the species.

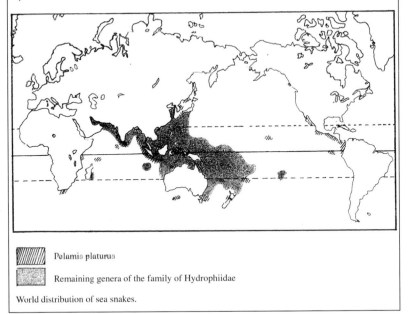

▨ Pelamis platurus

▨ Remaining genera of the family of Hydrophiidae

World distribution of sea snakes.

Glossina palpalis

Insects and other arthropods are responsible for the transmission of highly dangerous and widespread diseases. Many regions of Africa are infested with the bothersome **tsetse fly** (*Glossina* spp.), which is very aggressive and only minimally sensitive to classical insect repellents. In certain areas, this fly is a vector for the microorganism *Tripanosoma*, a protozoan that is transmitted with the bite of the fly, and which provokes the dangerous sleeping sickness. There is also an American tripanosomiasis, transmitted by winged triatominae insects.

Nearly everywhere in the Tropics, there is the risk of **malaria,** from plasmodia that can have varying resistance to the available prophylaxes and known therapies. The WHO (World Health Organization), a point of reference for today's most current and relevant information on such diseases, divides the tropical world into geographic areas of resistance against the various pharmacological preventatives, so it is prudent to be well-informed before planning a trip. Malaria is transmitted with the bite of the **mosquito** of the genus *Anopheles,* while mosquitoes of the genus *Aedes* are the principal vectors of **yellow fever.** In addition to the use of the pharmacological prophylaxes, it is important to try to avoid getting bitten—even if not every *Anopheles* or *Aedes* will prove to be a carrier of malaria or yellow fever—by using repellents, light clothing, and, during the night, antimosquito netting on the tents. The humid, half-shaded tracts of the mangroves are infested with mosquitoes even during the daytime, but other tropical environments generally have mosquitoes only during the evening and night, and not in especially dense concentrations (certainly less than those of the summer months in the temperate and boreal latitudes).

Fleas, mites, and ticks can transmit typhus or typhoid fever, and it is appropriate to wash frequently, using antiparasitic soaps, powders, and lotions, and to inspect one's body, especially after excursions that involve sleeping out in the open.

Dangers in the Sea

The many dangers of the sea deserve special attention. In the multicolored and dazzling universe of the coral reefs, there are many dangerous or un-

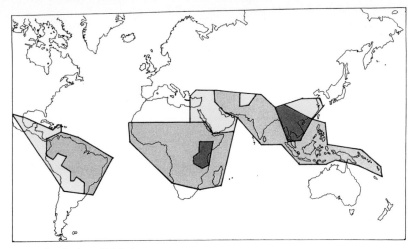

World distribution of Malaria.

□ Risk generally low and seasonal. Nearly zero in many areas and in the cities.
Plasmodia absent or sensitive to chlorochine prophylaxis.
Suggested prophylaxis: chlorochine.

▨ Risk generally not elevated in most parts of Africa, scarce or absent in many urban areas or at significant altitudes.
Plasmodia resistant to chlorochine.
Suggested prophylaxis: chlorochine in combination with proguanile.

▨ Elevated risk in the majority of areas in Africa, less serious in Asia.
Plasmodia resistant to chlorochine.
Suggested prophylaxis: meflochine or doxicycline, or chlorochine in combination with proguanile if the others are unavailable or contraindicated.

Note: Because of continuing discoveries of new areas of resistant strains of plasmodia, it is suggested that these data be considered indicative, and that any traveler refer to competent national or international health authorities for current, precise information.

desirable organisms. Apart from the sharks—which are very rarely encountered in shallow waters or among the corals, and if so, then only those of smaller dimensions—there are many other fish, mollusks, crustaceans, and invertebrates of various classes, orders, or families that ought to be carefully avoided; and in order to be able to do this, you must be able to recognize them.

Dangerous to Eat. Some species are dangerous to eat because they have **ichthyotoxins,** or **ciguatoxins,** from *ciguatera,* which means poisoning resulting from the ingestion of fish or seafood. Sometimes these poisons are not thermolabile, meaning that they are not destroyed with the heat of cooking, and some of their effects can be powerful and dramatic, such as those deriving from the *Arothron stellatus* fish, diffuse in the Red Sea. The ancient Egyptians recognized such poisonous properties, and remains of these fish have been discovered many times within their sarcophagi and tombs.

Two families comprising many toxic species are those of the puffers (Tetraodontidae) and the moray eels (Muraenidae). Certain puffers can cause death from their simple ingestion. Their poison, tetrodotoxin, is concentrated within certain organs, so that an expert cook can actually prepare them and serve them without danger. Notwithstanding this possibility, there are still many cases of intoxication and death from their incorrect preparation.

Some fish families have some edible species and some toxic species, as in the case of the surgeonfishes (Acanthuridae), so that it is necessary to be able to recognize each individual species in order to be certain of avoiding risk. In many species having toxicity, it is the liver that concentrates the majority of the toxin, so that it is a good precaution always to avoid eating that. Even species with excellent flesh, such as groupers and barracudas, can accumulate toxins in their tissues because of eating herbivorous prey that feed on poisonous algae.

Besides ciguatera, another form of intoxication from seafood is referred to as **hypervitaminosis A,** which is easily induced by the ingestion of shark liver, and there are further risks of poisoning from other water-soluble, thermoresistant toxins that can infect the flesh of sharks and rays, deriving from accidental contact with their gonads or viscera, where the toxins are highly concentrated. In order to reduce risk, it is always useful to trust the experience of the locals and never to lower the threshold of attention and caution.

Much more numerous than those that are poisonous, however, are the marine species that are **dangerous to touch.** The great majority of the many thousands of living beings to be found in a coral reef are safe and absolutely inoffensive, so there is no reason that an underwater diver or simple bather need go into the water oppressed by fear or panic. Once again, as with terrestrial environments, it is a question of knowledge and responsibility.

Jellyfish have always been noted for their stinging wounds, even in tropical latitudes, but particularly dangerous—to the point of being deadly—is the *Chironex fleckeri,* called the **killer box jellyfish,** which can be very widespread in the Great Barrier Reef of Australia during certain years. Jellyfish, hydroids, sea anemones, and corals are some of the most classic members of the phylum of Cnidarians (coelenterates). All possess **nematocysts,** meaning stinging cells, in varying quantities, but not all are dangerous for humans. Only the "syringe" type can cause punctures and consequent ill effects, because these are capable of perforating the human skin, and the sting can be more or less dangerous, depending on the strength of the injected poison.

During diving or snorkeling, it is useful to wear a protective garment, such as a rubber suit, to prevent accidental contact with hydroids or corals. The **fire corals** *(Millepora),* with their delicate forms and straw-yellow color, will inflict some very painful wounds.

Among the mollusks, there are certain snails that can be extremely dangerous, such as some species of **cone shells** belonging to the family Conidae. In the Red Sea alone there are about forty species that are dangerous or irritating for humans. Only three species in the world can provoke truly serious consequences, namely, the *Conus geographus,* which is the most dangerous, the *Conus textile,* and the *Conus lividus.* Death by coma and

Some of the Least Charismatic Tropical Wildlife

Poisonous Snakes

Many snakes, such as African tree mambas or ground-dwelling vipers, blend mimetically into their surroundings, while others are brilliantly colored, like the South American coral snakes. Some of these species hide on the ground, among fallen foliage, or in the branches of bushes, or even higher up among the leafy branches of trees. Still others conceal themselves under stones or in large cracks of rocks or tree trunks (particularly the nocturnal varieties).

Flying, Stinging Insects

For the most part, these are mosquitoes and dipterans, such as horseflies and bloodsucking simuliids. Often a repellent and anti-mosquito netting on the widows are sufficient to avoid contact. Light-colored clothing has a certain repellent effect. Tropical bees and wasps are known to be particularly aggressive when someone walks close to their hive or nest.

Bloodsuckers (leeches)

In order to avoid the aquatic variety of bloodsuckers it is sufficient to abstain from immersing oneself in stagnant waters (which are also dangerous because of possible infections from microorganisms). Bloodsuckers of the jungle, though, are much more bothersome, and because of the elevated humidity and rains in the Tropics, they can resist lack of contact with water, among the leaves of the ground litter. Their bite is not known to transmit any disease, as contrasted with that of their aquatic cousins. The small forest species (2–4 cm, or 0.75–1.6 inches) remain quiescent, saving energy until they are awakened from their torpor by the ground vibrations of an approaching animal. This causes them to move, stretching themselves forward, caterpillar-style, in the direction of the vibrations.

Their capacity for orientation is remarkable. In some regions, the forest floor is often infested with bloodsuckers, some of which, such as the Asian *Haemadipsa zeylandica,* have a completely painless bite, in contrast to the *H. picta.* The wounds bleed abundantly because of anticoagulant liquids, but the quantity of blood ingested by the bloodsucker itself is minimal. One of these hirudineans can survive for months on just a few milliliters. Bites from forest bloodsuckers are prevented by wearing special canvas legwear, such as the so-called leech socks that fit over trouser legs, tying snugly under the knee. Since bloodsuckers climb slowly up the legs in search of a segment of unprotected skin, it is necessary periodically to inspect oneself and to remove them. If you detach them quickly and throw them onto the ground, there is no danger of getting bitten during the process.

Certain bloodsuckers fix themselves to the leaves of bushes and small trees, waiting to attach onto animals (or to excursionists) that bump into them. They may also "rain" down upon their prey from above—although this is more rare—being dragged from their leaf or branch by the rains. During an excursion through a forest where bloodsuckers dwell, it is useful to inspect one's clothing well (including the pants pockets) and frequently, especially the shoes. (This will avoid the risk of carrying them into the bedroom—or even into the sleeping bag.)

Insects Parasitic to Humans

Some insects use humans as a host for their larvae. Among these, the species of the genus *Dermatobia* deposit their eggs under the skin, where the larvae develop, breathing atmospheric oxygen from the outside using a siphon that protrudes through the skin. As the larvae develops, little by little the pain from the wound increases, and this is the signal to intervene. Use a cutaneous disinfectant or mask the part with a covering substance that impedes the insect's respiration in order to kill the larva and remove it.

Ants

The tropical forest, like the savanna, is traveled long and wide (and high) by ants. Many sting if disturbed, and the warriors can be a real nuisance if one of their legions ends up invading your tent or sleeping bag. Giant tropical ants, which can exceed 2.5 cm (1 inch) in size (e.g., genera *Dinoponera* and *Paraponera*), inflict very painful bites.

Stinging Caterpillars

Many butterfly caterpillars have stinging hairs capable of inflicting painful pricks with after-effects for several days.

Spiders

The largest tropical spiders are wolf spiders and mygalomorph spiders. Wolf spiders (family Lycosidae) have long legs and a relatively narrow body, while mygalomorphs have thicker, shorter legs, a large abdomen, and a thick fur that covers them entirely. They all can inflict poisonous bites, but an ordinary amount of attention is sufficient to avoid them. It is only if very irritated that they will bite something that is not prey for them. It is possible to have a mygalomorph spider as large as the palm of your hand walk along your arm without running any real risk—you just need to overcome the first impression! Certain of the South American species hold the records for the largest in size; one very large example is the bird-eating mygalomorph *(Eurypelma soemanni),* which can reach over 18 cm (7 inches) from leg to leg. All these species are primarily nocturnal and can wander accidentally into your tent unless it is well closed.

Scorpions

Nocturnal, some specimens in the Tropics are enormous, exceeding 10 cm (4 inches) in length from the head to the stinger. The most toxic species are the smallest in size. After their nocturnal excursions, they may decide to take refuge among your clothes or shoes if these are abandoned outside the tent.

Scolopendras

Whereas the dark and slow millipedes feed primarily upon plant detritus, centipedes or scolopendras are rapid predators armed with large mandibles having chelae. They can bite and leave a deep pain. One Central American species, the *Scolopendra gigantea,* can reach up to 28 cm (11 inches) in length.

respiratory blockage can occur within a few hours. These cones possess a sharpened point, positioned at the top of a retractile, extensible siphon that functions either like a "lance," as it can be maneuvered into any direction, or like a "blowgun," as it is capable of expelling poisoned darts (another incredible example of adaptation!).

Among the echinoderms, the **sea urchins** are dangerous because of their movable spines that drive easily into tissues and end up being difficult to extract, as in the case of the *Diadema,* which has extremely long spines and is widespread throughout all the tropical seas, or the *Asthenosoma varium,* which has spines equipped with poisonous sacs.

Starfishes, as well, must be handled carefully, and often they protect themselves with spines or thorns of various natures. The sea star *Acanthaster planci,* famous for being a voracious devourer of corals, distributed widely in the Indo-Pacific Ocean and the Red Sea, is one of the few that is truly poisonous. Some holothurians, or sea cucumbers, contain toxins known as olothurins, which are dangerous if ingested or provoke strong irritations upon contact with mucous membranes, such as those of the eyes, mouth, or genitals.

Among the marine animals that are dangerous to the touch, there are some species that increase the possibility of an accidental contact with

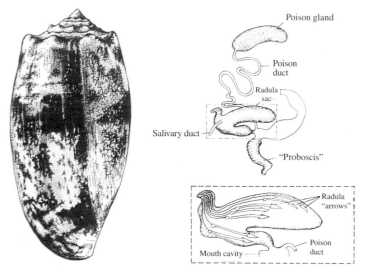

Geographic cone, *Conus geographus*

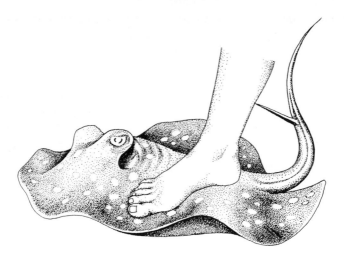

Reef stingray, *Taenyura limna*

them, because of their habit of concealing themselves within the top layer of sand under the water, whether for aggressive or defensive mimicry. Among these are the **rays** (order Rajiformes), one example of which is the beautiful *Taenyura limna*. Its splendid golden coloring with turquoise spots would render it very magnificent, indeed, if it did not have its day-time habit of resting covered by a thin layer of sand. If stepped upon, it strikes rapidly with its caudal sting, which has poisonous glands, causing stabbing pains.

Electric rays of various species have the capacity of launching electric discharges, which can reach up to 200 volts and 2,000 watts in large in-dividuals. The fish make use of these shocks to stun or to kill their prey or to defend themselves. If you approach inadvertently, you may notice their presence only because of the electrical shock that diffuses through out the surrounding water, causing a sudden, pervading chill. The danger is real only for direct or extremely close contact, with animals of larger dimensions. It is better, though, to recognize the phenomenon, to avoid torturing oneself with doubts and questions about the possible causes for such a trauma.

Dangers are not always signaled according to the classically understood messages of human communication. The stonefish *(Synanceia verrucosa),* a large scorpion fish, is dangerous and can even be deadly, but it is often virtually invisible because of its perfect mimicry. Once detected, it encourages anyone to abstain from touching it, because its aspect is repellent and menacing. A contrary example, perhaps, is that of the lionfish of the genus *Pterois,* which hides extremely dangerous stingers among its magnificently colored stripes and among the lovely and sinuous appendages

Saponin

Abundant in tropical plants, these are used by certain Amazonian Indios to "poison" the water, in order to capture fish in wells or bends of rivers.

Cyanogenetic Glycosides

It is well-known that cyanide is a deadly poison. Many plants contain molecules of cyanide combined with organic substances. Once ingested into the organism of an animal, the organic part is destroyed, freeing the cyanide to develop its toxic action. The manioc, for instance, contains these compounds in its roots, for which reason it must be well washed or cooked before being consumed.

Cardiac Glycosides

These are compounds active in relation to the heart and can be fatal even for healthy individuals. They are used for pharmaceutical purposes in appropriate concentrations.

Terpenoids

Abundant in many plants, these are substances having significant repellent, fungicidal, or insecticidal effects.

Toxic Amino Acids

Some plants, among which are many leguminous plants, contain amino acids that are unsuitable to be used in the synthesis of proteins, but rather they interfere with the process at the basis of life, being exchanged for the true, essential amino acids. Canavanine, for example, chemically resembles the essential amino acid argenico, and it produces a toxic effect when it is substituted for that. L-DOPA, by virtue of the same mechanism, can be highly hallucinogenic.

Calcium Oxalate

When calcium oxalate comes into contact with a mucous membrane (mouth, eyes, genitals) it produces a burning effect. Climbing philodendrons and many Araceae (those having the large leaves that normally tempt herbivores) contain calcium oxalate.

Besides chemical substances, which are dangerous in case of prolonged contact or ingestion, many tropical plants offer other perils, no less bothersome or dangerous, against which it is necessary to guard oneself with attention. These are pricks, thorns, or little hooks that can cause stabbing pains and often be difficult to extract or likely to provoke consequent infections. Leaves, branches, and even trunks can be armed with these mechanical defenses.

that embellish all its fins. In this case it is actually the special coloring and contours of the body that provide the warning signal for other animals. Humans, however, are often attracted to these beautiful specimens, and the desire can arise spontaneously in many of us to approach, or even worse, to touch one, thus provoking terrible pain and possibly serious consequences.

Intimidatory Rituals of Sharks

Encountering a shark in the water certainly raises emotions—more or less intensely, based on each person's personal experience. The most frequent shark sighting is the observation of a shark's retreat upon our approach. It often happens that those who know little about the behavior of sharks confuse aggressiveness with intimidatory demonstrations that are motivated by a sensation of fear, preoccupation, or irritation—and these are emotions that belong to sharks as well. The territory of a shark is a "no entry" area immediately around its body, rather than a specific portion of the sea—a sort of defense area that constantly follows the movements of the fish. In case of "border crossings" by intruders of a certain size that remain for prolonged periods (for example, scuba divers), the shark could stage a demonstrative ritual that consists in:

a) "wrinkling the nose" and lifting it;
b) lowering the pectoral fins;
c) arching the back;
d) bending the body laterally.

If the intruder's response is simply to go away, it is extremely rare for an aggression to follow.

Comparison between normal behavior in swimming (above) and an intimidatory display of "exaggerated" swimming that demonstrates excitation or anxiety, possibly being a prelude to an attack.

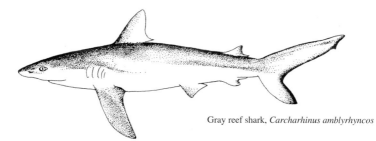

Gray reef shark, *Carcharhinus amblyrhyncos*

Above and facing: Some of the shark species most commonly observable inside or near coral formations. Only the gray reef shark is noted for having attacked humans, but almost always because of stimulation with prey (transporting dead fish under the water) or aggressions on the part of the skin divers.

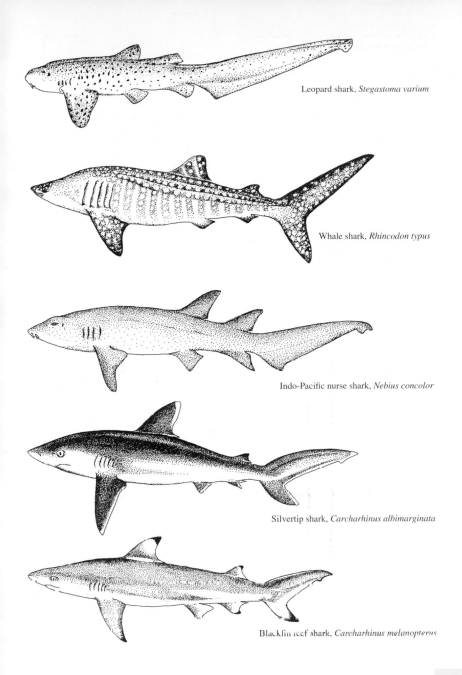

Leopard shark, *Stegastoma varium*

Whale shark, *Rhincodon typus*

Indo-Pacific nurse shark, *Nebius concolor*

Silvertip shark, *Carcharhinus albimarginata*

Blackfin reef shark, *Carcharhinus melanopterus*

Tropical Dangers and Precautions   287

57. The author with a game tracker on the Okavango delta.

It is obvious that it is sufficient to be forearmed against this type of accident. Avoid touching organisms that you do not recognize, even when using gloves, and always wear rubber shoes when you walk along sand beaches or shallow lagoons. Moreoever, it is useless to provoke or tease any animal. A respectful and prudent attitude will avoid unnecessary aggressive reactions. The lionfish just described, for example, has movements that are typically slow and graceful, but if it is approached too closely, it is capable of charging rapidly to sting.

The delicate and showy **surgeonfish** (family Acanthuridae) has a narrow, short channel on the portion of the tail between the dorsal and ventral fins, somewhat disguised by the dazzling coloration of its body. From this innocent-looking opening, the surgeonfish extends its terrible weapon as needed (caution when handling live!), a sharp, blade-like "scalpel," actually an osseous appendage, that is capable of inflicting quite serious wounds: hence the name surgeonfish.

There are many other species that have spurs, and in some cases these are accompanied by poisonous secretions, which causes them to be particularly painful or seriously dangerous. These weapons of defense in a fish are generally located between the dorsal and pectoral fins, toward the pelvic or anal areas.

Dangerous to Encounter. There are some marine animals that are dangerous even if they are just nearby. Sharks and barracudas are the only two

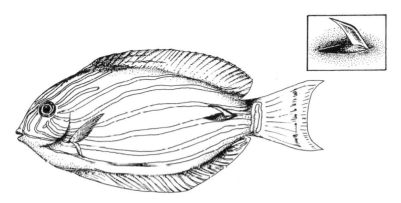

Surgeonfish, *Ctenochaetus striatus*

Geographic Summary of Risks for Tropical Travelers

Tropical Africa
Diseases transmitted by arthropods:
Generalizing the risk of malaria to the falciparum form, present everywhere below 3,000 m (10,000 ft) altitude, with the exceptions of the Seychelles, Cape Verde, and Réunion. Also present are filariasis, onchocerciasis, and yellow fever, but not in all countries. Particular risk of leishmaniasis in the arid zones. Human tripanosomiasis is rather localized and should be distinguished from the animal version, which is not dangerous.

Illnesses transmitted through alimentation or water:
Schistosomiasis, or bilharzia, is present everywhere, with the exceptions of Cape Verde, the Seychelles, and Réunion. The risk of contracting typhoid fever, hepatitis, cholera, dysentery is present everywhere.

Tropical Central and South America
Illnesses transmitted by arthropods:
Malaria is present everywhere below 3,000 m (10,000 ft) altitude (within Costa Rica, Panama, and Mexico, limited to a few zones), even in the falciparum form. In the Caribbean, Haiti, and the Dominican Republic only. Leishmaniasis is present everywhere, even if sometimes it is little common, while yellow fever is very rare. American tripanosomiasis is extremely rare in the Caribbean, very localized in Central America, and widespread in South America. Filariasis and arbovirus are present but localized, for the most part.

Illness transmitted by alimentation and water:
Amebiasis, diarrheic illnesses, viral hepatitis and helminthiasis are widespread. Schistosomiasis (bilharzia) is found in Brazil, Surinam, and Venezuela.

Tropical Asia
Illnesses transmitted by arthropods:
Malaria is present everywhere, even in the falciparum form, with the exception of Singapore and the Maldives. Filariasis is widespread everywhere.

Illnesses transmitted through alimentation or water:
Amebiasis, cholera, dysentery, helminthiasis, viral hepatitis, and typhoid fever can be encountered everywhere. Schistosomiasis (bilharzia) is endemic to the Philippines, China, and certain areas of Sulawesi.

Tropical Oceania
Illnesses transmitted by arthropods:
Malaria is present in Papua New Guinea and to the south, on until the island Vanuatu. It is not present in the Fijis, nor in the islands to the north and east, to French Polynesia, Easter Island, and New Caledonia.

Illnesses transmitted through alimentation or water:
Typhoid fever, dysentery, helminthiasis are frequent.

groups of tropical marine animals that are truly aggressive, in determinate situations, and that look upon humans as a potential meal, and although it may not be very comforting to know, these dangers are restricted to certain species in each case. Often it seems that barracudas, particularly the larger specimens, seem to be more interested and attracted by the bubbles of underwater breathing apparatus or by the movements of snorkelers as they use their flippers, so it results that some awkward pursuits lead rarely to aggression.

Adult **sharks** prefer deeper waters, and it is rare to encounter them in shallow coral formations. The reef sharks (genera *Charcarhinus* and *Triaenodon*) are the sharks most frequently found among coral reefs, and once in a while even a formidable tiger shark *(Galeocerdo cuvieri)* may penetrate those labyrinths, swimming mainly on the surface, dorsal fin completely emerged, and taking advantage of channels and passages among the corals.

In evaluating the possible dangers from the various species of sharks, the scenario becomes complex, and motives for a shark attack can often be attributed to factors and stimuli other than predation. It is certain, however, that a great white shark *(Charcarodon charcarias)* that is longer than 5 m (16 ft) in length has absolutely no problems treating an underwater diver on the same level as a tuna of one or two quintals (220 to 440 lbs).

Whether on land or in the sea, the possible dangers to a traveler must be recognized and understood. This is the best method for avoiding harm without renouncing the enjoyment of the great and magnificent natural world of the Tropics. Indeed, it often happens that many of the beings posing potential dangers for humans are actually some of the most fascinating to observe.

Suggested Reading

Geography, Biogeography, Climate, Soils, and General Ecology

Collins, M. *The Last Rainforests*. London: Mitchell Beazley, 1991.

Cox, C. B., and P. D. Moore. *Biogeography: An Ecological and Evolutionary Approach*. Oxford: Blackwell Scientific Publishers, 1985.

Darde, J. N., and J. Kahane. *Paesi e climi: guida per il viaggiatore*. Milan: A. Vallardi-Garzanti Editore, 1990.

Gaston, K. J., and J. I. Spicer. *Biodiversity: An Introduction*. London: Blackwell, 1998.

Goudie, A. *The Nature of the Environment*. London: Blackwell, 1989.

Huggett, R. J. *The Fundamentals of Biogeography*. London: Routledge,1998.

Martyn, D. *Climates of the World*. New York: Elsevier, 1992.

McDougall, J. D. *A Short History of the Planet Earth*. New York: John Wiley & Sons Inc., 1996.

Mittermeier, R. A., P. R. Gil, and C. G. Mittermeier. *Megadiversity: Earth's Biologically Wealthiest Nations*. CEMEX, 1997.

Myers, N. *The Primary Source*. London: W. W. Norton and Co., 1984.

Newman, A. *Tropical Rainforest*. Oxford: Facts on File, 1991.

Nieuwelt, S., and G. R. McGregor. *Tropical Climatology*. New York: John Wiley & Sons, 1998.

Prance, G. *Biological Diversification in the Tropics*. New York: Columbia University Press, 1982.

Reading, A. J., R. D. Thompson, and A. C. Millington. *Humid Tropical Environments*. London: Blackwell, 1995.

Rihel, H. *Climate and Weather in the Tropics*. London: Academic Press, 1979.

WCMC. *Global Biodiversity*. London: Chapman and Hall, 1992.

Wilson, E. O., ed. *Biodiversity*. Washington, D.C.: National Academy Press, 1988.

Young, A. *Tropical Soils and Soil Survey*. Cambridge: Cambridge University Press, 1976.

Vegetation and Flora

Blombery, A., and T. Rodd. *Palms*. London. Angus and Robertson Ltd., 1982.

Blundell, M. *Collins Guide to the Wildflowers of East Africa*. London: Collins, 1987.

Burley, S., and B. T. Styles. *Tropical Trees: Variation Breeding and Conservation.* London: Academic Press, 1975.

Chapman, V. S. *Coastal Vegetation.* Oxford: Pergamon Press, 1976.

Craven, P., and C. Marais. *The Namib Flora: Swakopmund to the Giant Welwitschia via Goanikontes.* Windhoek, Namibia: Gamsberg, 1986.

Gentry, A. H. *A Field Guide to the Families and Genera of Woody Plants of Northwest South America (Columbia, Ecuador, Peru).* Chicago: University of Chicago Press, 1996.

Ghazanfar, S. *Savanna Plants of Africa.* New York: Macmillan, 1988.

Graf, A. B. *Exotic Plant Manual.* East Rutherford, N.J.: Roehrs Co., 1970.

Henderson, H., G. Galeano, and R. Bernal. *A Field Guide to the Palms of America.* Princeton: Princeton University Press, 1995.

Lotschert, W., and G. Beese. *Collins Guide to Tropical Plants.* London: Collins, 1988.

Meijer, W. *A Field Guide to the Trees of West Malaysia.* Lexington, Ky.: University of Kentucky Press, 1974.

Menninger, E. A. *Flowering Vines of the World.* New York: Hearthside Press Inc., 1970.

Moleswort, Allen B. *Common Malayan Fruits.* Singapore: Longman Malaysia, 1975.

Noad, T., and A. Birnie. *The Trees of Kenya.* Nairobi: T. C. Noad and A. Birnie, 1989.

Polunin, I. *Plants and Flowers of Malaysia.* Millbank Books, 1991.

Reinmold, R. J., and W. M. Queen. *Ecology of Halophytes.* London: Academic Press, 1974.

Sohmer, S. H., and R. Gustafson. *Plants and Flowers of Hawaii.* Honolulu: University of Hawaii Press, 1987.

Steetoft, M. *Flowering Plants of West Africa.* Cambridge: Cambridge University Press, 1988.

Sutton, S. L., T. C. Whitmore, and A. C. Chadwick. *Tropical Rainforests: Ecology and Management.* Oxford: Blackwell. 1983.

Walter, H. *The Ecology of Tropical and Subtropical Vegetation.* Harlow, Essex: Oliver and Boyd, 1971.

White, F. *The Vegetation of Africa.* Paris: UNESCO Press, 1983.

White, M. E. *The Flowering of Gondwana.* Princeton: Princeton University Press, 1990.

Whitmore, T. C. *Tropical Rainforests of the Far East.* Oxford: Clarendon Press, 1975.

Van Wyk, B., and P. van Wyk. *Field Guide to Trees of Southern Africa.* Cape Town: Struik Publishers, 1997.

Fauna

Alderton, D. *Turtles and Tortoises of the World.* London: Blandford Press, 1988.
————. *Crocodiles and Alligators of the World.* London: Blandford Press, 1991.
Bernard, H. U. *Southeast Asian Wildlife: An Insight Guide.* Insight Guides, 1991.
Dunning, J. S. *Portraits of Tropical Birds.* Newton Square, Pa.: Harrowood, 1986.
Eaton, R. L. *The Cheetah : The Biology, Ecology, and Behavior of an Endangered Species.* Malabar, Fla.: Krieger, 1987.
Eltringham, S. K., ed. *The Illustrated Encyclopedia of Elephants.* London: Salamander Books, Ltd., 1991
Estes, R. *The Behavior Guide to Africa's Mammals.* Berkeley, Calif.: California University Press, 1992.
Forshaw, J. M., and W. T. Cooper. *Parrots of the World.* Neptune, N. J.: TFH, 1973.
Goodall, J. *The Chimpanzees of Gombe.* Cambridge, Mass., and London: Harvard University Press, 1986.
Grenard, S. *Handbook of Alligators and Crocodiles.* Malabar, Fla.: Krieger, 1991.
Humann, P. *Reef Creature Identification: Florida, Caribbean, Bahamas.* Jacksonville, Fla.: New World, 1992.
Israel, S., and T. Sinclair. *Indian Wildlife: An Insight Guide.* Insight Guides, 1988.
Kitchener, A. *The Natural History of the Wild Cats.* London: Cristopher Helm, 1991.
Kruuk, H. *The Spotted Hyena.* Chicago: University of Chicago Press, 1972.
————. *Hyena.* Oxford: Oxford University Press, 1975.
Mattison, C. *Frogs and Toads of the World.* London: Blandford Press, 1987.
Moss, C. *Elephant memories: Thirteen Years in the Life of an Elephant Family.* New York: W. Morrow, 1988.
————. *Portraits in the Wild.* London: Hamish Hamilton, 1981.
Morrel, R. *Common Malayan Butterflies.* Harlow (Essex), London, and New York: Longman, 1960.
Napier, P. H., and P. H. Napier, Jr. *The Natural History of the Primates.* Cambridge: Cambridge University Press, 1985.
Reynolds, J., and D. Odell. *Manatees and Dugongs.* Facts on File, 1991.
Sale, P. F. *The Ecology of Fishes on Coral Reefs.* San Diego: Academic Press, 1991.
Schaller, G, *The Serengeti Lions.* Chicago: University of Chicago Press, 1972.

Scott, J. *Painted Wolves: Wild Dogs of the Serengeti-Mara.* London: Hamish Hamilton, 1991.

Spinage, C. *The Natural History of Antelopes.* New York: Facts on File; London: Croom Helm, 1986.

Stotz, D. F. *Neotropical Birds: Ecology and Conservation.* Chicago: University of Chicago Press, 1996.

Sutty, L. *Seashells of the Caribbean.* New York: MacMillan, 1990.

Tartabini, A. *Il mondo delle scimmie.* Padua: Franco Muzzio Editore, 1992.

Thapar. V. *Tigers: The Secret Life.* London: Hamish Hamilton, 1989.

Vine, P. *Red Sea Invertebrates.* London: Immel, 1986.

Webb, J. E., J. A. Wallwork, and J. H. Elgood. *Guide to Living Birds.* London: MacMillan, 1979.

———. *Guide to Living Mammals.* London: MacMillan, 1979.

Wolfheim, J. H. *Primates of the World: Distribution, Abundance, and Conservation.* Seattle: University of Washington Press, 1983.

Fauna: Field Guides

Alderton, D. *The Atlas of Parrots of the World.* Neptune City, N.J.: TFH, 1991.

Bradley, P. *The Birds of the Cayman Islands.* IBIS, 1985.

Bregulla, H. *The Birds of Vanuatu.* Oswestry, Shropshire, U.K.: A. Nelson, 1992.

de Graaf, F. *Enciclopedia dei pesci marini tropicali.* Primaris, 1976.

du Pont, J. E. *South Pacific Birds.* Delaware Museum of Natural History, 1990.

Edwards, E. P. *A Field Guide to the Birds of Mexico.* Edwards, 1989.

Eisenberg, J. F. *Mammals of the Neotropics.* Vol. 1, *The Northern Neotropics: Panama, Colombia, Venezuela, Guyana, Suriname, French Guiana.* Chicago: University of Chicago Press, 1989.

———, and K. H. Redford. *Mammals of the Neotropics.* Vol. 2, *The Southern Cone: Chile, Argentina, Uruguay, Paraguay* (1992), and vol. 3, *The Central Neotropics: Ecuador, Peru, Bolivia, Brazil.* Chicago: University of Chicago Press, 1999.

Emmons, L. H., and F. Feer. *Neotropical Rainforest Mammals: A Field Guide.* Chicago: University of Chicago Press, 1997.

Emmons, L. H., B. M. Whitney, and D. L. Ross Jr. *Sounds of Neotropical Rainforest Mammals: An Audio Field Guide.* Compact discs (2) and booklet. Ithaca, NY: Laboratory of Ornithology, Library of Natural Sounds, 1997. Distributed by the University of Chicago Press.

Estes, R. D. *The Behavior Guide to African Mammals.* Los Angeles: University of California Press, 1991.

———. *The Safari Companion.* Johannesburg: Russell Friedman Books, 1993.

Guggisberg, C. A. W. *Birds of East Africa.* London: Collins, 1990.

Haltenorth, T., and H. Diller. *A Field Guide to the Mammals of Africa including Madagascar.* London: Collins, 1980.

Harrison, C. S. *Seabirds of Hawaii.* Ithaca: Cornell University Press, 1990.

Hilty, S. L., and W. L. Brown. *A Guide to the Birds of Colombia.* Princeton: Princeton University Press, 1989.

Juniper, T., and M. Parr. *Parrots.* Sussex: Pica Press, 1998.

King, B., M. Woodcock, and E. C. Dickinson. *A Field Guide to the Birds of Southeast Asia.* London: Collins, 1986.

Langrand, O. *Guide to the Birds of Madagascar.* London and New Haven: Yale University Press, 1990.

Lieske, E., and R. Myers. *Coral Reef Fishes of the Indo-Pacific and Caribbean, including the Red Sea.* London: Collins, 1994.

Merlen, M. *A Field Guide to the Fishes of the Galapagos.* Merlen, 1988.

Murphy, W. L. *A Birder's Guide to Trinidad and Tobago.* Peregrine Enterprises, 1987.

Myers, F. R. *Micronesian Reef Fishes: A Practical Guide to the Identification of the Coral Reef Fishes of the Tropical Central and Western Pacific.* Guam: Coral Graphics, 1989.

Payne, J., C. M. Francis, and K. Phillips. *A Field Guide to the Mammals of Borneo.* Kuala Lumpur, Malaysia: The Sabah Society, 1985.

Penny, M. *The Birds of the Seychelles.* London: Collins, 1986.

Pratt, H. D., P. L. Pruner, and D. G. Berret. *A Field Guide to the Birds of Hawaii and the Tropical Pacific.* Princeton: Princeton University Press, 1987.

Randall, J. E. *Red Sea Reef Fishes.* London: Immel, 1983.

Ridgely, R. *A Guide to the Birds of Panama, with Costa Rica, Nicaragua, and Honduras.* Princeton: Princeton University Press, 1989.

Serle, W., G. J. Morel, and W. Hartwig. *A Field Guide to the Birds of West Africa.* London: Collins, 1984.

Stiles, F. G., and A. Skutch. *A Guide to the Birds of Costa Rica.* Christopher Helm, 1989.

Taylor, K. *A Birder's Guide to Costa Rica.* Taylor, 1987.

Van Perlo, B. *Birds of Eastern Africa.* London: Harper Collins, 1997.

Vemoux, J. *Coral Fishes of the West Indies.* Latanier, 1992.

Voous, K. H. *Birds of the Netherlands Antilles.* De Walburg, 1983.

Walker, C. *Signs of the Wild.* Cape Town: The Struik Group, 1988.

Woodcock, M. *Collins Handguide to the Birds of the Indian Subcontinent.* London: Collins, 1984.

Wye, K. *The Mitchell Beazely Pocket Guide to the Shells of the World.* Mitchell Beazely, 1989.

Zaluomis, E. A., and R. Cross. *A Field Guide to the Antelopes of Southern Africa.* Wildlife Society of Southern Africa, 1987.

Habitats

Adam, P. *Australian Rainforests.* Oxford: Oxford University Press, 1992.

Bagnis, R., and E. Christian. *Underwater Guide to Tahiti.* Millbanks Books, 1992.

Balfour, D., and S. Balfour. *Etosha.* London: New Holland, 1992.

Beani, L., and F. Dessì. *La natura nel mondo. Savane africane.* Verona: Edizioni Futuro, 1985.

Bradt, H. *Guide to Madagascar.* Bradt, 1990.

Castner, J. *Rainforests: A Guide to Research and Tourist Facilities at Selected Tropical Forest Sites in Central and South America.* Gainesville, Fla.: Feline Press, 1990.

Caufield, C. *In the Rainforest.* Chicago: University of Chicago Press, 1984.

Cloudsley-Thompson, J. L. *Key Environments: Sahara Desert.* Oxford: Pergamon Press, n.d.

Cole, M. *The Savannas.* Orlando, Fla.: Academic Press, 1986.

Colfelt, D., and C. Colfelt. *Barrier Reef Traveller.* Hale, 1990.

Collins, M. *The Last Rainforests.* London: Mitchell Beazley, 1991.

Coughlan, R. *Tropical Africa.* Life World Library, Time Inc. Pub., 1963.

Cranbrook, The Earl of. *Key Environments: Malaysia.* Oxford: Pergamon Press, 1984.

Daturi, A., and C. Violani. *La natura nel mondo. Africa meridionale.* Verona: Edizioni Futuro, 1985.

Dorst, J. *The Amazon.* Austin, Tex.: Steck-Vaughn Co., 1992.

———. *Southeast Asia.* Austin, Tex.: Steck-Vaughn Co., 1992.

Edwards, A., and S. Head. *Key Environments: The Red Sea.* Oxford: Pergamon Press, 1983.

Elklis, R. *Guide to Mauritius.* Bradt, 1988.

Emmons, L. H., and F. Feer. *Neotropical Rainforest Mammals: A Field Guide.* Chicago: University of Chicago Press, 1997.

Goudie, A. S., and A. Watson. *Desert Geomorphology.* Harlow (Essex), London, and New York: Longman, 1980.

Goulding, M. *Amazon: The Flooded Forest.* London: BBC, 1989.

Griffiths, M. *Indonesian Eden.* Louisiana State University Press, 1990.

Hobson, E., and E. H. Chave. *Hawaiian Reef Animals.* Honolulu: University of Hawaii Press, 1989.

Hutchings. P., and P. Saenger. *The Ecology of Mangroves.* Penguin, 1987.

IUCN. *Global Status of Mangrove Ecosystems.* IUCN, 1983.

Mjoberg, E. *Forest Life and Adventures in the Malay Archipelago.* Oxford: Oxford University Press, 1988.

O'Brian, P. *Joseph Banks: A Life.* Chicago: University of Chicago Press, 1997.

O'Hanlon, R. *Into the Heart of Borneo.* London: Penguin, 1985.

Schreider, H., and F. Schreider. *Exploring the Amazon.* Washington, D. C.: National Geographic Society, 1970.

Shelford, W. R. *A Naturalist in Borneo.* Oxford: Oxford University Press, 1985.

Skutch, A. F. *A Naturalist in Costa Rica.* University of Florida Press, 1971.

———. *A Birdwatcher's Adventures in Tropical America.* Austin: University of Texas Press, 1977.

Smith, A. *Explorers of the Amazon.* Chicago: University of Chicago Press, 1994.

Vine, P., and H. Scmid. *Red Sea Explorers.* London: Immel, 1987.

Wallace, A. R. *The Malay Archipelago.* n. p., 1869.

Waterton, T. *Wanderings in South America.* London: Century, 1983.

Dangers and Precautions

Bettini, S. *Handbook of Experimental Pharmacology.* Vol. 48, "Arthropod Venoms." Berlin: Springer Verlag, 1978.

Campbell, J. A., and W. Lamar. *The Venomous Reptiles of Latin America.* Ithaca: Cornell University Press, 1989.

Caras, R. A. *Dangerous to Man.* Philadelphia: Chilton Books, 1964.

Halstead, B. W. *Dangerous Aquatic Animals of the World.* Princeton, N. J.: Darwin Press, 1992.

Halstead, B., and D. Campbell. *A Color Atlas of Dangerous Marine Animals.* Boca Raton, Fla.: CRC Press; and London: Wolfe, 1990.

Nichol, J. *Bites & Stings.* New York: Facts on File, 1989.

Organisation Mondiale de la Santé. *Recommandations pour les voyageurs.* OMS, 1988.

Phelps, T. *Poisonous Snakes.* London: Blandford, 1989.

Vine, P. *Poisonous Snakes.* London: Blandford, 1986.

———. *Red Sea Safety.* London: Immel, 1986.

Visser, J. *Dangerous Snakes and Snakebites.* John Visser, 1987.

Conservation

Collins, M., ed. *The Last Rainforests.* London: Mitchell Beazley, 1991.

Collins, N. M. *The Conservation Atlas of Tropical Forests: Asia and the Pacific.* New York: Simon and Schuster, 1991.

Cowell, A. *The Decade of Destruction: The Crusade to Save the Amazon Rain Forest.* New York: H. Holt, 1990.

Diamond, A. W., and T. E. Lovejoy. *Conservation of Tropical Forest Birds.* ICBP, 1985.

Ferguson Wood, E. G., and R. E. Johannes. *Tropical Marine Pollution.* New York: Elsevier, 1975.

Food and Agriculture Organization of the United Nations. *An Interim Report on the State of Forest Resources in the Developing Countries.* FAO, 1988.

———. *The Tropical Forestry Action Plan.* FAO, 1987.

Frankel, O. H., and M. E. Soulé. *Conservation and Evolution.* Cambridge: Cambridge University Press, 1986.

Gartlan, S. J., C. W. Marsh, and R. A. Mittermeier. *Primate Conservation in Tropical Rainforests.* Oxford: Pergamon Press, 1988.

Goldsmith, F. B. *The Tropical Rainforest: A Wider Perspective.* London: Chapman and Hall, 1998.

Gradwohl, J., and R. Greenberg. *Saving the Tropical Forests.* London: Earthscan, 1988.

Hansen, M. *Alternative to Pesticides in Developing Countries.* ICPR, 1987.

Heaney, L. R., and J. C. Regalado Jr. *Vanishing Treasures of the Philippine Rain Forest.* Field Museum of Natural History, 1998. Distributed by the University of Chicago Press.

Hoage, F. J. *Animal Extinctions: What Everyone Should Know.* Washington, D.C.: Smithsonian Institution Press, 1985.

IUCN. *The Future of Tropical Rainforests in Southeast Asia.* IUCN, 1985.

———. *Plants in Danger: What Do We Know?* IUCN, 1986.

Mitchell, A. *A Fragile Paradise: Nature and Man in the Pacific.* Collins, 1989.

Myers, N. M. *The Sinking Ark.* Oxford: Pergamon Press, 1980.

Newman, A. *The Tropical Rainforest: A World Survey of Our Most Valuable Endangered Habitat with a Blueprint for Its Survival.* New York: Facts on File, 1990.

Prosser, R. *Disappearing Rainforest.* London: Dryad, 1987.

Reid, W. V., and K. R. Miller. *Keeping Options Alive: The Scientific Basis for Conserving Biodiversity.* Washington, D.C.: WRI, 1989.

Richards, F. J., and R. P. Tucker. *World Deforestation in the Twentieth Century.* Durham, N.C.: Duke University Press, 1988.

Soulé, M. E., and A. Wilcox. *Conservation Biology: An Evolutionary-Ecological Perspective.* Sunderland, Mass.: Sinauer Assoc. Inc., 1980.

Wells, P., and M. Jetter. *The Global Consumer: Best Buys to Help the Third World.* London: New Consumer, Victor Gollancz, Ltd., 1991.

World Resource Institute. *Tropical Rainforests: A Call for Action.* Washington, D.C.: WRI, 1985.

———. *World Resources.* Oxford: Oxford University Press, 1990.

Index